D1195593

The Blue and the Gray on the Nile

THE BLUE AND THE GRAY

ON THE NILE

By William B. Hesseltine and Hazel C. Wolf

 THE UNIVERSITY OF CHICAGO PRESS

DT106
.H4

DT106
.H4

Library of Congress Catalog Number: 61-8644

The University of Chicago Press, Chicago 37
The University of Toronto Press, Toronto 5, Canada

© 1961 by The University of Chicago
Published 1961. Composed and printed by
The University of Chicago Press
Chicago, Illinois, U.S.A.

wwwwwwww

To Margaruite Graves
Granddaughter of "The Bey"

186898

Acknowledgments

For courtesies in making manuscript materials available to us we are especially grateful to the staffs of the Library of Congress Manuscript Room, the Louisiana State University Library, the Foreign Office Archives in London, the Khedivial Geographic Society in Cairo, and James M. Patton and the staff of the Southern Historical Collection in the Library of the University of North Carolina.

Many people have kindly furnished us with material or have helped us in our search for information. We wish to thank Miss Margaruite Graves, of Rome, Georgia, and Columbia, South Carolina, for her many courtesies, for permitting us to use the invaluable letters of her grandfather, Charles Iverson Graves, and for her personal reminiscences of her grandfather. Miss Annie Barringer, of Charlottesville, Virginia, Colonel William Couper, of the Virginia Military Institute, and Mr. Ezra J. Warner, of Douglas, Arizona, were most helpful in making materials available to us. We are indebted to Mrs. Elizabeth Hilderbrand, of the Peoria Public Library, for invaluable help in locating illustrative material.

Professor Robert Ferrell, of the University of Indiana, and Professor Lenoir C. Wright, of the University of North Carolina in Greensboro, gave us sound advice and suggestions for the handling of our materials. As research assistants at the University of Wisconsin, Professor Clifford Griffin, of the University of Kansas, and Professor W. Fletcher Thompson, of Wisconsin State College in Oshkosh, were helpful beyond the call of duty. Mrs. Elsie Crabb, of Madison, was both

Acknowledgments

patient and persevering in the onerous task of typing our manuscript. We are grateful to Mrs. Helen Hart Metz, of Elmwood, Illinois, for her work on the Index.

In Cairo, we are indebted to Professor Shafik Gorbal, of the Arab Institute; Dr. Naguib Hassem, Minister of Education; Dr. Hatti, of the University of Cairo; the Archivist of the Abdin Palace Archives; and William A. Lovegrove, Cultural Attaché, American Embassy. Mr. E. K. Gannett, of The Institute of Radio Engineers, and Mr. William Ellery Stone, of the American Cable and Radio Corporation, both of New York, helped us in our search for information on the family of Charles Pomeroy Stone.

wwwwwwwww

Table of Contents

wwwwwwww

Illustrations

PLATES (*following page 68*)

wwwwwwww

Introduction

In the 1870's half a hundred Union and Confederate officers went from the United States to Egypt to train and direct the armies of the Khedive Ismail. They were in the vanguard of many thousands who, in the next three-quarters of a century, would carry American knowledge, skill, and imagination to the far reaches of the earth. The problems they faced in dealing with a people of a different culture, of imposing American technical advances upon deep-rooted and established systems, of resolving their own internal conflicts, were the problems which increasing numbers of later generations of Americans would confront. Their successes set a record which might hold up the highest standards to their successors. Their failures could give pause and carry lessons of caution.

The men who went to Egypt had a high degree of technical excellence, superior training, and a rich experience. They were, for the most part, graduates of West Point and Annapolis. Many of them had perfected their training with experience on the high seas or on the American frontier. They were skilled navigators, skilled and experienced engineers. They had fought Indians and Mexicans and each other—gaining experience in the management of men, in the logistics of supply, in the tactical requirements of armed combat. They brought to Egypt the experience of four long years in the hardest-fought, best-equipped, and best-directed war the world had seen.

The Union and Confederate officers who put on the khedive's uniform were not an "official mission," but they were recommended for the service by the head of the American army. General William Tecumseh Sherman, who had had some of them in his own ranks and who had gained high appreciation of the merits of others against whom he had fought, recommended most of them to the Egyptian ruler. He released a few of the younger officers of the American army so that they might round out their Civil War experience in the land of the Pharaohs. In the Union and Confederate service they had held rank from major general to lieutenant. They had been in the Seminole wars, the Mexican War, and in the battles of Bull Run and Champion's Hill, the Wilderness and Atlanta, Vicksburg and Fredericksburg during the Civil War. They had campaigned with Grant, and Lee, and with Sherman himself. They were experts in the organization of armies, in the conduct of war. They were experts, too, in frontier exploration, in surveying, in building forts, railroads, and dams.

They were not, as it turned out, specialists in public relations or in international politics. They had no viable experience in dealing with people of a different culture and with a different religious background. Although some among them were expert linguists, they were to have difficulty communicating American concepts of efficiency, order, system, and law to Egyptians. They knew little enough of American politics, or even of economics, and they suffered from intrigues, which they never understood, among native politicians and foreign bankers.

And they had problems, too, in adjusting themselves to one another. No conflict arose between them over the issues of the American Civil War, and wearers of the Blue and of the Gray dwelt peaceably together; but they were men of varied personalities and different interests, and harmony was not always possible between them. Some had come out of the Civil War with a shadow upon them; some bore resentment at the fate that seemed to have deprived them of glory in the American campaigns. Some were youths eager for adventure, some were restless in peace after the excitements of war, some were wastrels, some were misers. Two were men, had fate willed otherwise, who might have been Stonewall Jackson. In Egypt one proved that he could have been, the other that he had not the qualities to have been Lee's most trusted lieutenant. Over them all was Charles Pomeroy Stone, a suspicion of treason resting upon him, who proved in Egypt that he was incapable of disloyalty.

Altogether, the Americans who served the khedive chalked up some remarkable accomplishments. They made contributions to Egyptian education, brought engineering skill to the aid of a progressive khedive who was trying to modernize his country, made significant geographical discoveries, and conducted extensive physical and sociological surveys on distant frontiers. Paradoxically, it was only in the area of military affairs that they had but limited success.

Perhaps their careers in Egypt threw some light on their services in the American Civil War. Certainly their deeds and their difficulties foreshadowed some of the problems that later Americans would face as they carried American technology to distant places.

I

wwwwwwww

Soldiers of Misfortune

Some day he would build the pedestal for the Statue of Liberty. Some day men would refer to him as the "American Dreyfus" and would dwell upon the outrage to liberty and freedom which his imprisonment had represented. Some day his own conduct would remove the taint of treason which evil men, for evil purposes, had put upon his name.

But that some day of triumph and vindication lay twenty years in the future, and in the last months of 1869 General Charles Pomeroy Stone, who claimed to have been the first of the millions who formed the great army of United States Volunteers who won the Civil War, was a civilian and none too happy with his post as superintendent of a coal mine in western Virginia. He was a soldier by profession and the unjust taint upon his record and his name rankled in his bosom. He sought eagerly an opportunity to remove the blot and to demonstrate by great deeds that he was indeed loyal to the code in which he had been trained. He welcomed the opportunity to enter the army of Ismail, the khedive of Egypt.

The opportunity for vindication came to a man who should not have needed to seek renown under a foreign flag. At the beginning of the Civil War, Charles Stone, a graduate of West Point with a distinguished record in the Mexican War and a career as a banker and as a surveyor in California and Mexico, was in Washington and ready to offer his services to the nation. It was, in fact, on the last day of 1860 that old General Winfield Scott asked Stone to organize the defenses of the capital. Stone accepted the task, built forts, gathered and

4

drilled the pitifully inadequate militia of the District of Columbia, and had them ready to stand guard when two months later Abraham Lincoln took his inaugural oath.

He was an attractive man with a broad forehead and balding temples, with straight eyebrows and bright, deep-set eyes both penetrating and frank. He wore an imperial beard and sweeping handlebar mustaches which hid the straight line of his mouth. He looked, in that romantic day, the very picture of the ideal soldier in whom an embattled nation could place its confidence. His speech was forthright, his bearing and manner that of a gentleman. He made it a point to get along well with his superiors. Presidents Buchanan and Lincoln liked him, General Scott trusted him, and rumor had it that Stone was the old general's second choice for the high post that Robert E. Lee refused. George B. McClellan found him "a most charming and amiable gentleman; honest, brave, a good soldier."

Unfortunately, Stone's personality was a contributing factor to his undoing. His superiors misjudged his talents, giving him responsibilities beyond his capacities. Scott used him properly as an inspector general and as an ordnance officer, locating posts for the defense of Washington. He could, of course, teach the manual of arms and the movement of platoons, learned on the West Point parade ground, to the militia companies of the District. He did well enough in organizing the inaugural parade and arranging for the President's security. But he had never commanded troops in battle, never directed so much as a skirmish in Mexico or on the Indian frontier, never found the necessity of winning loyal support from subordinate officers or men in the ranks. He had, moreover, no comprehension of the political storm clouds that were gathering to darken his skies. He and his superiors were alike unaware that being a good soldier and a charming and amiable gentleman were not enough to warrant a general's star.

A great part of Stone's undoing stemmed from his genius

for antagonizing those with whom it was vital for him to get along. Early in the war, when troops in Washington under his command seized the telegraph office, he won the enmity of the press. Reporters champed at his restrictions as they frantically sought to wire their papers the story of how Massachusetts' militia clashed with Baltimore hoodlums. He failed to display enthusiasm for freeing the slaves and became a target for the sniping of Radical Republicans. Unfortunately, too, he had little respect for the civilian soldiers who made up the armies of the Civil War. He was a bit of a martinet, a stickler for the rules, as he tried to whip his men into conformity with regular army standards. His men and his subordinate officers gave him respect but no affection. They were, moreover, bored with guard duty, drilling, and target practice, and eager to get at the army across the Potomac.

Indeed, it was this eagerness for gunfire and Confederate blood that brought climax and personal tragedy to Stone's Civil War career. On October 21, 1861, on orders from McClellan, Stone sent four regiments up the Potomac to make a demonstration and a reconnaissance. Two regiments were under Colonel Edward D. Baker who, impatient with the caution which he, like the Radical politicians, believed was the weakness of the professional soldier, crossed the river. He took no precautions for either retreat or reinforcements. Once over, the colonel found himself facing a superior hidden foe. He had no alternative but to try to fight his way out. Bravely —romantically, in white plumed hat—he placed himself at the front of his troops. Immediately nine balls pierced his body. The Confederates killed two hundred and captured seven hundred of his men.

Stone was in trouble. In civil life Colonel Baker was a handsome, glamorous, and popular figure, a close friend of the Lincolns. There was drama in his tragic death, and the Radicals in Congress, boasting that they would learn the true reasons for such Union defeats, quickly established a Committee on the Conduct of the War to begin its work with an investigation of the catastrophe at Ball's Bluff. The committee promptly looked for a scapegoat.

The press had already pointed to the guilty man. Baker was popular; Stone was not. Soon the press was charging Stone with responsibility. The committee took its cue from the press and summoned some of Stone's officers to give an account of Stone's activities. They co-operated readily and built a case against Stone. Twice Stone himself appeared before the committee, but its chairman, the venomous Radical Ben Wade, blandly denied that there were actual charges against Stone. The committee was only inquiring, he said. In the midst of the investigation, personal tragedy struck. Stone's frail wife died, leaving one small daughter to the distraught father. Soon Ben Wade sent to Secretary of War Edwin M. Stanton the demand of the committee for Stone's arrest. On February 8, 1862, at midnight, fitting the dark deed to the dark hour, an officer appeared at Stone's door to seize him and to conduct him in close custody, without communication, to Fort Lafayette. Neither superior nor subordinate rose to defend him.

Stone immediately demanded a court-martial. No one paid attention to him. He demanded charges, specifications, a chance to confront his traducers, an opportunity to present the facts against malicious error. He got no answer. For forty-nine days he remained in solitary confinement in a cell intended for enlisted men. Then, on the advice of a physician, he was sent to Fort Hamilton and had the "freedom of the prison." But he never saw a charge against him, never learned who his accusers were. After six months in prison, Stone was released as capriciously as he had been confined. With no knowledge of who had ordered him freed, with no orders, he had a shadow upon his reputation and a bitter sense of injustice within his soul. Even in Washington, where he went seeking justice, he found none. Neither did he find a hearing or an assignment to duty.

For months Stone hung around Washington seeking vindication by a court or the opportunity to vindicate his impugned loyalty by an assignment to the field. Both McClellan and Joseph Hooker asked Stanton for Stone's services. Neither got him. Then in the spring of 1863 the War Department sent him with General Nathaniel P. Banks, Massachusetts politician turned soldier, to Louisiana. Banks, assigned to clear the rebels from the lower Mississippi, needed the competent guidance and advice which a professional soldier could give and welcomed Stone as his chief of staff. It was the kind of assignment that Stone should have had from the beginning.

For almost a year Stone stayed with Banks, serving efficiently, faithfully, if without distinction. In March, 1864, in New Orleans, he met again his old friend General William Tecumseh Sherman. The latter had come down the river and en route had picked up as a prisoner Professor David F. Boyd, of the Louisiana State Seminary of Learning, over which Sherman had once presided. Seeking to ease his prisoner's lot, Sherman turned Boyd over to Stone, who, as Sherman knew, would treat him kindly. In Louisiana Stone married for a second time, his bride the daughter of a Louisiana judge named Stone, and for a moment his star seemed to be rising again.

But however much Stone may have won the support of his associates, his very success worked against him. Secretary Stanton had only ill will for the man he had persecuted. Banks's campaign was no success, and Stanton was willing enough to load the onus of its failure on Stone. In March, suddenly and as capriciously as it had two years before, the insulting wrath of the War Department fell again on Stone. Out of the blue came an order addressed to "Colonel" Stone, ordering him to report to Cairo, Illinois, to his old regiment. A few days later, still without explanation, another order unceremoniously mustered him out of his brigadier commission in the Volunteer Army. Stone made no protest. As a good soldier he obeyed orders. But Stanton, half in justification, half in hope he could yet pin a crime on Stone, called Ulysses S. Grant's attention to charges in a Chicago newspaper that Stone had mishandled Banks's campaign.

It was near the end for Stone. In August General Gouverneur K. Warren put him in command of a brigade in his corps in Virginia, but Stone no longer had any zest for service. He waited a month and then, sick, frustrated, and disgusted, resigned from the army. The first soldier of the Volunteer Army was gone.

In all the host of veterans of the Civil War, there were few men under greater psychological compulsion to prove their military worth. Charles P. Stone had a cloud on his reputation; as a soldier he could not rest until it was dissipated. He was a competent engineer and readily found employment. Work as a mining engineer was congenial to him, but his success in business did not remove the shadow the venomous Stanton and the hysterical Committee on the Conduct of the War had cast upon his reputation.

When in 1869 Thaddeus Mott, agent for the viceroy of Egypt, sought Civil War veterans for service in the Egyptian army, he consulted General Sherman. Among the first to whom the commanding general pointed was the old friend of his California days. Stone welcomed the opportunity to leave his Virginia mine and don the uniform of Egypt. He was ready to return to his profession, eager to prove on the Nile that he had been shamefully used on the Potomac.

Charles P. Stone was not the only veteran of the Civil War to whom the viceroy's offer spelled hope and opportunity. He was not the only soldier whose career in the war had been blighted. There were others who had just grounds for believing in their hearts that fortune had passed them by and that the authorities who controlled such things had not exercised either good judgment or impartiality in selecting men for high command. Nor were the ranks of the discontented filled only by those who had fought under the Stars and Stripes. There were Confederates, too, whose early promise had not been fulfilled and who might look for redemption and vindication on another continent and in another cause.

Such a man was "Old Blizzards" Loring, a major general in the Confederate Army, a soldier by profession, and a warrior who had a fair claim to having been under fire more times than any other living man. William Wing Loring was not a man to bear deep resentment and nursed no grudge against the one-time leaders of the Lost Cause. But he was sensitive, as a soldier should be, of his honor, his valor, and his judgment, and certainly the leaders of the Confederacy had not accorded him the responsibilities and the opportunities that an officer of his experience and accomplishments could rightly expect.

Few officers resigned from the United States Army to enter the Confederate service with a richer experience than Loring. In May, 1861, he was six months past his forty-second birthday and had been soldiering since he was fourteen. He had been in Seminole wars in Florida at a time when most of his later associates were learning parade-ground tactics on the fields of West Point. Later he studied law, and when Florida became a state Loring sat in the state legislature. Then, when the Mexican War called for valorous men, the twenty-seven-year-old Loring abandoned law and politics forever. He became a captain, a major, a lieutenant colonel. He won brevet promotions for gallant and meritorious conduct. At Mexico City he led an assault on Belen Gate and lost an arm. Thereafter his empty sleeve bore its eloquent testimony to his courage and gallantry. When the war ended, Loring stayed on in the army.

For a dozen years young Loring proved that the army made no mistake in keeping him in the service. No product of West Point looked more like a soldier than he. He was five feet nine inches tall, sturdy—even stout—in build. His carriage was erect, commanding. His hair and imperial-cut beard were coal black, matching his jet-black eyes. His nose was large, his complexion swarthy. His head—his whole bearing, in fact—struck men as Napoleonic. And his deeds confirmed the impression his appearance gave. He led his regiment, with six hundred mule teams, for twenty-five hundred miles across the mountains to Oregon without losing a man. A generation later it was called "the greatest military feat on record." He commanded the Department of Oregon. He fought Indians on the Rio Grande and on the Gila in Arizona. He fought Mormons in Utah. He went to Europe to study the military systems of the continent. He came back to command the Department of New Mexico. At thirty-eight he was the youngest line colonel of the American army. When he entered the Confederate service, even his enemies bore him tribute: a man of "unflinching honor and integrity," said the Federal officer who replaced him in his western command.

But whatever his record of gallant and meritorious conduct, his obvious ability as a fighter, and his unsullied honor and integrity, Loring carried into the Confederacy other traits born of long experience. He did not work well in harness. He had had independent command too long to adjust himself easily to the control of superiors. His days in the Southern service were marred by a tendency to make up his own mind. Had he gone to West Point instead of learning his tactics in the Everglades, he would have been taught that subordination is the first duty of a soldier.

William Loring had other traits that worked against his success. He was no martinet, no stickler for the niceties of military etiquette. He was no drillmaster. He was a fighting soldier who led rather than commanded his men. In camp he was genial, almost jovial, friendly with his officers and with the men in the ranks. Withal, he had a quick and fiery temper, and his flashing eyes and lashing tongue were more terrifying to cowards and incompetents than were the more refined and sadistic punishments approved by the Manual of Discipline. But these, too, events would prove, were traits little appreciated by more conventional officers.

Loring entered the Confederate Army as a brigadier general and served in the desultory actions in western Virginia in the fall of 1861. Then toward the end of the year the Richmond authorities assigned him to Stonewall Jackson's command in the upper reaches of the Shenandoah Valley. From the beginning there was conflict between the two generals, and in the end the Richmond authorities removed Loring to areas where his traits of forthrightness and independence could not disturb the Virginia general.

Thomas Jonathan Jackson was six years Loring's junior and already well on his way to becoming famous. His military experience and background were far less impressive than Loring's. He had graduated from West Point and won citations for heroism as an artillerist in the Mexican War. But while Loring was fighting Indians on the frontier, Jackson had been winning for himself a "character for singularity" as a teacher at the Virginia Military Institute. Apart from his duties on the parade ground, his only military activity after the Mexican War came in 1859. Then he led the school's battery of light artillery to Charles Town to guard from molestation the officers of Virginia as they hanged John Brown. His next military act came on April 21, 1861, when he escorted the Institute's cadets to Richmond to act as drillmasters for a camp of Virginia volunteers.

Within a few months fame came to Brigadier General Jackson. At the battle of Bull Run, Jackson's brigade occupied the center of the line facing the Federal troops. At his right was General Barnard Bee with a South Carolina command. In midafternoon the Federals massed their attack upon the flanks and pushed back and shattered Bee's line. Desperately Bee appealed to Jackson for assistance, and one of his officers heard him cry in anguish, "There's Jackson standing like a stone wall instead of coming to my aid." A few minutes later Bee led a forlorn charge and fell dead. Then Jackson charged, and his timely action, though too late to save Bee, turned the tide of battle. After the battle, men in the exultant Confederate camp remembered Bee's words differently. They thought he had said, "There's Jackson standing like a stone wall. Rally behind the Virginians." Jackson's men promptly adopted the name the South Carolinian, either in admiration or disgust, had given him. Thereafter they were the Stonewall Brigade, and their commander was Stonewall Jackson.

Perhaps the men of the Stonewall Brigade were a little arrogant in their pride over their reputation. Certainly Loring's officers were irritated by the implied superiority of the men of Jackson's command, and they did not take well to the discipline upon which Jackson insisted. Moreover, they did not relish being suddenly taken on a midwinter campaign in the mountains of West Virginia. Loring's own skepticism over the wisdom of a winter campaign was thinly veiled in the words with which he acknowledged the orders to join Jackson at Winchester. "I shall go into it with a spirit to succeed," he told the War Department, and his command, he said, would if necessary "cheerfully endure all the hardships of a winter campaign." So saying, on Christmas Day, 1861, Loring reported to Jackson. Although the experienced soldier was technically second in command, Jackson did not condescend to ask his advice.

The expedition did not go well. On New Year's Day, 1862, Jackson started his troops north toward a Federal outpost at Bath, forty miles away. The day was balmy, the sun shone, and clouds of dust raised by the marching men floated lazily across the dry brown fields. But before darkness fell on the short day, a biting wind rose, bringing freezing rain and snow before the night was over. The men had marched without tents, rations, or blankets, and the baggage wagons, hampered by ice, could not overtake them. Among Loring's troops, who did not share the aura of the Stonewall Brigade, there was slight inclination to "cheerfully endure" the rigors of the campaign. On the next night, when Jackson ordered Loring to halt until after the Stonewall Brigade had settled down in the houses of a village for the night, Loring exploded to Jackson's staff officer who had brought the message. "By God, Sir," he swore, "this is the damndest outrage ever perpetrated in the annals of history, keeping my men out here in the cold without food."

Nor did later events soften Loring's asperity. The campaign was futile, and the Federals at Bath slipped away while Jackson's men were advancing over the icy roads. By the time the Confederates caught up, disaffection among Loring's troops was so great that Jackson did not dare order them to pursue the enemy. Instead, he ordered Loring to go into winter quarters in Romney, while he took his prize brigade back to the comparative safety and comfort of Winchester.

Left in an exposed position where, in his judgment, he could easily be cut off, Loring was thoroughly unhappy. Some of his officers, led by his senior colonel, wrote a letter of protest which, with due military punctilio, Loring sent to Jackson. Equally punctilious, Jackson forwarded it with his indorsement of disapproval to Richmond. Others of Loring's officers went on furlough to Richmond and personally solicited relief for the command. Others wrote directly to Richmond officials. In Richmond, Secretary of War Judah P. Benjamin listened to the stories, studied the situation, and ordered Jackson to bring Loring back to Winchester. Loring himself advised Benjamin that unless his men were treated better they would not re-enlist. "We came," he added sadly, "cheerfully to co-operate."

The situation had clearly become unendurable for all parties. "With such interference I cannot be of service," snarled Jackson, and promptly sent in his resignation. Then he appealed to Major Thomas B. Rhett, adjutant to General Joseph E. Johnston, to have Loring sent back to Romney. He appealed to his friend, fellow townsman, and fellow Presbyterian deacon John Letcher, governor of Virginia, for indorsement and support. Solemnly and in righteous anger, he filed charges against Loring and demanded his court-martial. "God, who has so wonderfully blessed us during this war," he said, "had given great success, [until Loring returned to Winchester from Romney]."

The Confederate government was in a quandary. In a controversy between a popular hero with influence both in Richmond and in Heaven and a commander of long experience and proven worth—albeit no Virginian and not even a West Pointer—the only solution was to separate the contestants. Benjamin ordered Loring to Richmond. "Leave none of Loring's troops with Jackson," he commanded. The solution, however sensible it may have been, marked the end of whatever hope Loring may have had for distinction.

Thereafter, while Jackson went on to give substance by brilliant campaigns to his legend, Loring found himself only in subordinate roles. No word of jealousy ever escaped him as less experienced generals won their laurels. He performed his duty and fought bravely as a soldier should, but he never won popularity with the Southern people. He had challenged the judgment of Stonewall Jackson and had lost. His failure clouded his career.

After a couple of months the Richmond government promoted Loring to major general and sent him to command the Department of West Virginia. It was an unhappy assignment. His duties were half those of a constable, silencing the disaffection of Unionists in the mountain counties, and half those of recruiting officer, trying to get mountaineers to accept conscription gracefully. Once, in September, 1862, he made a raid through West Virginia's Kanawha Valley. He met the enemy and defeated them. His cavalry overran several towns, crossed the Ohio River, and rode twenty miles along its northern bank. He took Charleston, capital of the newly forming state; seized stores, supplies, and salt works; issued a proclamation to the loyal people; and complimented his army in bombastic, near-Napoleonic phrases. He marched five hundred miles, took three hundred prisoners, and reclaimed forty thousand square miles. He sent dispatches to Richmond stressing the speed of his movements, the great significance of his conquests. Perhaps he had Jackson's Valley Campaign in mind, and perhaps he was inviting comparisons. But Richmond was not impressed.

Somewhat greater success met him in the western theater of

war. Late in December, 1862, Loring joined the forces of John C. Pemberton in defending Vicksburg against Ulysses S. Grant's stubborn advance. At the head of the Yazoo, guarding the approaches to Vicksburg, he built Fort Pemberton—a fieldwork constructed of cotton bales—and mounted three guns on it. And here on March 11 he won momentary fame. A Federal flotilla of nine gunboats, twenty transports, and forty-five hundred men came against Loring's fifteen hundred defenders. Loring opened fire. Standing on his cotton-bale parapet, exhilarated, excited by the breath of battle, he directed the blazing guns of his little battery. "Give them blizzards, boys! Give them blizzards!" he shouted. And blizzards they gave until the enemy retreated up the muddy stream. Like the savage braves he had fought from childhood, William Wing Loring, thereafter "Old Blizzards," had won his name in battle.

His fame was only momentary, and soon more criticism followed a new demonstration of his tendency to make independent decisions. In May, after Grant had crossed the river below Vicksburg and moved toward Jackson, Mississippi, Pemberton called a council of war. Loring advised attacking the troops that Grant had left behind on Big Black Lick. Half accepting the advice, Pemberton moved out from Vicksburg, concentrated his forces at Edward's Depot, and sent Engineering Colonel Samuel H. Lockett, who had designed the defenses of Vicksburg, to select the ground and arrange the Confederate forces for an attack. But Pemberton, confused and vacillating, did not remain in the place Lockett had selected. Instead, on May 15, he crossed Baker's Creek and bivouacked for the night. The next day Grant attacked. At first the assault fell on Loring's command on the Confederate right, but Grant moved to the left, turned the flank, and moved the battle away from Loring. Badly pressed, Pemberton's left and center crossed the creek on a bridge that Lockett had built. But the Federals pressed so close that Loring could not get to the bridge, and he found himself, in fact, in the rear of the

Union Army. Pemberton, cursing Loring for not covering his retreat, fled into Vicksburg, while Loring, separated from his commander, struck out to the south. He abandoned his artillery—which caused Grant to believe that Loring's division was "dispersed in every direction"—and made his way to Joseph E. Johnston near Jackson. Johnston welcomed the unexpected reinforcements, but thereafter Pemberton blamed Loring for his defeat.

Until the end came in North Carolina, Old Blizzards Loring followed Joe Johnston. He was in the Atlanta campaign, and when General Leonidas Polk was killed on Pine Mountain, Loring took command of Polk's corps. He might have kept it, and Johnston might have kept him in command, but fate again ruled against Old Blizzards' fame. Alexander P. Stewart took command of Polk's corps, and soon Jefferson Davis replaced Johnston with John B. Hood. Loring stayed with his division through Atlanta and then went into Tennessee with Hood. Early the next year he was back with Johnston in the Carolinas and fought at Bentonville in March. A month later Johnston surrendered to Sherman, and Loring's service came to an end. It had been, altogether, a frustrating experience, and he might well have believed that the Confederate high command had made bad use of its most talented and experienced men.

With the end, Loring had no career. His profession was gone. He had been a soldier, a fighting man of experience and fame, when he entered the Confederate Army, and he had come out of the war with the shadows of Romney and of Baker's Creek darkening his record. He turned his steps to Florida, where long ago he had fought Indians, practiced law, and served in the legislature. But Florida was in enemy hands and undergoing reconstruction, and while there was perfunctory welcome, there was no job for a tarnished hero. At the age of forty-seven he had no place to turn. Eventually he drifted to New York, and old army friends helped him to find employment. The routine was dull for one who once had been a warrior. He was in the "banking business," a petty consultant on minor matters of Southern investments.

There he was in late 1869 when the rumor came that the khedive of Egypt was seeking American officers for the Egyptian army. Hard upon the rumor came Thaddeus Mott, armed with authority to enlist Americans and with passage money to send them to Cairo. Loring met him, heard the viceroy's plans, and received Mott's first offer. It was an opportunity to return to his profession. Perhaps it was an opportunity to win on foreign soil the fame denied him in his native South. Old Blizzards agreed to go.

The agent who dangled tempting offers of strange commissions to such soldiers of misfortune as General Loring was himself a veritable soldier of fortune, equally at home in the Orient and in the Western world. His connections were good, his personal record of valor unimpeachable, and his promises might well be taken at face value.

Thaddeus Mott was indeed an adventurer who had seen much of men and of warfare. His father, Valentine Mott, was a famous New York surgeon who years before had successfully performed a delicate cranial operation on the august head of the Turkish sultan Abdul-Aziz. The sultan was grateful, rewarded the doctor handsomely, and smiled approval when a Western-style romance developed between Dr. Mott's daughter and one of the young officers of the court. The sultan graced the wedding with his presence and years later sent Blacque Bey, with his American wife, as the first Turkish minister to Washington. Thaddeus, son of the doctor, stood high in the sultan's affections.

But Thaddeus Mott was not content with being a favorite at the Turkish court. He set out to win his spurs in his own right. For fifteen years he saw the world. While still in his teens he was in the Mexican War; in 1848 he went to Italy to fight beside the zealous patriots who battled to rid the land of the Caesars of foreign lords. In Constantinople, he married the daughter of a wealthy Turkish landowner. He learned the rudiments of seamanship, saw the world as an officer on American clipper ships calling at ports in the Far East, and sped supplies to California's coast for mid-century gold seekers.

After that came the Civil War, and a month after Fort Sumter, Thaddeus Mott was a captain in a New York battery of light artillery. He fought in the Peninsula campaign and down in Louisiana where Charles P. Stone was N. P. Banks's chief of staff. He became a colonel of cavalry, with something of the record so becoming to cavalry officers—a reputation for gallantry, a bit of derring-do, and more than a little dash.

In 1868 Mott was back in Turkey, and there he met Ismail, khedive of Egypt. Mott's career, his bearing, his command of the Turkish tongue, and his excellent connections in both Constantinople and New York impressed the khedive. Within a year Mott was Ferik Pasha, equivalent to a major general, gracing the khedive's court during the ceremonial opening of the Suez Canal and persuading Ismail to add more veterans of the American Civil War to the khedivial entourage.

The khedive was convinced. As the guests at the opening of the canal departed from Cairo, Mott left for the United States. He lost no time in consulting William Tecumseh Sherman, who, since Ulysses S. Grant was President, was now General of the Armies. Perhaps no man in America knew more officers of the old army than "Cump" Sherman, and certainly no one was in a better position to know the needs of old soldiers, graduates of West Point and veterans of many a battle, who might continue their careers under a foreign flag. Soon Sherman guided Mott to Loring and to Stone.

Under Sherman's guidance, Mott also selected Henry Hopkins Sibley, who, like Loring, was an old army man with long experience on the frontier. He had graduated from West Point in 1838 and gone off immediately to chase Indians in the Florida Everglades. His great contribution to the United States Army, with all of his years of service on the frontier and in the Mexican War, was the invention of a single-pole conical tent which the army adopted as standard equipment. During the Civil War, valiantly fighting for the Confederacy, he had lost New Mexico. After the war, jobless and disorganized, he had gone back to his native Natchitoches in Louisiana, until Sherman rescued him from his hopeless inertia.

Soon there were rumors spreading throughout the circles of the old army that three Confederate generals, P. G. T. Beauregard, Joseph E. Johnston, and E. Porter Alexander, would soon depart for Egypt. Soon, too, men who would welcome the opportunity to serve the khedive wrote Sherman or Mott, setting forth their qualifications.

On the other hand, there was at least one forlorn soul, a New York doctor, who was the hapless victim of a confidence game. He met a self-proclaimed agent of the khedive who assured him that a deposit of one hundred dollars would insure the proper arrangements. The doctor paid, received a letter from the agent saying he had been accepted, married on the strength of his prospect, took his bride to Cairo, and reported for duty before he learned he had been swindled.

In the next five years four dozen other Americans accepted commissions in the Egyptian army. For a time Mott selected them, with his brother, a New York merchant, and General Fitz John Porter, who had been court-martialed and cashiered from the Union army, to help him screen the applicants. Then, after Mott quarreled with General Stone and left the Egyptian service, Stone and General Sherman made the selections. The resulting group was a fair cross-section of the profession of arms in pre–Civil War America, with the members matured by their wartime experience. In America they had ranged in rank from major general to cadets and midshipmen; in Egypt they ranked from captain to brigadier general. In many different ways they brought varying talents and training and experience to the land of the Nile.

Among them were men who had wearied of trying to find a place for themselves as civilians in postwar America. Iowa's

Colonel William McEntyre Dye had tried farming; Virginia's Ensign Cornelius Hunt had written a none-too-successful book on the exploits of the C.S.S. "Shenandoah"; Cornelius Vanderbilt's grandson Vanderbilt Allen had found nothing to excite his jaded spirits since Appomattox; and Charles W. Field, Confederate brigadier in Lee's army, had found an unprofitable business in Baltimore dull indeed. And there were the romantics. William P. A. Campbell had distinguished himself by stealing from under the noses of the British authorities the Confederate cruiser "Rappahannock," which was being fitted out in a Thames shipyard. To Thomas G. Rhett and Walter H. Jenifer everything about army life smacked of excitement and adventure. Rhett was a son of Charleston's fire-eating editor and had been chief of staff for General Joseph E. Johnston. Jenifer was a cavalry officer who had designed a saddle during his career as an officer of the famed Second Cavalry. He had been in the battle of Ball's Bluff and had helped bring Stone to disaster. Another was Chancellor Martin, who quit the army after exciting battles in the Indian country, tried his hand at business, studied medicine at Columbia, and had almost resigned himself to practice in Bellevue Hospital when Stone offered him a commission in Egypt.

There were others—men of ability, of experience, of adventurous spirit. Some would prove failures in Egypt; some would make fundamental contributions to the land of the Nile and to the advancement of civilization; one and all, they agreed to serve Egypt in any war except one against the United States. Their pay was approximately that of similar grades in the United States Army, and for those who served in any of the distant provinces, an additional 20 per cent. In general, the men from the Confederate service took a grade no lower than they had had in the army of the Lost Cause. The khedive paid transportation costs between New York and Cairo. Should a man become ill during his term, he could accept two months' severance pay and resign. The heirs of any man who died in service received a full year's pay, and the widow of any who died in battle or of battle wounds would receive benefits—unless she remarried—until the majority of her youngest child.

The status of these officers was unique in military annals. They were something more than the traditional and romantic soldiers of fortune who appear on the battlefields of the world. They were something less than a military mission loaned by one state to another for the purpose of instructing the armies of the host. General Sherman interested himself in the project, recommended men, and even gave leaves of absence to junior officers to enable them to gather experience in Egypt. Perhaps his interest, especially after his own visit to Cairo in 1872, led him somewhat beyond the bounds of strict propriety, but the group of Americans never received anything approaching official status. Once the House of Representatives asked the Secretary of War about the officers released from the army for Egyptian service. The Secretary made a factual report on Eugene Fechet, Robert M. Rogers, Charles F. Loshe, and Dr. William Wilson, and Congress dropped the matter. The Americans were professional soldiers, employed under contract to perform a variety of military services. Perhaps we should class them with the wandering knights of the Middle Ages who sold their services to petty princelings. Among these knights-errant were many of proved capacity and experience. A little more than half of them came from the Confederate Army, and more than half were graduates of the service schools at West Point and Annapolis. Nine were engineers, six were cavalrymen, and two were artillerists. Three were adventurers whose previous careers had taken them into many parts of the world. Some had served in the western armies, fighting Indians on the frontier. All of them welcomed the opportunity to use their military training and experience.

They left America with high hopes—and with a great curiosity. Their hopes were for vindication, for adventure, or for wealth. Their curiosity was about Ismail Pasha, the monarch whom they had agreed to serve.

II

wwwwwwww

The Vision of Ismail

Ismail Pasha, khedive of Egypt, belonged to a fabulous mid-nineteenth-century generation whose far-ranging ambitions, flamboyant personalities, and exuberant behavior startled a staid world. The generation of Ismail Pasha first broke the restraining conventions of the Victorian age with the glittering assortment of parvenus assembled at the court of Napoleon the Little. In their personal characteristics, they ranged, these giants of mid-century, from the swashbuckling bravado of Sam Houston of Texas to the suavity of the Count de Mornay, but they shared common visions of empires to be gained, fortunes to be amassed, and worlds to be conquered. Before their day ended—say, perhaps by the 1890's—they transformed the face of the earth and from the steppes of Russia to the bayous of Louisiana altered the ancient relations of man to man. They opened the mines of Kimberley, probed the riches of the Comstock Lode, scooped out the Suez Canal, laid twin strips of iron in crisscross patterns over Europe and America, unified Germany and Italy, made a consolidated nation of the federated states of America, freed slaves and serfs, and from the Ganges to the Missouri bound millions of men with the chains of a new industrial order. These were the men of progress, and in their ranks marched Cecil Rhodes, the empire builder; Ferdinand de Lesseps, the builder of canals; Cornelius Vanderbilt, the ferryboat man who made a railroad empire; John D. Rockefeller, the oil monopolist; and Nathan Meyer, Baron de Rothschild, the broker. They were robber barons. They were men of genius. They were demigods—

compounded of monstrous human frailties and magnificent Olympian vision. And not least among them—in truth in some ways the greatest of the lot—was Ismail Pasha, khedive of Egypt.

Of all his generation, Ismail had dreams grander than most and accomplishments as wide as any. He dreamed of transforming Egypt, an appendage of backward Turkey, into a modern nation—a Western power equipped with such profit-making gadgets of progress as mines, factories, railroads, and armies. Before his career came to an inglorious end, he had doubled or tripled the size of his empire, built hundreds of miles of railroads, erected factories, founded schools, sponsored scientific expeditions, improved harbors, built palaces and forts, and, momentarily at least, had the dubious distinction—based on highly dubious calculations—of being the richest man in the world. Like the other giants of his generation, Ismail dreamed lustfully of power and wealth.

His ambition, both for himself and for Egypt, was a heritage from his energetic, far-sighted grandfather Mehemet Ali, who between 1805 and 1848 managed Egypt's internal and external problems to his own advantage. The son of a minor official in an unimportant Balkan village, Mehemet Ali had risen in the service of the sultan until, when Napoleon Bonaparte led the army of the French Directory into the delta of the Nile, he could lead Albanian "volunteers" to war upon the invader. Once there, he played one faction of Turkish subordinates against another and emerged from a round of intrigues and conflicts as master of Egypt. In 1805 the Sublime Porte recognized the facts and invested the adventurer as head of the Egyptian government.

Mehemet Ali was ambitious. Behind him lay the blood-stained traditions of centuries of oriental despotism. For forty-four years the Egyptian ruler worked to substitute his own power and his own system for that of the Ottomans. He began by confiscating privately owned land and reducing the deposed property owners to dependence on government annuities. He seized the lands of the mosques and added them to his personal holdings. He established state monopolies in agriculture and in manufacture. His economic power became the basis for political expansion. He began to build an army. He imported French military advisers to train the conscripted and reluctant fellahin. He built a navy along European lines. With it all, he solved the problem of internal revolt; he kept the peasantry—the fellahin—so impoverished and so miserable that they had no time, energy, or opportunity to rebel.

With a new army and new power, Mehemet Ali began to expand Egypt as if the country were independent. In order to capture the caravan trade that came out of the distant Sudan to the ports of the Red Sea, he pushed his control a thousand miles up the Nile and founded the outpost of Khartoum. Opposite it, on the Red Sea, he seized the ports of Suakin and Massawa. Over the interior regions between these tenuously held outposts, over Sennar and Nubia with its treacherous desert, and to the west of Khartoum in the vast region known as Kordofan, he established claims and exercised a spasmodic control. By 1841 Mehemet Ali had sufficient power to force the sultan to recognize the governorship of Egypt as hereditary in his family.

Meanwhile, Mehemet Ali had attended to the physical improvement of his dominion. In 1819 he started excavating the Mahmudiyeh Canal to insure a safe channel between Alexandria and the Nile. Constructed by conscripted labor—the *corvée*—the project cost the lives of some twenty thousand fellahin workmen, but as a result European merchants came with their trade to revive Alexandria as an important seaport and to re-establish by way of Egypt the overland trade route between Europe and India. In 1847 he laid the barrage across the Nile at the beginning of the delta. By then, except for the moderate tribute which the Porte required, Mehemet Ali had virtual independence in an empire extending from the Sudan to the Mediterranean. In this empire order was perfect. The Nile and all public highways were safe for all transportation, even that of Christians. The Bedouins had turned to peaceful pursuits. Egyptians took a new interest in science, and student missions went to Europe for study. The government established a number of technical schools. In addition, Mehemet Ali had started a great cotton industry. But most of all, he had recognized the advantages of European science and had left as a legacy to his successors the weakened ties between Egypt and her Turkish overlord.

Under his first two successors, Ibrahim and Abbas, the administrative system deteriorated. Then in 1854 Said took over the reins—and with him came a new infiltration of European influence. Said, thirty-two years of age, was convinced that in Western civilization lay the means to his and Egypt's advancement. Under his rule began a long process of modernization as he opened—just a trifle—the floodgates to European influence. In his first year as viceroy he granted a concession to the Eastern Telegraph Company and permitted Englishmen to establish the Bank of Egypt. In 1856 he gave Ferdinand de Lesseps permission to build the Suez Canal. For his personal expenses he availed himself of another Western practice. He borrowed from the Germans, and so began Egypt's financial indebtedness to the West. Well intentioned but lacking in strong character, Said was handicapped by poor health. In 1862 he fell ill and lay for some time at the point of death. Shortly after the opening of the new year he died.

In early 1863, beneath the official mourning for Said, all Egypt chuckled at the discomfiture of an English telegraph operator. According to the yarn going the rounds, the operator sat beside his instrument for three days and nights awaiting news of Said's demise and hoping to be the first to carry the tidings of his succession to a new viceroy. Finally, exhausted by his vigil, he lay down to sleep, giving his Egyptian assistant strict orders to waken him if the expected word came. Hardly had he dropped into his weary slumber when the telegraph sputtered out the news. But the assistant did not disturb his master. Instead, he himself took down the message and scurried off to the palace of Said's nephew Ismail, the heir apparent. In accordance with ancient custom Ismail heaped largess upon the bearer of the glad tidings, whereupon the assistant, hiding his wealth, returned to the telegraph office, roused his master, and told him of Said's death. His rested eyes glistening in anticipation, the Englishman hurried in his turn to Ismail but received only scorn as the bearer of stale news.

The new viceroy, Ismail, who ascended the throne on January 18, 1863, was European in educational background and cosmopolitan in interests. He had lived in France during the days of the dazzling Second Empire and dreamed of the day when he might enjoy a similar life in Egypt. This he might well do, for he had already inherited a number of buildings in Cairo and Alexandria, in addition to thousands of acres of sugar plantations in Upper Egypt. With the shrewdness of a good business man, he had returned from Europe intent upon managing his ancestral estates, increasing his wealth, and living in the style of his Parisian friends. During the reign of his predecessor, Ismail had stayed completely out of affairs of state and directed all of his efforts toward the acquisition of additional land and the cultivation of his constantly increasing holdings. He had a shrewd eye for agricultural improvement. He imported plants and seeds, experimented with new products. He laid out, in a manner reminiscent of Thomas Jefferson's Monticello but more in imitation of Versailles, the gardens about his palaces. Even before his accession Ismail had become, so it was said, the richest—and the thriftiest—prince in the Orient.

When he became viceroy, Ismail used his new office, title, and prerogatives to expand further his personal fortune. Shortly after his accession, to make sure there would be no family complications over property, the new viceroy bought out the holdings of his half brother Mustafa, his closest rival for the throne and next in line of succession should untoward events bring his reign to a sudden end. Having dispossessed his relative, he "permitted" him to leave the country. Mustafa went in silent, sullen mood to Constantinople, where he watched hopefully as Ismail's vaulting ambitions brought strained relations between Egypt and Turkey.

From the very beginning fortune smiled on Ismail. There was war in America, and the fatuous policy of the Southern Confederacy in withholding cotton from European mills combined with the effectiveness of the Federal blockade of Southern ports to bring a windfall to Egypt's ruler. The delta of the Nile, rich beyond the dreams of planters along the Mississippi, made possible Egyptian cotton to supplant the fleece from Dixie in the looms of Lancaster and Manchester. In Egypt the fellahin rolled in a sudden wealth. Many, seeing a tempting vision of opulence, mortgaged their holdings to acquire more land, hoping to rise above a bare subsistence level. But their master Ismail, quick as any contemporary entrepreneur in France or America to recognize an opportunity for profit, turned moneylender, bought up mortgages, foreclosed on many, and added more land to his personal domain. Within ten years after his accession, through his financial operations and his reclamation projects, Ismail held as his personal property nearly one-fifth of all the cultivable land in Egypt.

Moreover, Ismail's ambitious vision extended beyond the mere acquisition of acreage. He was tireless in his efforts to demonstrate that Egyptian production of all kinds could be geared for a whole new economy for the nation. He first turned his broad interest in botanical matters to the development of Egyptian agriculture and introduced on his lands improved varieties of maize, rice, cotton, sugar cane, and indigo. To increase his own wealth as well as to encourage industrial development, the viceroy established upon his own estates cotton mills, some fifteen refineries with fifty mills for crushing cane, and two hundred and fifty miles of railroad with forty locomotives and considerable rolling stock. In addition, intrigued by the gadgets of industry, he imported machines for farm work, hoping thereby to increase production and to reduce the need for continued use of the *corvée* on his own estates.

Ismail was just thirty-two years old when he became viceroy of the ancient land of Egypt. His physical appearance gave no hint of his energy and of his vision. He was short, broad-shouldered, almost pudgy; his dark hair and skin were only slightly darker than that of many Europeans. He wore his beard close-cropped, and a great mustache almost covered his straight lips. His dark eyes—"piglike," said his scornful enemies—were ordinarily half-closed, and when he concentrated on some problem in conference, discussion, or interview, he habitually closed the right eye and surveyed his surroundings with the left. Ismail looked the part, therefore, of the mysterious potentate Europeans and Americans pictured. When shortly they began to hear fantastic stories of his wicked extravagance and his incredible cunning, they knowingly assured themselves that they knew the type. But Ismail's cunning was not of the kind his detractors so willingly ascribed to him. The characteristic his critics called cunning was a cleverness born of innate intelligence and nurtured by ambition—both of which, developed by education and travel in the Europe of the Second Empire, rested on his cognizance of the challenge posed by Western civilization. He was one with the European and American entrepreneurs—dreamers of vast dreams, robber barons of an expanding age—who were changing Western civilization.

If Ismail's physical appearance designated him as completely oriental, his dress, his manners, and his interests set him apart as a true cosmopolite. He wore Western trousers, but his single-breasted coat or stambouli was a concession to Eastern custom. On his head he wore a red fez or tarboosh. He was friendly, soft-spoken, and endowed with a fine sense of humor. He conversed in Arabic and fluent French. He urged other Egyptians to adopt Western customs. He insisted that the use of forks and knives at meals supplant the Egyptian practice of eating with their fingers from a common dish. He urged Egyptian women to put their clothing in Western-style bureaus. He installed clothes closets in his own harem. He made no objection to Egyptian women—in timid ventures toward westernization—riding in open carriages. He approved the substitution of a thin face veil for the traditional heavy covering. Ismail may have looked the part of the oriental, but his ability, his observation of life outside Egypt, his varied interests, and his ambition for his country made him unique even for the age in which he lived. There was more truth than humor in the reply he gave an English newspaperman who told him that people said he heard with his closed right eye and saw with his alert and gleaming left one. "Yes," answered Ismail, "and I think with both."

He had need to think with both. His interests were broad, and he brought to the task of administering the government of Egypt all the zeal, energy, and attention to detail with which he had managed his own estates. Like his grandfather Mehemet Ali, he was convinced that his government would be honest and efficient only if he held personal control over the entire administration. His method of organization, therefore, put every department of government under his direct supervision and made every official subject to direct orders from the viceroy. He kept meticulous records on every penny of income and personally supervised each expenditure from each government account. He worked, moving toward his goals for Egypt and his dreams for himself.

Impressed by the great projects completed or nearing completion in America and other parts of the world, Ismail determined to modernize his native land. It was the railroad age, and he built some twelve hundred miles of railways, strung up a thousand miles of telegraph lines, arched streams, gullies, lakes, and estuaries with five hundred bridges, beckoned the night-overtaken mariner with fifteen lighthouses, and for his safety built quays and breakwaters. He dug miles of new canals for navigation and an additional twelve thousand miles of irrigation channels. He improved the port at Suez, planned, surveyed, and built an addition to the city of Cairo and a harbor for Alexandria, and provided both cities with gas, water, and drainage systems. In addition he reorganized the collection of customs, purchased—with a loan—the post office from private operators, and revamped the schedule of postal charges. He established steamer service on both the Nile and the Mediterranean and set up Egyptian land banks to keep the fellahin from dealing with foreign moneylenders.

At the same time he gave his attention to the intellectual and cultural problems of his people. He imported a Swiss educator as chief inspector of schools, and under his direction Egypt established a handful of primary schools roughly resembling the common schools of the United States. In addition, the viceroy decreed special government schools for the study of medicine, mechanics, and technical work. He set up a few preparatory schools to bridge the gap between the special schools and the primary school. Promising students went to Europe for study at the expense of the Egyptian government. There was nothing too small for Ismail's attention, nothing so ancient or so sacred that it must be preserved at the expense of modernization. He adopted such Western institutions as the metric system and the Gregorian calendar. He discouraged the old custom of the doseh, an annual religious ceremony in which celebrants rode horseback over the backs of prostrate, writhing fanatics who believed that death in such manner sent them to a special reward in Paradise.

When Ismail's rule began, the world situation favored Egyptian prosperity. Along with English speculators in cotton and dealers in martial hardware—to say nothing of enterprising French bankers—the viceroy became a profiteer on the American Civil War. He fostered cotton cultivation in Egypt. He convinced himself that without slavery the American cotton crop would never regain its former dominance of the world market and that before it again became a competitor Egyptian cotton culture would be firmly established. Moreover, he moved toward a goal which the embattled Confederates had never reached. His eye fell upon the plight of Lancaster and Manchester mill owners deprived of cotton, and he determined to set up his own mills to turn the fleecy staple into yard goods.

It all cost money. The railroads, bridges, telegraphs, gardens, palaces, roads, agricultural improvements, and sugar refineries cost more than Egyptian revenue produced. But European moneylenders realized Egypt's economic potential. Indeed, Ismail's predecessor Said had had little trouble borrowing. In 1862, with the approval of the sultan, Said had contracted a loan for £1,200,000 through German bankers. At the moment Egyptian securities were in such high repute that the agents who managed the transaction reported that they had ready customers for five times the amount. Two years later Ismail borrowed £11,890,000, and in 1870 he contracted for another £7,000,000. Obviously, foreign moneylenders either shared Ismail's faith in the future of Egypt or relied heavily on their own governments' abilities to collect their debts for them.

Ismail's dalliance with the moneychangers aroused the suspicions and even the jealousy of his suzerain, the sultan of Turkey. When the viceroy was negotiating for his second loan, the sultan, who had ample reason to suspect the vultures of the countinghouses, formally protested to the British authorities against any financial arrangement affecting Egyptian revenues without the express consent of the Porte. Clearly the sultan regarded his viceroy as a babe in the woods of international finance. Neither the British nor Ismail paid heed to the sultan's assertion of sovereignty, and the British did not deign to reply.

The warning note and the jealous eyes on Egyptian finances were only symptoms of the sultan's growing suspicion of Egypt's ambitions. As far back as 1856, during the reign of Said Pasha, the sultan had shown his distrust by withholding his approval of the contemplated Suez Canal. A decade later, the island of Crete revolted and appealed to the Western nations, particularly to the United States, for sympathy and help. From sundry libertarian groups and from the U.S. Senate the rebellious Cretans got resolutions of sympathy, but they got no aid. Yet, since the Turkish effort to suppress the Cretan revolt was unpopular, Ismail, with an eye to maintaining the good opinion of the Western world, gave only token help. He sent an Egyptian contingent to the Turkish punitive expedition, then withdrew it the moment it became evident that the strength of the rebellion was spent. The sultan was indignant at the desertion.

Yet the sultan could only fume. Ismail blandly explained that he could not afford the expense. The explanation was coupled with an offer—with strings attached—to increase Egypt's annual tribute to the Porte. For some time Ismail had been pressing for a change in the rule of succession to the Egyptian viceroyalty. Taking advantage of his master's exigent need for men and money, Ismail bargained. Out of elaborate oriental deliberations the two negotiators hammered a new firman. Henceforth Ismail would bear the ancient Persian title of khedive and the succession would pass, not to the eldest male relative, but to the son of the ruler. In return Ismail raised his annual tribute from 80,000 to 150,000 Turkish purses.

The new arrangement was no evidence of rapprochement between Moslem master and liege, and each attempted to turn the situation to his own advantage. The new khedive used the firman to strengthen his position both in and out of Egypt. As quickly as possible he acquired the properties of his uncle Halim, putative successor under the old Ottoman law. He had already purchased his brother's property, but Halim, personally popular among Egyptians, proved obdurate. When Halim refused to sell or to vacate his palace of Shubra near Cairo, Ismail ordered the roads leading to the palace destroyed. Thus isolated, Halim sold out and went to join Mustafa in Constantinople, where they could hope to conspire against Ismail. The sultan, Ismail's enemies gave out, was disgusted with the khedive. His shabby treatment of Halim reflected unfavorably on the Ottoman Empire.

Outside the empire Ismail attempted to make his new title bring a new status. Soon newspaper reports alleged that Ismail was sending out agents to ask if the leading governments would favor his complete independence of the Sublime Porte. The rumor was false; Ismail planned to go himself. In 1867 he went to Paris and London to feel out the situation. He shopped in Paris, spending lavishly, but Paris was no longer the center of continental diplomacy. In London he received the usual treatment accorded visiting dignitaries—half complimentary, half advice on how to run his domain according to the best British taste. Queen Victoria conferred on him the Grand Cross of the Bath, but the British Anti-Slavery Society managed to force the khedive to listen to a harangue on the evils of slavery. Ismail turned even this ungracious gesture to his own advantage by informing the antislavery men that the key to slavery was the slave trade, and if he were only permitted to act against European-supported slave traders he could end the evil. Unfortunately, he explained, he was forbidden the right of search in his own waters. Perhaps, he thought, if the British consulate at Khartoum were abolished, he might have a freer hand.

Lest Ismail's personal appeal for power and influence have effect, the sultan himself followed the khedive to the European capitals and everywhere made it clear that the title of khedive indicated a subordinate rank. British officials, treading warily, taxed their ingenuity to pay proper honor to each, but in such a way that neither could be offended. The British as well as the rest of Europe were looking forward to the day when the Suez Canal would be in operation.

Indeed, running through the whole story of Ismail's ambitions for independence, his vision of a Europeanized Egypt, and his dreams of wealth was the Suez Canal. And through the building of the canal, too, ran the story of European diplomacy, the rivalries of France and England, and even of

Russia, as they sought advantages in the cold war each intermittently waged against Turkey, the "Sick Man of Europe." Each of the powers was interested in the Suez, in the canal which would drastically reduce the expense and the time between the Eastern and Western worlds. Each played a part in the destiny of Ismail Pasha, khedive of Egypt, who wanted to be free from both Turkey and the Powers.

Ismail's first troubles came from France. When Ismail came to the Egyptian throne in 1863, Ferdinand de Lesseps' French canal company had barely a good start on the Suez. Almost at once the new ruler encountered difficulties with the canal builders. By the terms of the original concession, De Lesseps claimed, Said had agreed to supply at no cost to the company the manual labor required to construct the canal. The company, therefore, made no provision for labor in calculating its expenses. Hence, when Ismail announced that the *corvée* could not be used for the canal, the contractors were frantic. At the moment the work had not progressed far enough to convince skeptics that the project was feasible, and the company had already exhausted its ability to borrow. For De Lesseps the situation was grave.

With the judicious use of "connections" at the court of Napoleon and of his distant relative, the Empress Eugénie, De Lesseps relayed the story that English influence had prompted Ismail's objection to furnishing the *corvée* for a foreign company. The English, he explained, were jealous of the French and their advantage in Egypt and would go to any lengths to drive them out. Thereafter De Lesseps and the French diplomats pressed Ismail to agree to submit to arbitration the whole matter of the *corvée*. Yielding reluctantly, the viceroy pronounced himself willing to submit the question to the Emperor Napoleon. Napoleon appointed a commission which immediately proceeded to consider Ismail's alleged breach of contract not only in refusing to furnish the *corvée* but also for insisting that the company return to the Egyptian government certain lands bordering on the canal.

The decision was foregone, and Ismail suffered his first disillusion with his European friends. Napoleon shortly announced that for breaches of contract Ismail should reimburse the company in the amount of £3,000,000.

The award was a keen disappointment to Ismail. His uncle Said had made Egypt a satellite of France. Ismail himself had admired the French empire and French manners and customs. Napoleon III had been his friend. The penalty pronounced shook his faith in such friendships. Moreover, at the time of the *corvée* dispute he had some fifteen French officers in his army. These men had been establishing French military organization and training Ismail's forces according to the French manual. In disgust, Ismail decided to free himself of these remaining connections with the French. In the weeks following the breach of contract decision he methodically mustered out his French officers and laid his plans for acquiring other foreign advice and assistance in military affairs. His searching eye began to watch developments in the American Civil War.

Ismail's dismissal of his French military advisers began an ever deepening estrangement between Egypt and France. It came at the moment when Napoleon III faced serious continental problems and a world-wide loss of prestige. French intervention in Mexico in 1864—a mission for which Egypt had supplied token auxiliary forces—had resulted in 1867 in a dishonorable withdrawal at the demand of the United States. The day of Napoleon III was drawing to an end, and Ismail's dismissal of his French officers was only one new incident in the emperor's declining fortunes.

Yet Ismail was not quite ready to sever the ties he had with France. However weak French influence became, the ambitious viceroy still needed a friend on the European continent. More to be feared than the declining power of France was the ever waxing influence of England and the ambition of Englishmen to dominate Ismail's Turkish suzerain. In 1853–55 England and Napoleon had battled Russia in the Crimean War, and their victory had substantially assured

English dominance in the affairs of the Ottoman Porte. Thereafter England's traditional policy was to bolster Turkish rule in repeated crises which threatened the Porte's authority either at home or abroad. At every turn Ismail found himself hampered or blocked by the hidden influence of Great Britain. At the very moment he was losing his French connections he found his nominal overlord gaining strength through England's constant and aggressive backing. Moreover, as England bolstered the waning Turkish empire, the sultan became increasingly suspicious of Ismail's ambition. Early in 1869, in a gesture whose symbolism was not lost on observers, the sultan conferred high office on Mustafa Pasha, whose bitterness against his brother Ismail was becoming increasingly vocal. Observers noted, too, that rumors of war were increasing and that Ismail was said to be planning to arm Egypt. But the rumors, thoughtfully weighed, seemed to stem from Constantinople and might well have been Turkish propaganda designed to stir up prejudice against the viceroy.

The troubles, however, did not remain long in the realm of subtle rumor. Ismail's ambitions to secure monarchical rights and royal rank, to free himself from paying monetary tribute to the Porte, and to rid Egypt of the necessity of furnishing men to Turkey, were apparent as the day drew near for the opening of the Suez Canal. His observations led him to believe that the time would come when enemies would again attack Turkey. Then he, the guardian of the great route to the East, would be in a position to demand consideration from the Western powers. He planned the ceremonies of the canal opening with an eye to commending himself to the Western world, and the sultan took the opportunity to call his obstreperous underling to heel.

To Ismail, with his knowledge of Western manners and customs, the canal opening presented a golden opportunity to display to the world the new Egypt wrought by his extensive modernization program. Familiar as he was with the story of the Erie Canal celebration and with the world-wide

The Blue and the Gray on the Nile

interest in the Crystal Palace erected as the show place of the British International Exposition of 1851, Ismail saw in the canal festivities the making of an effective advertising campaign for his country and her future rapid development.

Ismail planned the canal celebration as carefully as ever a late-nineteenth-century businessman launched a sales campaign for a new product of some young and thriving industry. With the festivities set for November, 1869, Ismail went in person to Europe to issue invitations. Promptly the sensitive sultan became indignant. He refused to permit the viceroy to issue invitations and protested when European nations received Ismail with honors usually given to crowned heads—honors, he explained, that were not due one who was "only the greatest Pasha in the Empire, bound to pay a subsidy and do homage." It looked for a moment as if a crisis were brewing, but the European powers had no intention of permitting Turko-Egyptian affairs to lead to hostilities. They officially accepted the invitations and prepared to send delegations to the ceremonies. In pique the sultan announced that orders for armaments which Ismail had given during his trip—sixteen thousand rifles from Berlin and a warship from Trieste—should not be executed. The *Levant Herald*, an English-language newspaper published at Constantinople, loyally reported that Ismail's tour was "the most miserable of fiascoes" and his treasonable ambition had been "rudely rebuked." The rebuke, however, was apparent only to the Sublime Porte's bedazzled sycophants. When Ismail asked permission to visit Constantinople to offer proof of his loyalty and to extend an invitation to his lord, the sultan refused to permit the visit. Instead he sulkily announced that he would not attend the opening of the Suez Canal.

Ismail invited not only the monarchs of the civilized world but also countless men of accomplishment in science, literature, journalism, and the art of business. All could come at Egyptian expense, have board and lodging for so long as they chose to remain in the country, and enjoy railroad travel and admission to all of the functions connected with the canal opening. In addition, the khedive's master of ceremonies supplied guests with the services of carriages, donkeys, and dragomen. One Englishman later claimed that a visitor might have lived a splendid two months in Egypt with scarcely a penny of expense from his own pocket.

First among Ismail's guests was the beautiful Eugénie, empress of France, and the khedive centered the entire celebration about her. On November 16, 1869, she witnessed the inaugural ceremony at Port Said. On the following day she boarded the vessel "Aigle," lead ship of a fleet representing many nations, which was to make the first through trip to Suez. Eugénie reached Ismailia the same day and remained for the great ball in her honor, for which Ismail had built a special palace on the banks of Lake Timsah. Her arrival at Suez on November 20 was the signal for the canal to receive regular traffic of the world's commerce. In her honor, too, the khedive built a city of tents near the palace and for three days kept open tables for thousands of visitors who gorged upon the delicacies of food and drink Ismail had imported from all over the world. In Eugénie's honor he staged pageants and processions and ordered fantastic displays of fireworks. Ismail was the unbelievably thoughtful and generous host. Throughout the civilized world men marveled at the riches, the splendor, and the culture of the new Egypt.

In the Turkish capital the overlord of Egypt also heard and read of his vassal's show. The Porte was not pleased. On the eve of the festivities the Grand Vizier filed in a long letter the sultan's list of grievances against Ismail. The viceroy had invited monarchs without consulting the Ottoman emperor; he had treated directly with European governments without consulting Turkish representatives; he had bought arms for his army and ordered ironclads for his navy. The sultan could not permit the Egyptian treasury to be ruined by such expenditures.

"It is a truth everywhere recognized," intoned the Grand

Vizier, "that luxury being not the cause but the effect of civilization, true progress consists in the accomplishment of the reforms which produce that civilization." From unctuous platitudes, the Grand Vizier quickly became peremptory: "You will henceforward concentrate all your efforts upon the development of the prosperity of Egypt and of the security of the lives and property of its inhabitants."

To add to the insult the Turkish government gave the letter to the press, and for a moment there was a stir in European capitals. There was no disposition anywhere to come to the aid of Ismail. Moreover, at the moment Ismail could not expect, without allies, to defeat Turkish troops in a war. There was nothing for him to do but write a humble letter protesting that his "fidelity and devotion are unalterable." It was a humiliating gesture, and it took much of the edge off the festivities of the canal opening. Furthermore, following up his advantage, the sultan ordered Ismail to turn over the ironclads to the Turkish navy and then, in quick succession, announced that Ismail's revenues must be collected in the name of the sultan and his annual budget submitted for his master's approval.

Ismail's retaliation was necessarily mild. He proclaimed at a high point in the canal celebrations that the Suez would be forever neutral. The sultan promptly protested that this was another trespass on his sovereignty. Ismail let rumors circulate that he would not pay his annual tribute, but this, in his weak military position, he did not dare attempt. For the moment Sultan Abdul-Aziz held all the trumps.

But perhaps it need be only for the moment. Clearly, if Ismail were to realize his visions of independence and greatness, he needed to prepare his defenses and train his army. Clearly, too, as his experiences in the six years of his reign had shown, he could not depend on European allies. In the situation, the khedive's eyes fell upon the United States. At the court of the sultan, Ismail had met Thaddeus Mott, veteran of the Civil War and friend of America's William

Tecumseh Sherman. At the canal festivities he had met Nathan Appleton, financier and promoter of grandiose schemes as great as Ismail's own. With Appleton was Nathaniel P. Banks, the major general who had commanded— with the aid of Charles Pomeroy Stone—far-flung expeditions in the valleys of the Mississippi and the Red. The khedive had given attention aplenty to the American Civil War and to America. He had had interests in cotton, in the new ironclad vessels the war had produced, and in Mexico, whence his forces, along with Napoleon's, had been ousted by American influence. He had seen, too, along with the rest of the world, the Americans locked in the greatest war the world had ever known and had seen them emerge with factories purring, mills grinding, and furnaces belching flame and smoke. They were probing the earth for precious ores, linking the coasts with bands of iron. They were a race of giants.

Ismail talked with Thaddeus Mott.

III

The Land of the Pharaohs

In Thaddeus Mott the Khedive Ismail had an adviser of wide experience and excellent connections. He understood Ismail's problem and was able to use his connections in the United States to select Americans for Egypt's army. The khedive needed soldiers who could organize, instruct, and drill an army; he needed engineers who could survey, build forts at strategic points, prepare maps, and organize the complete logistics of war; he needed commanders and, even more, he needed men of lesser rank who could perform lesser tasks and in doing them could instruct their Egyptian associates. These things Mott understood, and he knew the men in America who could guide his selections.

Neither Mott nor the khedive understood the difficulties that lay before them. Each was a cosmopolitan, understanding both the Orient and the Western world, and thoroughly adjusted to the conflicting cultures and mores of two different societies. The khedive was modernizing Egypt, and he hoped the American officers whom he employed would quicken the adjustment of Egypt to European civilization. Mott, who was as much at home in Constantinople as in New York, had no comprehension of the deep provincialism of the Americans who were willing to take commissions in the Egyptian army. Perhaps, too, neither Mott nor his master recognized the depth of the resistance Egyptians were prepared to offer. The failure of everyone to foresee the difficulties, even the refusal of everyone to make adjustments, would trouble the days of the Americans on the Nile.

In those days it took three weeks or a little less to go from New York to Cairo. Most of the veterans of the Blue and the Gray sailed from New York to Liverpool, traveled across England (only changing trains at London's Charing Cross) to Dover, crossed the channel, and on to Paris. Here some of them spent a little time sightseeing, but most of them tarried only from midnight to morning sun, then boarded a train which sped them through France, across the Alps, and along the length of Italy to the port of Brindisi on the Adriatic— "through Rome even," mourned Samuel H. Lockett, Confederate engineer and sometime schoolteacher, "as if it were any other way-station." Four days later, by steamer across the blue Mediterranean, they saw the shores of Africa.

The first sight might well have dismayed them had the shock not been softened by American officers, earlier arrivals, come to greet them. General Mott personally accompanied General Loring and General Sibley, his first recruits, to Egypt. He sent his second group, but Loring and Sibley journeyed to Alexandria to meet them at the boat. After a time Loring, who was stationed at Alexandria, generally managed to meet the arriving Americans and to ease the first shock of their new land.

The shock was indeed great. The harbor of Alexandria had inadequate depth for large vessels, and the natives turned the lack of quays and docks to their own advantage. As the Americans prepared to debark from the liner, Arabs in lighters and shore boats scrambled for the privilege of taking them ashore. Confusion of shouts, fights between contending escorts, and the jostling of boatmen left the unescorted Americans bewildered and apprehensive. But this was merely an initiation into a confusing, even terrifying, society.

When General Stone and a group arrived unexpectedly in the summer of 1870, they received a demonstration of unfriendliness which indicated how thoroughly unwelcome they, or any foreigners, were to the native Egyptian. An official designating himself as "Ali Bey" summoned them to appear before him. Assuming the officer to be a man of some importance, the Americans went to his house, where no one met them, and they were left to cool their heels. After a time one of the group began to storm loudly about the indignity. Thereupon the bey appeared, haughty and displeased. He told the Americans there were too many of them and that most must be sent home. Those permitted to remain would have to accept reduction in rank and pay. When James Morris Morgan, who was twenty-four, announced he would be a captain with an American captain's pay, the bey laughed in his face.

Insulted and nettled, Morgan, the son-in-law of the Confederate Secretary of the Treasury, proclaimed that he was going to Cairo to find out who had brought him seven thousand miles to be insulted. Then, defiantly, the hot-headed youngster declared he would either "get satisfaction" in a duel or horsewhip the deceiver. He spoke in English, but as it turned out the bey understood English perfectly. At Morgan's words his dark face blanched. He quickly turned to Stone, explaining that he was only expressing his own opinion and hoping, may it please your excellency, his words would go no further. The bey, it developed, was simply a minor official and his only instructions were to speed the Americans on the road to Cairo. He sent a servant to show them on their way.

Stone was gleeful at the bey's discomfiture. "Morgan," he said, "that was about as pretty a call-down of a bluff as it was ever my good fortune to witness." But the lesson was there: Americans were not welcome in Egypt.

Greeted by thinly veiled hostility, the Americans searched for landmarks or familiar scenes that would remind them of their homeland and to which they could tie their observations. The approaches to Alexandria reminded Lockett of New Orleans. The levees of Louisiana were here represented by a long line of stone docks, but the same forest of masts bearing the flags of all nations grew from the water's edge. Here, too, were stalwart blacks, stripped to the waist, glossy muscles shining in the hot sun; and for cargo there were cotton bales and sacks of rice. Swarming around the ship were natives in small boats offering oranges, bananas, figs, grapes, watermelons, and cantaloupes, a sight familiar enough to Louisiana eyes. But no experience in New Orleans or any American port had prepared the visitor for the noise, the babel of tongues, or the varied complexions and costumes of Egypt.

The children of the American officers were fascinated by the donkeys, whose riders' legs nearly touched the ground. They were less certain about the camels, whose rickety high-piled loads towered above them. They were startled by the clamoring natives. Their elders, especially if General Loring met them in Alexandria, soon learned to cry "Rue al Allah" —referring the persistent demands for baksheesh to the Lord. Loring assured his charges that the swarming Egyptians were both harmless and amiable, anxious to serve—"always providing the piastre is at once forthcoming," he explained. But many of the Americans were disposed to agree with a member of the British parliament who announced: "For knavery no place can touch the modern Alexandria. One word, however, is far from describing all the infamies of the city. It surpasses Cologne for smells, Benares for pests, Saratoga for gaming, Paris itself for vice."

In Alexandria, as in all their journeyings in Egypt, the American recruits to the khedive's army were tourists, seeing the land of the Pharaohs with the uncomprehending eyes of visitors. They gazed upon the wonders, made quick and superficial comparisons with the scenes of the United States, and arrived at naïve judgments compounded in equal parts of the provincial's repugnance for strange ways and of the credulity of the ignorant. They did not understand Egypt, and they made no effort to understand the Egyptians. At the moment, in the recently reunited United States, their fellows and former colleagues were compounding errors in their dealings with Negroes in the South and Indians in the West. The group that went to Egypt showed no greater aptitude in handling the human problems in the delta of the Nile than their fellows managing the Freedman's Bureau showed in the delta of the Mississippi. In both cases the American officers were outlanders, and those who worked for the reconstruction of Egypt faced the additional handicap of working with people of a different culture and a strange tongue. Only superhuman efforts could have overcome the obstacles before them. But the Americans in the khedive's army were not supermen. They were only professional soldiers, technicians in the arts of war, who would content themselves with obeying orders and amuse themselves by watching the bizarre ways of an alien land.

It was as tourists, eager enough for thrills and adventures, willing enough to witness the sights, that they saw Alexandria and then, guided by their welcoming escort, boarded the train for Cairo. As soon as the train ground to a stop in the Cairo railway station, the traveler alighted to a scene of the wildest confusion. Here was rush and scramble exceeding that of Alexandria. Porters, vying for luggage, rushed frantically about, the tails of their blue and white shirts flapping. They roared at each other and grabbed at bags and parcels. Fortunate were the Americans, for Stone and his staff had made arrangements for temporary accommodations for the newcomers. Even so, the escorting officer had to find the hostel representative, present his credentials, and climb aboard the hostel omnibus or two-horse carriage while the concessionaire saw to the accompanying luggage. The unofficial visitor who had no reservation had to find himself a porter, work out of the melee, and attempt to find lodgings, no mean accomplishment in a Cairo crowded with visitors.

Tourists in Cairo, especially Americans and Englishmen, usually thought first of Shepheard's Hotel. The hotel, standing on the west side of the Ezbekiyeh Gardens a short distance from the railway station, had once been a palace. A huge edifice, it surrounded a beautiful garden and was itself surrounded by two or three others. Its rooms were always comfortable and usually cooler than other buildings in Cairo. Its decor was Arabic. Behind the hotel guests could play tennis, walk in the lovely shaded garden, or wander through a palm grove. In front, stone steps led the visitor some six feet above the street to a platform, also of stone, before which natives congregated throughout the day to hawk their goods or their services. Across the street the donkey boys impatiently awaited hotel guests who required transportation for business or for sightseeing.

Although Shepheard's was and remained the central gathering place of American visitors to Cairo—three hundred Americans checked in at the office of the consul general in 1870— the American officers were to find rooms at the Grand New Hotel a block away. This hostelry, built and owned by the khedive, had every modern convenience and was surrounded by gardens that reflected Ismail's interest in horticulture. Here the American officers stayed while they prepared for their reception by the khedive and, if they were to remain in Cairo, until they found more permanent quarters.

The first event for the arriving American officers was an interview with the Khedive Ismail. For some of them it was the high point in their Egyptian service. For all it was a moment excitedly awaited and long remembered. Even the most blasé among them approached the reception wide-eyed and as embarrassingly self-conscious as a debutante about to be presented to Queen Victoria. Like the maidens who curtsied before the queen, the knights-errant needed proper clothing and basic lessons in court etiquette.

Clothing was important—and not one of the Americans had thought to bring along his dress uniform, Federal blue or Confederate gray. Perhaps Mott, or Porter, or Sherman himself had hinted that such regalia would be out of place in Ismail's court. Instead, each was to be garbed, as befitted his new role, in an Egyptian stambouli. On the morning after their arrival at the Grand New Hotel, an Italian tailor appeared to take their measurements. The "Effendi," explained the little tailor, wanted them in uniform when they appeared before him. "It was not conducive to a long life," someone suggested to young Morgan, "to keep Ismail waiting."

Perhaps the tailor feared to earn Ismail's frown, for no later than the next day he appeared with the necessary undress uniform—"an exact reproduction," snickered Morgan, "of the coat of a Presbyterian parson." It was black, single-breasted, and meant to be worn buttoned to the throat, with nine black buttons standing in a prim row. The trousers, too, were black, and patent leather shoes of glossy black completed the somber ensemble. The summer uniform, which they ordered later, was far more attractive. Its trousers were blue with two strips of braid running down the seam; its coat was gleaming white, double-breasted, with a standing collar with an even whiter cord braided around it and with white braid entwined in myriad loops from cuff to elbow. But, summer and winter, they wore on their heads a bright red fez—a tarboosh—complete with black silk tassel. A "red smoking cap," said Charles Iverson Graves in amusement. They looked for all the world like a row of red-crested vultures, as their escort, General Stone himself, led them from the Grand New Hotel to the even grander Abdin Palace.

Each new group of American officers received elementary instruction in court etiquette, but the khedive was no stickler for the niceties with his American recruits, and they were more observers than participants in the first reception. The road to the palace of Gezireh had its share of fascinations. It crossed the Nile over a magnificent iron bridge and for two miles led along beautiful avenues bordered with luxurious vegetation, past groups of Arabs with flowing gowns and capacious turbans, past strings of camels—a land of make-believe transported from the Arabian Nights. At the palace gate the officers left their carriages and walked through the grounds. It was a fairyland picture, thought Charles Iverson Graves of Georgia. There were rippling brooks and shady walks, flowers in profusion, and fountains springing crystal streams into the pure morning air. At the palace door Zulficar Pasha, the khedive's master of ceremonies, greeted Stone and his charges and led them through the ranks of the palace guard and the assembled beys and pashas. Through an arched doorway they went, down a long colonnade, up a broad stairway, into the resplendently draped audience chamber, and across the deep Persian carpet to stand beneath the great sparkling chandelier. "It seemed to me," Graves later wrote in awe, "that the East with its luxury and its magnificence and the West with its civilization and taste had here met, and acting in perfect harmony had combined to construct the most exquisite and perfect habitation for man since the Garden of Eden."

Then Ismail appeared at the end of the room, standing before a silk-covered divan. Slowly, Grand Master Zulficar bowed until it seemed he would fall on his face. He then advanced, escorting the Americans one at a time to within a dozen feet of the august presence. Zulficar's arm swooped to the floor as his knee bent in the grand salaam. His open hand scooped the imagined earth from before the khedive's feet and brought it upward to his heart, his lips, and his forehead. Each American performed in turn an abbreviated version of the salaam, bowing slightly, swooping lightly, and winding up with a sort of military salute.

Then Ismail spoke. With one eye closed and the other intently studying their faces, His Highness addressed them in fluent, precise French, thanking them for their prompt response to his invitation. He had invited them, he explained, because of their experiences in the Civil War and because their country had no selfish acquisitive interest in Egypt. Egypt needed them, and, he added, "I may say to you, in absolute confidence, that you are expected to see active service very soon."

He had more to say when he had led them to another room and seen them served with iced sherbet, coffee, and cigarettes. They could expect, he warned them, the jealousy of native army officers. "Bear it," he begged them, "with patience and indulgence," but if it became unsupportable, "do not hesitate to come to me for redress." He counted, he said, upon their discretion; he asked their devotion and zeal to aid in the independence of Egypt. And he promised to bestow upon them, when the mission was accomplished, his highest honors.

The Americans were impressed. They warmed to Ismail's personality, to his friendliness, to his outspoken yearning to free his country from a tyrant's yoke. They were romantics—else why would they be here?—responding to the noble phrases of nationalism, patriotism, and freedom. They resolved to show their worth, and almost without exception they served faithfully and with devotion.

It was not the last time the Americans would see Ismail. Most were to serve in Cairo, and all spent much time in the capital. Frequently they were guests at the khedive's lavish entertainments. Then, not in the dark stambouli but gorgeously caparisoned in blue coat with gold epaulettes and gold chevrons, gold sword belt, and bright red trousers with a wide gold stripe, they adorned the court, attending state dinners when Congressman Elihu B. Washburne, or General Sherman, or former President Grant came to Cairo, eating from gold plate and drinking from gold-rimmed crystal. They went to breakfasts at noon, formal dinners at seven, soirees, musicals, and dansants at ten o'clock, suppers at midnight. Accustomed to hearing of the elaborate goings-on in the brownstone mansions along Fifth Avenue, the Americans reveled in ornamenting Ismail's even more elegant, even more rococo, festivities. They marveled.

They marveled that he had built a theater, that he had commanded Verdi to write an opera, that he imported actors, singers, and dancers for the performances, and that at each performance a fire engine with steam up stood guard before the door. And perhaps their appreciation was enhanced by the khedive's practice of daily sending eight or ten tickets to the Citadel—most of them intended for the American staff. They marveled at the tales of the entertainment for the Empress Eugénie when the Suez Canal was opened. They saw with their own eyes, in the winter of 1873–74, the wedding celebrations for three of the khedive's children. For six weeks, while all Egypt took a holiday, silk-and-satin-lined pavilions covered a square mile, and entertainers performed. The pageantry was dazzling, surpassing the imagination. Colonel Dye's mind was filled with wonder and confusion as changing uniforms and scenes passed in procession. "Fantasia," "profuseness," "dazzling splendor," were the words that came to his mind. "Finally," he wrote, "the limits of the imagination were reached, everything dancing before the mind like a vision."

The celebration in conjunction with the opening of the Suez Canal cost $10,000,000; the weddings exceeded it by half. The British, who were infiltrating the Egyptian economy and the khedivial treasury, reacted with horror to Ismail's extravagance. They denounced Ismail as a barbarian, an "oriental potentate," an uncouth savage who sat cross-legged upon his divan, fingering his bare toes during an audience. So simple a monarch, wringing his wealth from the wretched fellahin and wasting it in oriental extravagance, needed curbs, the British said. But the Americans saw no evil in him. They saw instead the perfidious purposes of Englishmen. From the time of their first interview with the khedive they were, most of them, Ismail's men. They wrote home praising him. They inspired New York correspondents covering the Orient to slant their news in Ismail's favor. "This extraordinary man, who has placed himself so high above the foulness and abominations of the East," said a Loring-inspired reporter, "seeking to lift whole peoples with him in his elevation, deserves the admiration and sympathy of the world."

Against British moralizing the Americans set the evidence of progress. "The just and upright motives which prompted him were patent to all intelligent observers," Loring swore of the khedive. Ismail was interested in education, in ameliorating the lot of his people. He tried to abolish slavery; he set up schools, new systems of agriculture, cotton gins, sugar mills, steam pumps for irrigation. He planted forests; he built railroads, canals, telegraph lines; he improved harbors; he began a library. If the fellahin were not better off, wrote Loring, it was their own fault; and if perhaps Ismail was extravagant in entertainments for foreign guests, it was only suitable. And, added Charles Chaillé-Long as, later, he looked back over his days in Egypt, "if Ismail was prodigal, his prodigality nevertheless lent a remarkable impulsion to progress."

The Americans saw the khedive through American eyes. He was a sort of Jim Gould and Jim Fisk and Cornelius Vanderbilt and Uncle Daniel Drew—men of bold and audacious vision, with more than a touch of flamboyance in their nature. Looking with American eyes, they understood—or thought they understood—Ismail Pasha, khedive of Egypt. American eyes, at any rate, were good enough to see through Englishmen.

American eyes were not of much use, however, in seeing beneath the surface of Egypt. When the Americans, group following group for the next five years, left the khedivial palace after their first interview with Ismail, they became tourists again. Each of them, unless he was assured of immediate assignment outside the city, began to search for suitable quarters less expensive than the Grand New Hotel. Some found pensions, others took apartments; and some who had brought wives and children looked for houses. A few high-ranking officers like Stone got rent-free "palaces." The search gave them their first opportunity to see Cairo.

The city they saw spread over some four square miles of sloping plain between the east bank of the Nile and a spur of the Mokattam Hills. It was nine or ten miles south of the point where the river divided. The city was a center for trade in gums, ivory, hides, and ostrich feathers from the Sudan; cotton and sugar from Egypt; indigo, shawls, and carpets from India and Persia; sheep and tobacco from Asiatic Turkey; and machinery, hardware, cutlery, glass, woolens, and other manufactured goods from Europe.

Of prime interest to the American military men was the great white Citadel on a slope of the Mokattam Hills. Built near the end of the Mokattam spur by the Sultan Saladin in 1166, the mighty walled fortress was in effect a small community. Old Cairo, easternmost from the Nile, grew up around this stronghold. The Cairo which Ismail's American assistants saw was indeed a city in transition. Everywhere the khedive's occidental innovations sprang up beside the relics of Egypt's past. In Old Cairo, at the foot of the Citadel, the streets were still unpaved, discouraging carriage travel. In its Arab section the narrow lanes would scarcely permit two camel riders to pass. There, also, the projecting balconies of the harems nearly met, thus affording some protection from the glaring sun. Along these streets passed the great variety of humans who made up the population of the city, their brilliant and fantastically styled costumes making Cairo one of the most colorful cities in the world. Many a traveler felt himself caught in a tale of Arabian nights as he viewed and heard Old Cairo's polyglot crowd. Wrote one: "Ladies wrapped closely in white veils, women of the lower classes carrying water on their heads, and covered only with a long blue garment that reveals too plainly the exquisite symmetry of the young and the hideous deformity of the elders. . . ."

Lieutenant Colonel Graves, who had seen much of the world in the American and Confederate navies, was fascinated by the camels moving through the bazaars in single file with every kind of load—boxes of dry goods, hardwood, coal, grapes from the Oasis of Fayum, goatskins of water, chickens, and even sand and stone for buildings. "Camels are used here where we would use a wagon," he wrote. Through the same streets padded veiled women, many with infants astride their shoulders. Other women, mounted upon donkeys, wore black gowns whose gauzy balloon-like drapery floated out behind them as they moved. Turbaned Turks, black-robed mullahs, stately Arab sheiks, and Africans of every hue, from the yellow-brown of Egypt to the shining jet of Nubia, traveled afoot about their business. As prospective buyers dickered with the keepers of Old Cairo's open-air shops, the distinctive sounds of the city vibrated around them. From time to time the voice of coachman, donkey boy, camel-driver, or sais called out, "Take care of your foot, oh, man!"—words of warning to him who impeded the progress of carriage or animal. Beggars, a large percentage of them blind, hoped to incite compassion as they begged for alms, crying, "I seek from my Lord the price of a morsel of bread," or "I am the guest of God and of the Prophet." He who heard the beggar call "God will have mercy on you!" knew that some passerby had answered the mendicant's plea. Carriers, bent under the weight of a goatskin of water, offered a saucer or small bottle of water, crying, "May God recompense me," and looked hopefully for earthly reward from the drinker. Dervishes proffered "hemali," a water flavored with orange blossoms. Vendors hawked fruits and itinerant peddlers of sweets sold a thin jelly of wheat starch and sugar, accepting in payment nails or old pieces of iron. Wandering cooks carried portable kitchens and sold servings of hot meat puddings or of fish, and their customers squatted or sat cross-legged by the side of the street as they ate.

All in all, the Union and Confederate officers who reported for khedivial service could scarcely have found a more fabulous city—or a nation in a more exciting era—for adventure. Everywhere were the remains of Egypt's long history and everywhere were evidences of both the dreams and the energy of the Khedive Ismail. Reminiscent of the former were the bazaars just off the Muski, the principal business street of Old Cairo. Along both sides of narrow, dirty lanes were vari-sized rooms set some three feet above the ground level and open to the street. There merchants were grouped together either by nationality—Turkish, Syrian, Tunisian—or by trade—carpetmakers, shoemakers, brassworkers, silversmiths, fezmakers.

Sellers and buyers sat cross-legged before the displays, contentedly smoking and sipping coffee as they discussed prices. Heavily laden camels made their determined way through the crowds, sometimes completely blocking the thoroughfare with their bulky loads. Amidst deafening noise, hawkers lauded their commodities and elbowed stragglers; an occasional auctioneer, carrying on his shoulders the goods he hoped to sell, dashed up and down the lanes shouting the latest bid on some article or other.

There were antiquities—"So many associations connected with past ages, so many things daily to be seen to remind one of Bible stories," sighed Graves as he wished his wife back home in Georgia could join him. "How you would enjoy the sight of the grand and majestic Pyramids, the classic Nile, the ancient Citadel round whose walls the Crusaders vainly sought an entrance." Once Graves hurried up to the Citadel at night to see the Mosque of Mehemet Ali—"the finest in the world"—on the one night of the year when the tomb of the founder of the Egyptian dynasty was opened. Thousands of lights suspended from the dome brought out the rich beauties of the Turkish and Persian carpets, and two candles as large as a man's leg, in candlesticks of pure silver, lighted the tomb. That evening the Pyramids, too, were lighted up. The Americans drank in the sights of the city and repeatedly thought of the Arabian Nights. The contrast between Cairo's antiquities and Ismail's Western innovations was particularly noticeable to these tourists. The mortar was scarcely dry on some buildings, and at others workmen barely had a start on new projects. A whole new section was developing northwest of Old Cairo. There, in a triangular area on the east bank of the Nile, was the Ismaileyeh quarter. Near the center of a triangle formed by two canals and the Nile was the parklike Ezbekiyeh, a large octagon of luxuriant vegetation. It included an ornamental lake, well-kept shrubbery, shady walks, artificial grottoes, and rippling cascades. From a brilliantly lighted kiosk in the center of the garden a military band gave a concert each evening. Built at a point once the focus of Cairo's oriental trade, the Ezbekiyeh stood in the very midst of the city's principal hotels, consulates, cafés both European and native, attractive shops, and fine homes. Opposite its southwest corner stood the khedive's new opera house and beyond that, toward Old Cairo, lay Ismail's winter home, the horseshoe-shaped Abdin Palace. To the northwest of Cairo, beautiful Shubra Avenue, lined with sycamore and lebbek trees, led to Shubra village. Each day the fashionable of Mohammedan and of Christian society rode along the avenue. On Friday and Sunday evenings the ubiquitous donkey riders and carriages bearing ministers, consuls, merchants, and lightly veiled harem ladies, crowded the lanes. More frequently than not, the khedivial equipage was somewhere in the throng.

To the Americans who served the khedive in the 1870's, the native was as different from the occidental as the surroundings in which he lived were different from the sidewalks of New York or the prairies of the Midwest. In appearance the fellah was unlike the European or American, yet did not fit the Westerner's picture of the way an Oriental should look. Nor did he look like the Negroes whom the Confederates knew in the South. Most men of the fellah class were lean, broad-chested, and medium in height. Brown of skin, the fellah had a broad-browed, oval face, thick-lashed, brilliant black eyes kept half-closed against the glare of the sun, a straight, broad nose, thick lips, and gleaming teeth. Most had large heads and scant curly hair which they shaved but for a tuft at the crown. Most wore mustaches and beards. In the delta, the fellah's costume was a blue cotton smock. Those who lived in the Nile Valley wore a smock of brown wool and a loincloth for undercovering. Headgear varied with the wearer's means. Common was the white cap worn under the fez, around which the man wound a long strip of muslin to make a turban. Those who could not afford the muslin covered their heads with a thin cotton cap. The wealthy Egyptian wore a shirt of white silk or cotton and over it pulled a long striped robe bound at the waist by a thick girdle. For outdoor wear he added a cloth coat and, if the temperature required it, added a vest as an extra layer between the shirt and the robe.

The woman of the fellah class had fine skin and facial characteristics similar to those of the men. To the foreigner the contrast between the slender beauty of her youthful figure and the grotesqueness of her mature years was almost unbelievable. Customarily—to protect herself from the Evil One— she tattooed her chin, hands, arms, and the space between her breasts. Sometimes she wore rings at ears and nose and silver or copper bracelets on her arms. Her usual garb was the loose blue cotton gown. In chill weather those who owned two garments wore both. Her plaited hair was combed and rebraided only on bath day, and the coiffure added no beauty to her appearance. Henna rinses were fairly popular with those whose hair was gray. Some wore the head veil in such a way that it could quickly be drawn over the face at the sight of a man. Others, particularly women of the upper classes, wore a short black veil. In the southern provinces women wore gowns made of the same brown wool of which the men's smocks were made. Upper-class women—who were never so well dressed on the street as at home—darkened their eyelids and eyelashes and hennaed their fingernails and toenails.

The Egyptian's diet was simple but varied. He ate vegetables, black bread, salt-sprinkled cakes of unleavened flour, fruits, dates, and melons. He seasoned some foods with caraway, garlic, or raw onion. He frequently chewed contentedly on lightly roasted grain or legumes.

The health of the fellah, despite his miserable economic status, was excellent. There were occasional epidemics, but the Egyptian appeared to be immune from disease, and one American officer concluded that Cairo was, after San Francisco, the most healthful city in the world. The packs of hungry dogs that roved the streets acted as scavengers for the city's waste. Ophthalmia seemed to be the one Egyptian ailment and blindness the most common affliction. Americans attributed the inflammation to sand and glare, and the more careful of them adopted the practice of bathing their eyes several times a day. But there were no scavengers to consume the flies, and the Egyptian fly seemed to seek out the eyes. Someone explained to the wife of Colonel Samuel H. Lockett that the Arabs had a superstition about brushing off flies. One of her daughters had an attack of ophthalmia, but an American doctor cured her in a few weeks.

The Americans shared the general good health and marveled at it. Only a few claimed that their health suffered from their Egyptian adventure. Colonel Raleigh Colston broke down under the desert sun on an exploring expedition. Alexander and Frank Reynolds, father and son, died—one of a heart attack, the other of disease. One American died of sunstroke, another of malaria. Only Colonel Thomas G. Rhett, suffering paralysis, left the khedive's service because of his health. The other Americans were remarkably healthy, not even suffering from the usual bowel complaints of the tourist. Lockett reported, "I am in better health than I have been for years," and Mrs. Lockett added, "I really think my children have been healthier here than they were at home."

Perhaps it was the climate. There were but two seasons: the short, mild winter, which got down to freezing not more than once in twenty years, and the long, hot summer. Charcoal braziers carried from room to room kept the Lockett house comfortable in winter, while a retreat to the shade—the difference between sunshine and shade astonished the Americans—kept the family cool in summer. One could exercise freely out of doors, go for a donkey ride, or drive in a carriage along Shubra Road at all times of the year. "Who could think of dyspepsia or hypochrondriasis while beholding the lovely sunrises and glorious sunsets of Egypt?" cried one of General Stone's English visitors. The only sour note was struck by Lockett after he had spent some unhappy months nearer the equator: "I believe in cool air and high ground for the white man."

At any rate, neither climate nor indisposition restrained the Americans from enjoying the sights of Egypt. They saw the ruins, the pyramids, the markets and the fairs, and they watched, fascinated but uncomprehending, the varieties of religious observances that lent an air of excitement to a large part of each year. Indeed, the Americans in Egypt complained constantly of the great number of work days lost because the Mohammedans, the Christians adhering to either the Orthodox or the Roman church, and Egypt's numerous Copts celebrated their fast, feast, and holy days independently of each other. "Friday is the Mohammedan Sunday," reported Graves. "They give me Friday and I take Sunday," he added. Work days lost totaled some two months each year, and these were in addition to those lost during the thirty-day fast of Ramadan, when Mussulman Egypt ate and drank all night and fasted and slept during the day. Many of the observances, of course, called for elaborate celebration. One of these was the yearly recognition for the pilgrims who returned from Mecca. As the time of their return neared, many Cairenes journeyed out to meet the caravan and many more kept vigil at the place called "pilgrim's lake." The welcome for the pilgrims included a two-hour parade with a twelve-gun salute as the procession reached the open area before the Citadel.

The fast of Ramadan, the ninth month, commenced the day after the new moon appeared. On the afternoon of the preceding day, a special delegation left Cairo to go out on the desert where nothing would interfere with their observation of the celestial phenomenon. A multitude assembled at the Citadel, anxiously awaiting their report. As soon as the news arrived that the new moon had been seen, a procession of societies representing the trades of Cairo moved down into the streets. "Oh Blessing! Blessing! Bless ye the Prophet! On him be peace!" Thereafter for a month no Moslem ate, drank water, or smoked from sunrise to sunset. The nights were given over to feasting.

Aside from the pageantry and the strange excess of religious observances, the Americans saw little of interest in the Moslem faith. Unlike most Americans, Charles Iverson Graves, pious Episcopalian, found a reasonable word to say about the Moslems. "They worship the Living God and regard our Savior a great prophet, and in this respect are better than either the Jews or the Unitarians." More typical was Loring. When he arrived in Cairo he had been impressed with the mingling of Moslem minarets and Christian crosses, with the medley of the muezzin's call to prayer and the merry chime of the Christian bells, but he made no effort to understand the Moslem. Someone warned Morgan when he first arrived not to try to enter a mosque; the natives might not take kindly to infidel prying. The word was passed on to later arrivals, and the Americans restrained their natural curiosity. They saw the outward manifestations of Moslem piety and concluded that the whole was mere superstition. The Mohammedan religion, concluded Loring, was largely responsible for the Egyptian's "lack of intellectual stamina." The Koran was the final measure of his knowledge, dominated his life, and prevented his intellectual growth. "The true believer is possessed with the idea that modern science and improvements are but the devices of the infidel, instigated by the Devil." Their will, he said, was "chained by the rhapsodies of the Prophet," and "until some Arab Luther" came along, their religion would control them.

Unwilling to study the religion, the Americans were unable to understand a social system based upon the Koran. They observed the phenomena of Arab society, tested what they saw by the puritanical standards of American Protestantism, and recoiled. They had a prurient curiosity about the status of women under Moslem law and nursed a fond belief that the harem was a scene of lewd debauch. Colonel Dye heard and reported that Ismail kept nine hundred women in his harem, while the khedivial family had more than three thousand. The Americans, whose picture of a harem came from smatterings of *The Thousand and One Nights*, were never able to learn anything very definite about the lascivious go-ings-on. They settled in the end for the conclusion that indo-lence and ignorance—both as offensive as sexual immorality to right-thinking Americans—were the chief characteristics of the harem. Loring looked upon the harem with the prejudices of a Christian and a bachelor. The women, he said, lacked all intellectual stimulation. Their sole concern was with their own beauty and with producing sons. "When not making their toilettes, they lie around, smoke cigarettes, and eat sweets." The men tyrannized over them. They had no oppor-tunity to develop their "natural intellectual and social in-stincts," said Loring, and the men suffered in turn. They, too, sank into indolence and sluggishness.

Colonel Dye's judgment of the influence of the harem was far more caustic. "To this institution," he indignantly asserted, "with all its ignorance, superstition, envy, jealousy and in-trigue . . . may be traced lying, bakshish, blackmail, bribery, forgery, theft and corruption generally, high and low, and exorbitant taxes, cruelty and murder, emasculation and slav-ery, and all their concomitants!"

Colonel Graves even found that the horrors of racial equal-ity accompanied the harem system. Once, as he was busily engaged in a meeting of an important commission, "a long, lanky, elegantly dressed Nubian appeared at the door. It was evident," he went on, "that he was a very poor arithmetician, as the young widow bride said of her second husband, aged 64 (he couldn't multiply). As soon as Ali Pasha Moobarek saw him he rushed to him and salaamed in the most respectful manner, the other members of the commission rising to their feet and remaining standing until the eunuch, turning and motioning with his hand, said in the most gracious manner 'fad'le, fad'le' (be seated)."

While the pasha and the eunuch talked, the commission kept "still as mice," but Graves was growing more disgusted by the minute. Then the eunuch rose and everybody stood—everyone, that is, but Graves—and the eunuch smiled goodbye graciously. "Now this black Nubian negro," spluttered Graves when he got away from the meeting, "is the most powerful man in Egypt after the Khedive's own sons." He was, in fact, chief eunuch of the queen mother, had property to the amount of fifteen million dollars, and had such influence with the khedive's mother that "even Cabinet ministers are not powerful enough" to protect themselves against his "back door influence."

"I must explain"—it was the voice of Rome, Georgia, speaking—"that when he first entered the room I was surprised into rising to my feet by the sudden example of the others. I couldn't think it was in deference to this Negro, whose only education was the training he received to fit him to act the spy, the jailor, and the servant. . . . I kept my seat."

To Graves there was a lesson in it that must have been apparent to other than the Confederates in the Egyptian service. "All the efforts His Highness can make to civilize his people will be useless until he abolishes all the Harems and EUNUCHS FROM THE LAND!"

Equally repugnant to the Americans were the institution of polygamy and the ease of divorce. Loring had fought Mormons on the Utah frontier, and he was steeped in arguments against plural marriage. Once an Egyptian officer of "fine education and character," according to Loring, invited the American to be an honored guest at his second wedding. Loring, instead of feeling honored, was outraged. He proceeded to lecture the Egyptian on the virtues of monogamy. It would not, he argued, be fair to the first wife; indeed, it would be "cruel and brutal." Moreover, in Western countries women were on an equality with men, the law protected their rights, and they were "elevated, refined, and educated." And, bachelor Loring added, they were "always good, young and beautiful." Divorce, he said, was a crime and "an act of cowardice," and taking another wife was "morally wrong."

The Americans, as might be expected, were seldom invited to the homes of Egyptians. Loring's officer went ahead with his wedding, though later, having added a Xanthippe to his menage, he ruefully confessed that Loring might well be right. Yet the cultural gap between Christian Americans and Mohammedan Egyptians was too great to be bridged. Loring had one native friend who, having read Cooper's tales as a child, had absorbed a romantic interest in Indians and was delighted to meet an old Indian fighter. He had, in fact, injured his spine while playing Indian on the harem stairs and still suffered from the accident. He sought out Loring to practice his English. But few Egyptians had such an interest, and their social contacts with the American officers were few and formal. The Americans attended state functions where the khedive loved to have them on display. Pashas and ministers invited them to formal affairs, officers of the army entertained them on inspection trips, but few made friends of them. No daughter of an American officer found her groom in the delta of the Nile; no officer—and many were young and eligible—married an Egyptian girl.

They found, of course, plenty of entertainment in Cairo. From October until April the opera house and both the French and Italian theaters presented programs on alternate evenings. Some cafés offered music in the Greek or Roman style, and in others Bohemian and native performers played everything from Wagner and Strauss to discordant and plaintive Arabian airs. Visitors could obtain temporary membership in a club which an English nobleman had founded. There, in rooms overlooking the Ezbekiyeh Gardens, they could play cards or billiards or read from a great variety of magazines. All people were welcome in the library and reading room of the Khedivial Geographic Society. In the desert area beyond the Citadel visitors flocked to watch horse races, and in the establishments of Cairo the visitor could gamble at roulette or faro.

Among themselves, and apart to themselves, the American officers and their families, Federal and Confederate, gave neither word nor thought to the memory that less than a dec-

ade before they had been at war with one another. The ladies
drove together into the desert; officers and their wives went
in groups to visit the ruins. They gathered for parties, with
European toys for the children, on Christmas Eve. Federal
and Confederate, wearers of the Blue and the Gray, they
dwelt together peaceably on the Nile.

Excluded from Egyptian society by the religious and cultural gap, the Americans lived apart. Together with the consul general, the missionaries, a few businessmen, and a few
selected Englishmen and Frenchmen, they huddled in their
own group in polyglot Cairo. In Alexandria they mingled,
more or less freely, in the somewhat larger English colony.
Their children went to the missionary school or to a German
school where they learned French. No one studied Arabic.
They were in Egypt—they were never of it.

But perhaps their isolation was, in part at least, an aid to
their work.

IV
ⱽⱽⱽⱽⱽⱽⱽⱽⱽ

The Americans at Work

There was work to do. The American officers of His Highness' army may have been tourists in their naïve reactions to
the sights and sounds and smells of Egypt, but they were also
trained and experienced technicians, with duties to perform,
tasks to accomplish. They had sought and accepted employment where their talents and experience could be used; they
wanted to be useful, and for the most part they worked with
a will. Some among them accomplished much; it was only in
areas of human relations, where they had no training and
where the clash of cultures produced mutual misunderstanding, that they failed.

In the beginning they believed their primary objective was
to train an army that could wrest the freedom of Egypt from
Turkish tyranny. This was the story that Mott, who whispered as though he were privy to the inner counsels of some
vast conspiracy, told Loring and Sibley on the dark Atlantic.
It was the meaning that Americans read in the khedive's half-
closed eye as he welcomed his recruits to the land of the Nile.
Some of the Americans—more especially the Confederates
among them—saw in the delivery of Egypt some vicarious
redemption of the Lost Cause of Marse Robert and Jefferson
Davis. And the Yankees, too, saw the situation in an idealistic
light—had not their former compatriots offered their lives in
the battle to free the slaves and to spread the great truths of
democracy from Canada to the Gulf? The Americans saw
clearly the role they might play in bringing a new member
into the family of nations. "You will be called upon very soon

to take the field," Ismail had said. "I count upon your zeal and devotion to aid me in achieving the independence of Egypt. When this is accomplished, as it will be, *Inshallah*, I shall bestow upon you all compensation and the highest honors."

But for all of his ambition and his desire to free himself from Turkey, Ismail had no sure knowledge upon which to operate. He was not a military man. He had watched, uncomprehending, the course of the Civil War in America and the triumphal campaign of the Prussian army against his old friend Louis Napoleon in Europe, but he knew nothing, either at first hand or as an intelligent student, of modern warfare. He was willing to learn, however, and as his first act he assigned General Loring as inspector general of the army. A lesser man than Ismail might well have been appalled at the reports Loring began to send back to his new master and the Egyptian war office. They added up to an admonition that it would take long, slow, and careful training before the viceroy's army would be able to challenge his suzerain in Constantinople.

In his calm moments William Wing Loring was a man of experience and sound judgment. Under the tensions and excitement of campaign and combat he had stormed Belen Gate of Mexico City and lost an arm; in the Civil War he had impugned Stonewall Jackson's judgment and lost command; in the fighting above Vicksburg he had shouted louder than his own cannon; he had abandoned Pemberton and joined Johnston after Baker's Creek and become a figure of controversy. For all his reputation of having been under fire more times than any living American, he had not established a clear reputation for sound acts under emotional stress. But here in Egypt, for the moment working with freedom and without tension, he saw clearly and outlined concisely the military needs of the country.

The situation that he found was like nothing he had known before. The fellahin who made up the army were conscripts from the villages along the canals, agricultural workers without even a rudimentary knowledge of the duties of a soldier. In the army they were untrained, unkempt in their persons, inept in the uses of the tools of war. Their organization was feudal, even tribal, and bore no resemblance to the squads, platoons, companies, and battalions into which European and American armies divided and controlled their men. Loring met—though it can hardly be said that he understood at this early moment—the pasha system that was the rough equivalent in Egypt for the regiments, brigades, corps and armies of American military organization. Indeed, had he recognized its implications he might well have given voice to the unrestrained outbursts that characterized his emotional moments. Instead, he calmly recommended that the army needed complete reorganization, that the soldiers needed drill, training in the use of weapons, and discipline according to Western models. And, clearly, what the army needed immediately was more Americans, and at the head it needed a chief of staff and a complete general staff to supervise the work of reorganization. But this Ismail already knew; long before Loring made his first reports, Thaddeus Mott had gone scurrying back to New York to enlist more American recruits and dispatch them to Egypt.

Loring's duties as inspector general were not confined to advising on army reorganization. Together with Sibley he set about inspecting the fortifications that guarded Alexandria and Damietta and the approaches to the Suez. Without security on his Mediterranean shores, Ismail was only a dreamer of futile dreams. There was no longer a navy—the sultan had seen to that—and in its absence Ismail needed substantial coastal defenses more than ever. It took no more than a casual glance by an eye acute at Vicksburg and Atlanta to see that Egypt was completely undefended against possible attack by the Turks. Loring's report on these matters brought him a fresh summons to the khedivial presence.

There were, in fact, not one but several conferences with the khedive; with Stone, the chief of staff; and with Kassim Pasha, the minister of war. From these meetings emerged a new view of the problems of Egypt. Whatever the hopes of Ismail for immediate independence from Turkey, and whatever the ambitions of the Americans for martial glory, Egypt was in no condition to wage a war. Perhaps, too, it was clear to everyone that the European powers, ever tense over the Near East, would not permit Egypt to upset the delicate balance in the Arab world. Before Egypt could claim independence, she must earn it; she must have an army that could command respect, must have an economy that could sustain the shock and strain of war, must have resources, trade, and a broader territory over which the rule of the khedive was undisputed. This was not to be accomplished in a moment.

In time, however, it would not be impossible. Out of the conferences there emerged the outlines of a plan for the future. In this plan were many parts, and in each of them the Americans would have a major role. In a strictly military sense, as Loring's reports showed, the defenses of the country needed to be strengthened and the army reorganized, modernized, and brought under a single system of control. In a broader sense, the army and the Americans should be used to expand the territory of Egypt by exploration and by the conquest of lesser peoples along its frontiers. From the explorations and the conquests would come trade and supplies, and they would reveal the hidden resources of soil and minerals that could make a stable economy. Under the direction of Charles Pomeroy Stone the army would be reorganized and made fit. Under his guidance the veterans of the Civil War would explore the interior, map old trade routes, and survey the terrain for railroads yet to be built. Under Loring's direction the defenses would be strengthened in order that, behind the rising fortifications, the development and expansion of Egypt might go on.

The immediate result of the conferences was the assignment of General Loring to the command in Alexandria. In the presence of Stone and Kassim Pasha, Loring spoke persuasively to the khedive, arguing that a single responsible head should

Brigadier General Charles P. Stone, chief of staff at the Citadel, Cairo

Ismail Pasha, the khedive of Egypt

Shubra Avenue, Cairo (from Georg Ebers' *Egypt*, 1884)

Shepheard's Hotel, Cairo (from Georg Ebers' *Egypt*, 1884)

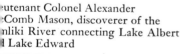

utenant Colonel James M. Morgan,
erpreter for General Loring

utenant Colonel Alexander
Comb Mason, discoverer of the
nliki River connecting Lake Albert
l Lake Edward

Colonel Charles Chaillé-Long, the
discoverer of Lake Kioga

Major General Thaddeus P. Mott,
agent of the khedive

Newspaper correspondents on the "Morris," on their way to Port Said
for the inauguration of the Suez Canal (*Leslie's Magazine,* November 20, 1869)

The Empress Eugenie, seated on a camel, as she appeared at Ismailia
for the opening of the Suez Canal (*Leslie's Magazine,* January 8, 1870)

Colonel Beverly Kennon, designer of coastal defenses

Major William P. A. Campbell, who went to Sudan with General "Chinese" Gordon

Guests arriving at Alexandria for the opening of the Suez Canal (*Leslie's Magazine*, November 27, 1869)

General William W. Loring, in charge of coastal defense

Colonel Raleigh R. Colston, on expedition to Kordofan

Major E. Sparrow Purdy, who explored Darfur

Egyptian troops at gun drill in an Egyptian port during British bombing of
Alexandria (*London Graphic*, July 8, 1882)

The Citadel, Cairo, under British occupation (*London Graphic*,
September 8, 1882)

General William W. Loring poses with visiting General Ulysses S. Grant at the Pyramids, 1878 (courtesy, Florida State Museum, Gainesville)

have complete control of all military units and establishments along the entire northern seacoast. Ismail sat quietly, studying him with his half-opened eye, interrupting to ask searching questions about forts, defenses, military organization. At last he spoke. He was persuaded and convinced. He turned to the minister of war, speaking slowly, first in Arabic and then in French. He placed Loring in complete command of the coast and ordered him to report directly, without the intervention of the officials in the Citadel, to the khedive.

Already Loring had moved to Alexandria. Now he took over the Gabbari, or "stranger's palace," a rambling, baroque, jerry-built structure of which he was inordinately proud. From here he directed the construction of coast defenses from Alexandria to Aboukir and on to Rosetta. Frequently he left his ramshackle palace with its gaudy grounds and furnishings to travel over his domain. He watched the fellahin soldiers, more accustomed to spades than to guns, dig the excavations for gun emplacements or drag stones for the battlements that stood above the blue waters of the Mediterranean. As he watched, he may have been reminded that the remote ancestors of these men had dragged across the desert the huge stones for the Great Pyramid just as their descendants were now erecting these monuments to Ismail. Turning from the laborers, Loring visited their officers, drank formal tea, smoked ceremonial cigarettes with his subordinates, and with more success than he had anticipated instilled some efficiency, pride of workmanship, and even a degree of patriotic devotion in them. At Rosetta, near the eastern end of his journeys, he halted to consult with General Sibley, who acted as a sort of chief foreman and district supervisor.

Loring and Sibley had come to Egypt together, and together they had devised the complete plans for the coastal defense of Egypt. At the western end of the Bay of Alexandria they built fortifications and mounted large caliber guns that could, they thought, withstand any naval attack. From Alexandria eastward they planned a line of hidden forts, stretching thirty miles to Rosetta, each of which would mount a single high-powered gun. The forts would be so close together that they could effectively cover the entire coast.

For the scheme itself and for its practical operation Loring was indebted to another Confederate officer, Colonel Beverly Kennon. The scheme was, in truth, grandiose enough to appeal to Kennon's imagination. During the Civil War Kennon had demonstrated his valor in combat as he pushed his ship, the "General Moore," into the battles below New Orleans. In addition he had demonstrated a prodigality that horrified his tightfisted superiors. In August, 1861, he had taken charge of the ordnance department at New Orleans and had shown aggressiveness, ingenuity, and imagination. He had found war material in such short supply that he could scarcely meet the local demand and had nothing for other naval bases. He promptly took matters into his own hands, set up a factory to produce cartridge bags and rifle shells, stockpiled tin and lead for casting cannon, and contracted for the repair of ships and the purchase of steamers for the navy. In his haste he ignored regulations for proper requisitions and for the approval of his superiors. "I knew if I allowed myself to be held down by rules," he told a congressional investigating committee, "I would never have done anything." The Secretary of the Navy was alarmed at the mounting costs of Kennon's ordnance station. He sent an investigator who, in his turn, was shocked, and recommended replacing Kennon with someone more mindful of regulations.

Egypt could use men of Kennon's imagination and energy, and it was not long after his arrival that he appeared as colonel of ordnance on Loring's staff in Alexandria. Here red tape and navy regulations were no longer in the way, and his commanding officer took no mean and petty view of his projects. Loring admired Kennon, and when the ingenious Virginian elaborated extensive plans for encircling Alexandria with a system of railroads, Loring set about building them. Then when Kennon devised his "disappearing forts," Loring gave him a free hand.

The distinctive feature of Kennon's forts was that they were to be completely hidden. He planned to sink them in the sand, hiding them so well that they would completely escape observation. Then he devised machinery that would lift to the surface the high-powered gun in each fort. Once fired, the gun would seem as suddenly to disappear into the earth. With Loring's enthusiastic support Kennon constructed his first fort with its jack-in-the-box, breech-loading cannon at Ras et-tin on the outskirts of Alexandria. To protect the fort from the shells of invaders, he topped it with a conical hood. Officers, Egyptian and American, came to observe and to admire it, and Kennon looked forward to lining the coast with his gun emplacements. But once again his ingenuity and aggressiveness were halted by pecuniary considerations.

The khedive, for all the world like the Confederate Secretary of the Navy years before, was operating with a dwindling treasury. He was having difficulties meeting his payments to European creditors and to his grasping superior in Constantinople, and he reluctantly stopped the building of the forts. Even so, he rewarded Kennon with a decoration—the Order of Medjidie, Third Class—"for ingenuity, activity and perseverance displayed." But the building of forts came to an end. Kennon stayed another year in Egypt and then, in 1874, bored with inactivity, resigned and returned to America. His fort remained, slowly choking with sand; but it was the only Egyptian battery to survive the British bombardment of Alexandria in 1882.

Despite the frequent calls for economy, Loring proceeded with the construction of coastal defenses. In addition to Sibley and Kennon, he had the services in various capacities of a number of the Americans. Two were father and son, Colonels Alexander W. Reynolds and Frank A. Reynolds of the Confederate Army. Both were West Pointers, the son having the dubious distinction of having outranked only George A. Custer in the graduating class of 1861. Frank Reynolds served three weeks in the United States Army, resigned for the Confederacy, and rose to a colonelcy before peace cut short his military career. His father, "Old Gauley" to his soldiers, had been in the old army and was mustered out of it when discrepancies developed in his accounts. In the Confederacy he was a brigadier general through the Chickamauga and Atlanta campaigns. After the war he joined his wife in Philadelphia— where she had sat looking after her property while her husband and son were in the Confederate Army—and sought suitable employment. Neither father nor son had found work fitted to their talents when the Egyptian offer came. In addition, Colonel Vanderbilt Allen, whose social position had given him a place on Sheridan's staff, worked for Loring as a topographical engineer.

Loring's staff consisted entirely of Americans. Loring himself studied diligently but never learned to speak Arabic, and his French was completely undependable. Old Blizzards could storm effectively only in English. Yet, despite his linguistic deficiencies, he was the only American officer in Egypt who had direct command of any considerable body of Egyptian troops. On his trips of inspection and on his ceremonial social contacts with his native subordinates he depended on interpreters. Sometimes he had more trouble with them than with any other part of his command.

For a time Loring's interpreter was the perennial juvenile, James Morris Morgan, who had the uncanny ability of getting into situations which pointed up the differences between Eastern and Western culture. Morgan was young, vigorous, and enthusiastic. A sixteen-year-old midshipman at Annapolis when the Civil War began, Morgan promptly transferred to a Confederate training ship. During the war years he strutted in the battles below New Orleans, went in high spirits to England to speed the freshly cut Great Seal of the Confederacy to the new government, cut a dashing figure as a gallant young officer in social circles in Richmond and Charleston, fell in love with the daughter of Confederate Treasury Secretary George Trenholm, and was one of Mrs. Jefferson Davis' escorts on the last flight from Richmond. After the war he married Helen Trenholm, who died. He failed as a cotton planter, failed again at raising potatoes. Then Egypt beckoned, and he rushed away impetuously, determined to astonish the Orient.

Perhaps Morgan's picture of himself as the Southern gallant would have brought him troubles anywhere in the world —including the defunct Confederacy—but in Egypt he showed a complete incapacity for adjustment to the mores of a strange people. He picked up a smattering of Arabic, just enough to make himself useful to Loring, but with it he acquired no useful understanding of the Egyptian way of life. Loring, in his capacity as inspector general of infantry, unwisely used him as an assistant. Morgan promptly went looking for trouble and as promptly found it.

One morning, in company with Loring, he inspected a regiment in the suburbs of Cairo. It was very early, and Morgan was amazed at the number of soldiers who were taking that hour for their morning devotions. Mohammedans, of course, could pray whenever they chose, and no man might interfere with them as they faced the east and addressed Allah. But Morgan, who had seen much of "soldiering," suspected that those men who were so devoutly seeking spiritual consolation at this hour were the very ones whose guns would not pass inspection. He reported as much to Loring, who in turn reported it to the minister of war, who took it up with the commander of the regiment.

The commander, unfortunately, was Arabi Bey, as devout a Son of the Prophet as any man in Egypt. Years later he would lead a nativist revolt in an attempt to overthrow the foreigners who infested his land. He was a large man, over six feet tall, lithe and active, gentle in manner, but reserved in the presence of foreigners. Above all, he was religious. Like Loring's Arab adjutant Lutfi Bey, he prayed five times each day. Strictly adhering to the rules, he approached the throne of

Allah only after washing himself—first the right hand and arm to the elbow, saying a prayer, then the left, then the right side of the face, the left side, the right foot and leg to the knee, the left foot—and with each ceremonial ablution the appropriate prayer; then, standing on his rug, eyes toward Mecca and arms uplifted to Heaven, another prayer; then another, with hands on knees, then with forehead touching the ground, and then, sitting on his ankles, another to complete the ritual. Loring had observed the bey's devotions but dismissed them as sheer superstition, as did Morgan. He little realized how offended his colonel would be at Morgan's imputations.

When the minister of war summoned Arabi, the pious bey promptly lost his amiable manner. The accusation, he said with high indignation, was gross evidence of the religious prejudice of the Americans. Unable to counter the charge, the minister of war called in Loring, and Loring carried to Morgan the message that if he expected to remain in Egypt he would have to drop some of his Christian intolerance. Morgan, as became a Southern gentleman, promptly flared in rage. Then he became amused. It was the first time he had been suspected of harboring an excess of Christian zeal.

But Loring was angry, too, and he ordered Morgan to inspect Arabi's regiment again the next day. Again Morgan went early in the morning, and again a large number of devout Mussulmen took the hour of inspection for the hour of prayer. This time Morgan seized a half-dozen guns and bore them off to the Citadel. The guns proved his point. They were filthy. But by this time the condition of the arms was the least of it. The minister of war was as angry as the storming Arabi, and Morgan got another lecture on religious tolerance. A few days later Loring sent him off to inspect rusty cannon at Rosetta.

Still, despite such incidents, Loring got along well enough with his command. He worked as steadily as finances would allow on the defenses of Alexandria, inspected his troops, and enjoyed his palace with its moth-eaten rugs, faded brocades, and ragged divans. Morgan, who thought the place had not been swept since the days of the Pharaohs, objected to the fleas, flies, and scorpions that shared the residence, but Loring was happy with it. He found his staff congenial, and he and General Alexander Reynolds never missed the Bairam fetes and the khedivial dinners in Cairo.

In Alexandria the Reynolds families—Mrs. Alexander Reynolds, whom Old Gauley always referred to as the duchess, and son Frank's wife and boy had come to Egypt—were the center of a cozy circle. In the spring of 1873, when Dr. Edward Warren, sometime surgeon general of Confederate North Carolina, arrived for a tumultuous career in Egypt, he found the Reynoldses living in the palace and keeping house for Loring. For three weeks Warren was a guest and was as impressed as Loring with the palace. Perhaps it was the iced champagne which, by his story, he drank steadily that led him to think it "gorgeous, with mirrors, marble floors, panels of porphyry, mosaics, divans, carpets, and all that can be conceived of Oriental luxury." He was impressed by the murmuring fountains, the fruits and flowers, and by the broad avenue of mimosa trees that led to the palace. There the Allens and Kennon and W. P. A. Campbell made a delightful company.

Charming, too, until disasters overwhelmed them, were the Hunts. Cornelius Hunt arrived in Egypt in the spring of 1870 and soon sent back to Connecticut for his fiancée. Sarah Keables arrived in November, and the union of the Virginia sailor and the Yankee maid was duly solemnized before the American consul, with all the officers in Loring's entourage and a goodly group from Cairo to sign the marriage certificate and to toast the couple in iced champagne amid the fountains at Gabbari Palace.

On the whole, those stationed in Alexandria were happier than were their colleagues in Cairo. And the khedive was pleased with the command on the Mediterranean. He promoted Loring, conferred decorations on him and his associ-

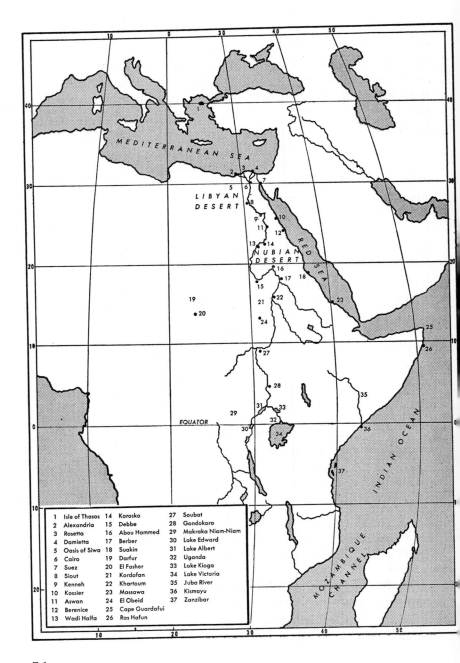

1	Isle of Thasos	14	Korosko	27	Soubat
2	Alexandria	15	Debbe	28	Gondokoro
3	Rosetta	16	Abou Hammed	29	Makraka Niam-Niam
4	Damietta	17	Berber	30	Lake Edward
5	Oasis of Siwa	18	Suakin	31	Lake Albert
6	Cairo	19	Darfur	32	Uganda
7	Suez	20	El Fasher	33	Lake Kioga
8	Siout	21	Kordofan	34	Lake Victoria
9	Kenneh	22	Khartoum	35	Juba River
10	Kossier	23	Massawa	36	Kismayu
11	Aswan	24	El Obeid	37	Zanzibar
12	Berenice	25	Cape Guardafui		
13	Wadi Halfa	26	Ras Hafun		

ates, and rested content in the belief that that part of his army and his country were in good hands and secure position.

While Loring and his staff in Alexandria were looking after the coast defenses of Egypt, General Charles P. Stone was undertaking the more extensive task of reorganizing the entire Egyptian army. In the beginning, when Loring and Sibley were newly arrived on the Nile, the khedive and General Mott undertook to direct their services. The khedive and Khahin Pasha, the minister of war, sent out Sibley as inspector of artillery and Loring as inspector general of the armies. The war ministry assigned new arrivals to their duties. Kennon, for example, went up the Nile on a hydraulic survey. But such a system of assignment was hardly a system, and Loring's first report called attention to its inadequacies. He proposed the appointment of a chief of staff, and shortly after Stone arrived in the spring of 1870 the khedive—with no understanding of the nature of such a post—assigned him to its duties. As they began to plan for the reorganization of the army and the expansion of the empire, Stone missed no opportunity of telling His Highness what a chief of staff and a general staff should do.

His way was made easier by Thaddeus Mott's fall from grace. Mott was on the khedive's personal staff and nominally a general of cavalry and artillery. He was the khedive's personal adviser in all that related to the American officers. But to some people Mott seemed to have additional interests. Lord Lyons, the British minister in Washington, watching with skeptical eye the migration of American officers to Egypt, suspected that Mott was involved in a speculative scheme for the selling of arms to Ismail. Partner in the speculation, Lyons suspected, was Massachusetts Congressman and ex-Major General Benjamin F. ("Beast") Butler. When Butler's nephew, Colonel George H. Butler, appeared in Alexandria as the American consul general, the British foreign office was certain of a conspiracy. Whatever the connection with General

Butler and a deal in arms might have been, it was shortly apparent that Colonel Butler and Mott were on the most friendly terms. But Butler was a true Butler, with a flair for controversy that resembled his Uncle Ben's. Within a month he was in a row with American residents in Alexandria, was pushing a dubious claim of dubious Americans against the khedive, and had won Ismail's disgusted enmity. When Mott defended Butler, the khedive lost confidence in him. When Khahin Pasha and Mott clashed over Mott's attempts to interfere in the assignment of Americans, Ismail lost all patience. Mott returned to America, sent back some more recruits, and, out of favor at court, quit the service. The beneficiary was General Stone, who had sided with Khahin. He replaced Mott as the khedive's adviser on military matters.

Stone's position depended as much upon his confidential relations with the khedive as upon his official position. He was loyal, and his devotion to his ruler made him completely trustworthy. Ismail appreciated him, confided in him, elevated him to the rank of Ferik Pasha, decorated him, and followed his advice. Slowly it dawned upon the officials of Egypt that a new power had unobtrusively risen in the land. Throughout the rest of Ismail's reign and through the days of his successor, Stone Pasha gave loyal advice and service.

Perhaps, indeed, only a man of Stone's background could have undertaken his double duties as confidential adviser and chief of staff. But Stone was determined to succeed and to remove the shadow that still darkened his Civil War record. Here in this foreign land he had a wholly new environment in which to prove his ability, judgment, and capacity for leadership. No item which might affect the fortunes of his new master was too small for his attention, no task too burdensome to tackle. Withal, he had to display the agility of an acrobat and the balance of a tightrope walker. He had to deal, at one and the same time, with the army, with Egyptians who suspected all foreigners, and with Americans who suspected all Egyptians. The confidence that Ismail bestowed on him was at once a source of strength and a cause of trouble.

The army over which Stone came to preside numbered perhaps 40,000 men in the ranks. They were conscripts drawn mostly from the rural villages. The ranks were kept filled by calling on the governors of provinces who, in turn, called on the sheiks of the villages for the number of recruits required. The sheiks, using force when necessary, gathered the fellahin from the fields. The more apt among the village rulers usually called for more than their quota and permitted the excess to purchase exemptions. The unlucky remainder went away to the army, linked alternately by their right or left hands to a chain, usually fifty feet long, which ran between the files. Once they were enrolled, they were to remain in the army, but some received indefinite furloughs for agricultural work, to be recalled to the colors when need arose. Thus there were, by the time the Americans came to Egypt, perhaps sixty thousand of these "trained" men in reserve.

In the army the soldiers received pay equivalent to one American dollar a month—which was perhaps as much as they might have saved beyond living expenses in civilian employment. Their food was adequate, their clothing better than they were accustomed to. Punishments were severe—hard labor in ball and chain or exile to service in the Sudan. With discipline good, and competent instruction in the manual of arms and in parade-ground marching, the units of the army made an impressive appearance. Observers were likely to exclaim that they looked to be the finest body of soldiers in the world. "They would charge the gates of darkness," exclaimed a visiting American—who was not, incidentally, a military man.

This was the infantry. Both the cavalry and the artillery were also likely to inspire favorable comments from uninformed observers. The cavalry was Bedouin, recruited from the desert and proud of its horsemanship. The artillery owed its distinction to careful selection. Ophthalmia, as has been said, was the prevailing disease in Egypt, and the average infantryman was afflicted with poor eyesight. Artillerymen, however, were chosen from the ranks for their power of vision, and in every battery there was at least one man able to sight a gun. Neither cavalry nor artillery was organized as a separate unit but was attached to the divisions.

The officers of the army in the higher ranks were Turks or Circassians, but Ismail had opened the lower grades, even those of colonel or bey, to the fellahin. Arabi Bey, who commanded the regiment which Morgan thought showed excessive religious zeal, and Lutfi Bey, Loring's adjutant, had been born in mud huts in distant villages and had risen to high rank through energy and devotion. Even Ratib Pasha, the commander of the army, had been born a slave. Only about one-third of the officers of all grades, Stone discovered, could read and write.

Stone's first job, and the first job of the early arrivals among the Americans, was to learn the nature and organization of the Egyptian army. The khedive, Mott, and Khahin Pasha assigned the first Americans to duties for which they were presumed competent. Old Gauley Reynolds found himself assigned as quartermaster, commissary officer, and paymaster general in an army where none of these functions had ever been performed by a single head. Loring started as an inspector general of infantry, Sibley as inspector general of artillery. Thomas Rhett, onetime aid and adjutant to Joseph E. Johnston of the Confederate Army, was chief of ordnance—and set about building a powder plant near Cairo. The younger Reynolds was momentarily a colonel of light artillery. Each of the officers reported to Stone, who was nominally chief of staff, but who, in fact, had no power to do anything more than co-ordinate the reports and make recommendations to his superiors. It was only after Stone replaced Mott in the confidence of the khedive that he was able to put his recommendations into practice.

Stone wanted, the Americans with him wanted, and the khedive thought he wanted a complete reorganization and

modernization of the Egyptian army. But in the way of reform stood the pasha system, to which every officer of the
Egyptian army was attached. Under this system each unit of
the army was an independent command and its commanding
pasha was free from all responsibility except to the khedive
and the minister of war. Within his unit he performed all
functions. He was commissary officer making requisitions and
purchases, quartermaster issuing supplies, commander issuing
orders, adjutant transmitting them, and judge advocate pun-
ishing their infraction. The commanding pasha was in a position of power, and he wanted no interference with his command. In battle his men fought, if they fought at all, through
loyalty, or interest, or fear of him. The general in chief,
Ratib, sat on commissions and in conferences when someone remembered to call him, but he never pretended to issue
an order. When Lieutenant Colonel Chaillé-Long received
orders to report to Ratib as an aide, he dressed himself in
his full-dress gold-embroidered uniform and reported for duty. Ratib was confused and more than a little annoyed by the
sudden implication that he needed a staff. "It is true that I
am general in chief," he said ruefully, "but I have no headquarters, nor yet a staff. If I should have want of you later, I
will write to you." Whatever work was done in the department was done by the minister of war, and orders that went
to the army were merely sealed by Ratib's Coptic clerks. The
minister himself, used to doing business in this way, regarded
all changes as infringements on his prerogatives.

The key to the organization of the Egyptian army lay not
in the pashas themselves or in the direct chain of command
that led from individual units straight into the Ministry of
War. The key was the clerk—a civilian, a civil servant, and
incidentally a Coptic Christian, whose peculiar merit was his
ability to read, write, and keep books. They swarmed in both
the army and the civil establishment, ubiquitous, scheming
like petty members of the bureaucracy to hold their jobs and
to advance in favor. Illiterate officers were completely de-

pendent on them, and lazy officers entrusted their duties to the clerks. Having entrenched themselves with their pens, they resisted with intrigues every reform that might threaten their position. With their ability to influence the pashas, they formed a solid phalanx against modernization.

Early in his career Stone realized that he could not expect to have his American officers in direct command of Egyptian troops. Loring was successful enough in Alexandria where he and his staff could direct engineering operations. But the Americans were better as instructors and inspectors. They were not fitted for positions in the line. For a time Colonel Walter H. Jenifer, who commanded troops in the Confederate Army and had been an inspector of cavalry along the Gulf coast, took over a command of cavalry in Egypt. But there was little indeed that a Maryland cavalier could teach an Arab horseman. Jenifer and the Bedouins did not get along, and when Jenifer complained to the Ministry of War about the unruly conduct of his fighting men, Stone realistically supported the Bedouins. Jenifer asked for and got a furlough to go home and went off in a huff. Back in Maryland he found another job, resigned his commission in Egypt, and ever after damned Stone for having betrayed him to his enemies.

Such experiences were enough to confirm Stone in his judgment that the Americans ought not to have line commands. Besides, in his judgment the American officers could be more effective as instructors, as staff officers, as technical engineers. For a time, at least until a new military crisis led to the importation of more fighting men, Stone selected and brought to Egypt only administrators, engineers, and men of proved competence in technical work.

His first task, and one at which he worked steadily during his dozen years in Egypt, was to build a general staff. A chief of staff clearly needed a staff through which all plans and programs for the army could clear. A general staff, Stone explained to the khedive and through him to all the army, could serve the army by relieving the commanders of the details of supplying ordnance and commissary, could serve as an intelligence division, could channel communications between commanders and subordinates, and could keep records. Moreover, as Stone went on to spell out the duties in detail, the general staff could train experts in map making, in engineering, and in bookkeeping.

The theory of the general staff was clear enough and, even though the minister of war regarded it with jealous skepticism, the khedive gave his approval. On paper Stone organized a general staff: a judge advocate's department, another concerned with inspection duties, and others for supply, for orders and correspondence, for general engineering, for mapping and surveying. In actual fact, most of the sections received only the most tentative organization. Stone was never able to get a supply section organized and implemented; the beys and pashas who purchased supplies for their separate and scattered regiments, and their Coptic clerks who profited with them in the contracts, were adamant in their opposition. Nor was a judge advocate's office feasible: there was no code of military conduct, certainly none that an American could understand, in operation in the Egyptian army. To Americans it seemed that military justice depended on religious rules that appeared absurd, or on favoritism and bribery.

Another section, devoted to engineering projects and training, had a nominal existence. In theory, Rhett's powder plant and Kennon's and Allen's engineering duties came within the jurisdiction of the Seventh Section; so, too, did the artillery training school at Aboukir under Cornelius Hunt, and the efforts of Edmund Parys to organize a signal corps. In fact, they fell under the general direction of the local commanders. The Americans duly made their reports to the general staff and took their orders from the commanders or directly from the ministry.

Gradually, only work of a highly specialized and technical nature was left to the general staff, and it fell under the direction of the Third Section. Strictly speaking, the Third Section was concerned with mapping and surveying, but it assumed a wider range of duties. Its first chief was E. Sparrow Purdy, scion of a governor of California, who had been with Stone on surveys of Sonora and Lower California, had fought the Civil War valiantly at a desk in the Military Department of the Pacific, and who had come with Stone from New York. He got some of the work organized before he went off for important surveys in the Sudan. For a time Colonel William McE. Dye had charge, and finally Samuel H. Lockett supervised the work of the Third Section—which by that time had merged with the engineering section. But, whatever the name, the work of exploration and mapping became the major work of the general staff. Stone gave it his greatest attention, and increasingly the graduates of the staff college moved into its program. Its best work was in exploration. Starting in 1873, Stone began to send out small exploring teams to map the far-flung holdings of the khedive. For the most part, the smaller expeditions were geodetic and astronomical surveys, but they also laid out routes for roads and railroads, for irrigation works, and for projected reclamation works, and they searched out artesian wells, oil, salt, and mines.

Two examples of the extreme ranges of the work of some of the Americans under the direction of the Third Section were the expeditions of two Confederate graduates of Annapolis, Colonels Charles Iverson Graves and William Ward. Ward, whose official title was lieutenant colonel of marines, proved himself generally useful in Egypt. He learned Arabic early and thereby drew some of the more interesting assignments. He was, for example, General William T. Sherman's guide and monitor when the American general visited Egypt in 1872. In the summer of 1875 he went to survey the island of Thasos, which Egypt owned, in the Grecian archipelago. Ismail hoped to extract a revenue from the island, and Ward made an extensive survey and presented an exhaustive report on the island's resources and opportunities. He looked into the ancient silver mines and suggested new methods for working them. He found possibilities for marble quarries, copper mines, timber production, and the growing of olives. He reported on the condition of the harbors and outlined the steps necessary to improve them. He submitted a map, supplementary information on the island's antiquities, and observations on its inhabitants. His report was a model, equal to the best that were coming from simultaneous explorations in Darfur and Kordofan.

Colonel Graves made almost the last survey and report contributed by the Americans in the service of the khedive. In 1878 he set out on a reconnaissance expedition to Cape Guardafui at the southern end of the Red Sea to find a place for a lighthouse to guide commercial steamers from the Indian Ocean into the Gulf of Aden. His reports and maps, filled with information on shipping routes, details of the coastline, observations on winds and currents, and containing plans for a lighthouse and garrison, delighted Ismail. For his efforts Graves received one of the last decorations given to the Americans.

Yet for all the effort Stone expended on getting a general staff organized for the Egyptian army and for all the success the general staff might claim for explorations—not only on the coasts but in the more important expeditions into the Upper Nile and the southern deserts—the general staff, the *état major*, was never successfully integrated into the Egyptian military establishment. Eventually the general staff became merely a repository of unpublished reports and, unable to combat the pasha system, degenerated into what Lockett described as a "miserable farce" in which all were "playing roles."

Realizing that a frontal attack on the pasha system involved a long and bitter struggle, Stone began an oblique assault upon it at its key position. The key was the Coptic clerk with the enormous power that literacy and a knack for bookkeeping gave him. From the beginning Stone had seen that education was the crying need of the Egyptian army and of Egypt in general. In August, 1870, well before he suggested the creation of a general staff, Stone began his long battle against the Coptic clerks. "What is wrong with the Egyptian army?" asked the khedive after Stone had made his preliminary surveys and read the reports of the inspecting Americans who had visited army outposts. Stone had the answer ready. "The worst evil," he replied promptly, "is that all the clerks, whether company or battalion, are civilians." All paper work, and therefore the entire administration of the organization, was done by them. If only the noncommissioned officers and the privates could read and write, civilian company clerks could be eliminated.

Ismail, who prided himself on his educational reforms, was impressed by Stone's opinion. He sent for the minister of war and with him drafted an order to the army. Henceforth no man, whether commissioned or noncommissioned, would be promoted unless he could read and write.

With this accomplished, Stone presented his solution to the problem. He proposed, and the khedive approved, the establishment of a school in each battalion in the army. One and a half hours each day, in addition to regular duties, were to be devoted to teaching the soldiers to read and write. The results, to the combined amazement and consternation of the Coptic clerks, were soon apparent. Within four years, Stone proudly reported, 76 per cent of the army was literate.

As the battalion schools got under way, Stone had another proposal. He suggested the establishment of a noncommissioned officers' school, drawing a sergeant and a corporal from each company. This made a school of fifteen hundred, organized in the barracks attached to the war office in Cairo. Here the men learned reading, writing, and arithmetic and, more important, the keeping of company and regimental books. Moreover, Stone saw that they were organized into two model battalions and instructed in drill and in what the Americans considered the rudiments of military discipline. As soon as the men were prepared, they returned to their regiments and their replacements arrived from the companies.

One unexpected development came from the noncommissioned officers' school. The arriving sergeants and corporals brought their families to Cairo with them and when they appeared in the classrooms their sons accompanied them. Instead of ousting them, the officers instructed the children as well as the fathers. Both Stone and the khedive were inspired by this eagerness for education, and Stone pressed for the establishment in each division of special schools for teaching the sons of soldiers. It would not be charity, Stone told the khedive, but it was a demonstration of "the express right of a soldier to have his son educated." Ismail was delighted, and in 1873 the schools were opened. New school buildings arose on the sun-baked plains near each division headquarters, and boys from the barracks, clad in clean clothes and fed a noonday meal, were instructed by officers of the army. The cost of the schools was low—the equivalent of $75,000 a year— and Stone and the American officers had high hopes that they would accomplish the "leveling" and "civilizing" of Egypt. From his office in the Citadel, Samuel Lockett often watched *les enfants militaires* at the nearby school. There were eight hundred of them between seven and fourteen years of age, dressed in white uniforms in European style. They were, he declared, "a great improvement upon the pig-tailed turbaned little rascals of the streets." In fact, he concluded, "the Army here is the great civilizer, and Generals Stone and Loring have been its teachers."

At the same time that Stone was attempting to encourage army schools, he was attempting to improve the army with a staff college and to improve the khedivial system of military schools from among whose top graduates he hoped to recruit students for the staff college. Soon after his arrival in Egypt in 1875, Lockett, West Point graduate and instructor who just before coming to Egypt had had his own military school, visited the academy in Cairo. He found the several schools for the engineers, cavalry, artillery, and infantry housed in a long, unattractive single-storied building surrounding a courtyard. The classrooms were large and airy and adequately equipped.

The students were "a very good-looking set of young Arabs, about the color of a genuine mulatto, straight, well-formed, and neat looking in their white uniforms." But what distressed Lockett was the complete lack of the military discipline for which American military schools were famous. "The professors sit crosslegged on their divans to hear recitations," he exclaimed, "smoke all the time, and frequently have a cup of coffee brought to them during a class." When one cadet recited, the others wandered around, lounged, talked, and paid no attention. "Yet in spite of all this they seem to learn something," Lockett admitted uncomprehendingly. He had, in fact, several of the graduates of this academy working with him on the staff, and he found them intelligent, good draftsmen, acquainted with geometry, and knowledgeable about instruments. The drawings of the engineers, to his surprise, were quite as good as he had ever got in his American classes. "The great trouble in the whole concern is that everything is loose and slack twisted."

Stone and the Americans tried to persuade the Egyptians to adopt the American system of military-school discipline, and they tried to import teachers who would instil in the Egyptian academies the strict codes of West Point, Annapolis, and the Virginia Military Institute. In 1873 Stone brought to Egypt as a professor of geology in the military academy Raleigh Colston, graduate of VMI, professor in the Institute, Confederate general, and head of two military preparatory schools. But Colston was more valuable as an explorer than as a teacher, and he never met a class. He tried to arrange the appointment of David Boyd, head of Louisiana State University and a friend of Lockett and Sherman, but the khedive refused to employ a man who did not have a complete mastery of French. In the end, the military academy failed to receive the benefits of American discipline.

It was in the staff college, to which the better graduates of the military academies were sent, that the Americans gave their instruction to the future leaders of the Egyptian army. There,

The Americans at Work

building upon the foundations already laid, the Americans gave the fledgling staff officers intensive work in practical mathematics, surveying, map making, and the planning and execution of supply and transportation. On leaving the staff college the graduates served on the staffs of American officers who closely supervised their further training. Loring gave "unremitting care and attention" (or so he claimed) to their proper indoctrination. Lockett undertook to lead his young men through the intricacies of draftsmanship. He found them intelligent and painstaking but slow and incapable of speed and independent judgment. Yet he and the others persevered—pressing on in the hope that these young staffers would reform the army.

Yet when the young staff officers returned to the army, eager to apply the lessons they had learned from the Americans, they found prolonged contact with the foreigners a disadvantage. Their less able classmates from the military academy had gained a year's seniority, and the pashas were suspicious of innovations. The graduates of the staff college came to believe themselves the victims of discrimination.

Despite some lingering doubts about the reception of the American trainees, the Americans were convinced that they had improved the condition of the Egyptian army. They had inspected and reported endlessly; they had instructed the artillery, the cavalry, and the engineers. They had raised the level of literacy in the army, replaced substantial numbers of civilian clerks, and improved the drill of the men in the ranks. "As far as I can see," declared Lockett after the Americans had been at work for five years, "the army, both officers and men, are pretty well up to the standard of that of our country." The soldiers, wrote Colston, were "the most orderly and quiet in the world. They never fight among themselves, never drink anything but water." They were strong, able to endure fatigue. To the Americans who looked at the troops after their first five years in Egypt, it seemed indeed that they had made an army upon the best European and American models.

V

wwwwwwww

Delta Days

The men who made up Stone's staff of co-workers had been
selected for their technical capacities. They had been educated, many of them, in the service academies of the United
States and had experienced the American Civil War. They
had not been selected because they were congenial one with
another or because their personalities were harmonious. In
fact, since their tasks were different, it was not surprising that
their tastes were different. They were men of various traits:
plodding technicians without imagination, romantics with excess imaginations and little technical competence, well-rounded
citizens with balance and judgment, and odd fellows who
would have been misfits in any society. In some respects they
resembled the assortment of eccentrics thrown together in a
frontier post in the days of the old American army.

As they would have done in a frontier army post, they
worked together—and in a strange and unfamiliar environment.
The general staff occupied a wing of the Citadel—the wing
which Mehemet Ali had set aside for the harem—and some of
the Americans thought that they could detect lingering reminders of its former occupants. Actually, the rooms in which
they worked were great barren spaces more reminiscent of the
outlying desert than of the trappings of oriental luxury with
which the general staff furnished them in their imaginings. To
the great fortress the Americans made their way each morning by nine-thirty. It was about a forty-five-minute walk
from the neighborhood of the Ezbekiyeh Gardens, and most
of the officers hired a donkey for the trip.

One officer reported, "My legs would have dragged the ground if the stirrups had not been short—and away we started, two wild Arabs following and urging up our steeds with all sorts of yells and screams. Away we flew through crowded and crooked streets, our brave and amiable little donkeys threading their way through motley crowds of people, carriages and camels, now almost running over an Arab baby, and now almost being run down by a huge camel. I gave that donkey my confidence from the first. I did not pretend to use the reins, but to indicate to him the street—all the dangerous and intricate details of the navigation he managed himself."

The workday ran from nine-thirty until noon and from one until five o'clock. For the most part they dealt with papers—maps and reports and the elaborate plans that passed over their desks, to rest, unimplemented, across the court in the offices of the minister of war. Each American had a seal ring with which he stamped documents. The ring worn by Charles Iverson Graves had his full name in Arabic, together with his rank and a rampant lion and a unicorn. He stamped it proudly on each letter he wrote home to his wife, but only one initiated into its mysteries would have been able to determine what the blue blobs signified. The seal was as important as the tarboosh in identifying them as high officers of the khedive.

In August, 1875, when Graves arrived in Cairo, the routine of work at the Citadel had long been established. On his first day he reported to General Stone, received a cordial greeting, and set forth to meet the other Americans on the general staff. There were ten officers stationed in Cairo, and another dozen were a part of Loring's command on the Mediterranean or exploring the boundaries of Egypt in the Sudan and up the Nile beyond Khartoum. This was the average number of Americans in the khedive's service at any one time and the normal distribution of men between the capital and the field. For the most part those in Cairo were only temporarily assigned to the Citadel; from time to time the personnel changed, with some officers going on scientific missions and others coming in to

186898

write their reports and draw maps of the lands they had surveyed.

Charles Iverson Graves had been selected for the Egyptian army because he was an experienced engineer. A native of Georgia, he had gone to Annapolis as an appointee of Alexander H. Stephens. He graduated, high in his class, in 1858, and took his first cruise on the "Iroquois." A handsome man, charming in manner, with a taste for literature and a flair for writing, he made the most of his talents on his cruise in European waters. He wrote charming letters for publication in the newspapers of Rome, Georgia, gained entree to society in European ports, and once met Garibaldi and brought back an autographed picture Italy's revolutionary leader had given him. On return from his first cruise he visited relatives in North Carolina and there met his cousin Maggie Lea, as beautiful as he was handsome. Before he returned to his ship there was an "understanding" between them. The understanding almost became a misunderstanding when Georgia seceded and there came no news that Graves had resigned from the American navy. He was, in fact, on a cruise in the Pacific, and it was months before he was able to return to Washington and make his way to Richmond to enter the Confederate service. Upon their marriage, Graves took his bride "Chichi" to the Gulf, where he was to serve on a ship guarding the entrance to Mobile Bay. He was next sent to England, brought back a blockade runner from France, and was assigned to the staff of the Confederate Naval Academy, a training ship anchored in the waters of the James. Chichi with her first-born joined him in wartime Richmond and on the flight from the doomed city accompanied Mrs. Jefferson Davis under a guard of naval cadets.

After the war Graves tried to farm and for almost a decade struggled to grow cotton. Four more children came, and cotton prices remained high, but in the spring of 1874 a flash flood wiped out his hopes. Egypt seemed an answer. He sought an appointment, accepted Stone's offer of a commission as a lieutenant colonel at $2,500 a year in gold, and went to Egypt, as he said, "for the same reason that Joseph's brothers went—to get corn for my family." The family, Chichi and her five children, went back to her mother in North Carolina.

In Egypt Graves did not lose sight of his purpose for a moment. He lived economically, drinking not at all and entertaining modestly, and went to the opera only when given a free ticket. Regularly he sent money home to reduce the mortgage on his farm. He reserved his severest strictures for those of his fellow officers who mismanaged their private finances. There were, as it turned out, a great many whose Egyptian careers were marked by extravagance and debt.

Immediately after leaving Stone and meeting his fellow officers at the Citadel, Graves set out to find a room. He found one in "a delightful part of the city" near the Ezbekiyeh Gardens. It was furnished with a single bed, a marble-topped bureau, three chairs, a washstand, a center table, and a divan. For it he paid $14.50 a month. He took his meals at a restaurant—"the cheapest respectable restaurant in Cairo"—for breakfast getting coffee, bread, four boiled eggs ("eggs are small in Egypt"), grapes, and "a glass of lemonade made with limes." Dinner, which he invariably took under the trees where he could listen to the band concert in the gardens, was on the same scale. For his meals he paid $17.10 a month. Board and room came to $31.60, and he calculated carefully in the hope that he could reduce it to $28. For his personal expenses he allowed himself $480 per year. In Rome, Georgia, his creditors were pressing, and in North Carolina his wife, whose allotment was $50 a month, was nursing the hope that if things went right with the mortgage she might join her husband in Cairo.

Graves wrote encouragingly. For three years he kept promising that next month, maybe—next quarter, certainly—he would be able to send for her. In the meantime he examined the living arrangements of other Americans whose families had joined them and made note of the expenses involved.

House rents, he discovered, were high. Vegetables and fruits were cheap, but butter and milk were intolerable in quality—and milk sold for twenty cents a quart! Sugar was ten cents, the best coffee twenty-three cents, bread five cents, and eggs twelve cents a dozen. But always there was an obstacle, and Chichi was not summoned from North Carolina.

In sharp contrast to Graves, whose sense of responsibility and careful economy led to penny-pinching, was Colonel Samuel H. Lockett, who came to Egypt only a few weeks later. Lockett and Graves were to be presented to the khedive at the same audience, but Lockett failed to reach the palace in time for the ceremony. Lockett was a man who summed up in his own person many of the mixed impulses that led veterans of the Civil War to Egypt. He was restless and ambitious, a man of ability who had a record of successive failures—a hopeful, ebullient romantic, who approached new tasks with enthusiasm and quickly became querulous and hypercritical when work became burdensome and the inevitable problems arose. He bore no rankling animosity for the mistreatment he received during the war, but he had a need to reaffirm his steadfastness under difficult circumstances. It was his undoubted ability that led to his call to Egypt. Loring and Stone and Sherman all knew Lockett's work and respected his talents. It was he who built General Loring's fort on the Yazoo and prepared the defenses of Vicksburg. A graduate of West Point in 1858, he had had only a short tour of duty before the war—teaching Spanish at the military academy and as "assistant professor" in the use of small arms. But General Albert Sidney Johnston, of the Confederacy, recognized his abilities and made him chief engineer on his staff at the Battle of Shiloh. After Johnston's fall, Lockett rallied a regiment from disordered retreat and led a new attack. He ended the war with a distinguished record as an engineer.

For a couple of years after the war Lockett taught mathematics and natural science in a college at Marion, Alabama, and for six years was professor of mathematics at Louisiana

State University. For four of those years he was also director of the state's topographical survey. He then became president of struggling Calhoun College at Jacksonville, Alabama. The next year he established a boys' school, the Hamner Military Academy, in Montgomery.

There was one fault to be found with each of these positions—they paid little money. Lockett left Louisiana because his salary was in hopeless arrears, and he left Calhoun College because he could not raise enough money to pay his bills. By the summer of 1874 Mrs. Lockett was supporting the family by giving music lessons, and Lockett was touring as a lecturer on popular science. He barely made expenses. It was then that he was offered a chance to go to Egypt, with a salary of $2,500 in gold. "What do you say to that?" he exuberantly inquired of his old friend David F. Boyd, who was struggling to keep the state university alive. "But for the little wife and babies," he added, "this would be splendid. I am very much tempted anyway."

For months he flirted with temptation. The thought of Egypt did not leave his head. He consulted with Sherman, and he got more details from General Stone in Cairo. Before long he had begun to find a number of reasons why he should take the Egyptian offer. Business had not recovered from the panic of 1873, the Democrats had won the congressional elections of 1874, and the ubiquitous "gentlemen-here-from-Washington-recently" were reporting uneasiness, expectations that the Democrats would try to impeach President Grant, and "actual civil war" between the factions. "Who knows," asked Lockett, "what this year and the next may bring forth?" Sometimes, he admitted, he was much troubled by the uncertainties of the times. Moreover, Mrs. Lockett was adding her bit. She was "all in the notion of going across the waters." Finally, in a long, soul-searching consultation with Professor Boyd, it came out. He was, he admitted, getting tired of "the miserable little petty annoyances of *keeping school.*"

In such a mood, he needed little persuasion. "The pay is

not brilliant," Stone wrote him, "and I wish I could offer you something more worthy of the talent and energy displayed in the defense of Vicksburg and Port Hudson." Egypt, wrote Stone in an appeal to Lockett's romantic streak, "needs solid, serious, earnest soldiers like you to aid the present sovereign in his magnificent efforts to restore her to more than her former glory." Lockett's spirits soared, but his financial condition proved a handicap. At last, dodging creditors while he tried to collect money owed to him, he raised a small amount. He sold his telescope, went to New York, and there scraped together loans from old friends. He got enough to take his family with him, and on July 17, 1875, they boarded a steamer for Europe.

It was a large party that set out. There were seven in the Lockett family. With them was Colonel William McE. Dye, who, after almost a year and a half in Egypt, had come back for his wife and children. There, too, was Colonel Charles Field with Mrs. Field and their children. Colonel Henry C. Derrick, also a Confederate engineer, and German-born Major Charles F. Loshe, whom Sherman was releasing from the army for a foreign stint, brought the number to seventeen. They were, said Lockett, who was no phrasemaker, "seeking the fleshpots of Egypt."

Perhaps the difference between Lockett and Graves was symbolized by their choice of phrases: the search for "corn" was not the same as a longing for the "fleshpots." Lockett had borrowed $1,000 in New York, and he had the Egyptian government's allowance of £75 for his expenses. When he reached Cairo, he had but $15 in his pocket. He went to the Grand New Hotel, where the rates were $4 a head, and before he could find a house for his family he owed more than $80. Again he had to borrow money. Then he moved to quarters on the lower floor of a three-story house. It had a salon, three bedrooms, a dining room, and kitchen, but not a stick of furniture.

While Mrs. Lockett surveyed the inches of dust on the floor, the colonel went searching for furniture. Guided by a dragoman who could speak little English, he made his way to the bazaars, where he made discoveries about Egyptian merchandising. One shop had bedsteads, one chairs, one tables, one washstands, one bedticking, another cotton to stuff the ticking; one had pans, one had frying pans, still another had dustpans. The dragoman produced a porter, who bore the first purchases on his head and followed Lockett from store to store. When the first porter was loaded to capacity, Lockett hired another, and another, and all trailed behind him until the shopping tour was completed. Back at the house the dragoman, now fully master of ceremonies, brought in men to sew the ticking, others to fluff the cotton, others to hook up the bedsteads, and still others to set up the furniture in the manner of the country. There were special workers to put up the water filters and special arrangements to be made with the water-bearers who would bring goatskins of water each morning. For this, Lockett borrowed $300 more, and by the time his family had moved in his debts amounted to $1,400. His rent came to nearly $45 a month, his servants to $15. Because Mrs. Lockett did not learn the mysteries of washing clothes with Egyptian equipment, a laundress was hired for another $15. With an estimated $125 a month for food, water, and fuel, Lockett had a monthly expense of $200—on a salary of $2,500 a year, and a debt of $1,400. "Lockett is beginning to realize," pronounced Graves, "that he made a grand mistake in bringing his family out here without knowing what to expect." And he added, "He and Mrs. Lockett think they're in a bad fix."

The living arrangements of other Americans were less complicated and less expensive. The Locketts' house had been occupied by Major and Mrs. Chancellor Martin, who were going on leave to Europe. The Martins were young, in their twenties, but he had fought Indians on the frontier and she once fought at his side in an all-day battle. They were well connected. His father had been a friend of Lincoln, Grant, and Elihu Washburne. Her people were the Sumners and

Warrens of Boston. For all her experience on the western plains, Mrs. Martin was "given over to fashion" and social pretensions and had a particular aversion to children. "So you may judge," Graves reported to his wife Chichi and his own five children, "that I was not enthusiastic over her!"

Disaster was to strike the Martins (or so it seemed to them), and the gossiping members of the American colony were to enjoy their discomfiture. In the summer of 1876 the Martins again went on leave, and there was a nodding of heads among the Americans in Cairo. In September their suspicions were confirmed: Mrs. Martin had given birth to a son in Switzerland, and she would not return to Cairo that winter. "She has not the courage to meet her friends here after such an affair!" added the knowing ones. And Mrs. Stone, a modest lady, was so amused that she confided the opinion that she knew Mrs. Martin "feels like scratching Major Martin's eyes out!"

More disastrous and far less amusing was the domestic menage of Wilburn Briggs Hall, a South Carolinian whose services to the Confederate Navy had been both dramatic and varied. He had graduated at the head of his class at Annapolis in 1859 and promptly set sail for African waters, where his ship captured a slave trader off the mouth of the Congo and rescued its seven hundred involuntary passengers. He had no more than got back from this cruise when South Carolina seceded, and Hall quit the United States Navy. In March, 1861, he began his Confederate career by purchasing the "Huntress" in New York and running it out of the harbor in the face of a severe gale, raising at its mast the first Confederate flag upon the high seas. For four years thereafter he saw varied service—rescuing the garrison from falling Port Royal, ducking in and out of the Federal blockade, and laying in Savannah Harbor the first submarine torpedoes for the Confederates. He was on the Mississippi, on the Red, and he was commander of the midshipmen of the Confederate Naval Academy, where Graves served on the staff. His postwar years were undramatic, and he sank into debt. When, early in

1874, the Egyptian opportunity came, he left his wife in Charleston and went to Cairo. There he held a number of different titles—chief of the First Section of the Ministry of War, chief of the Bureau of Military Construction, inspector of the education of the khedive's sons, inspector of khedivial military schools—but his duties were never more than those of a clerk. After a year he sent for his wife.

Harriott Horry Hall, connected with Horrys, Laurens, and Rutledges in South Carolina, was the daughter of Duncan Ingraham, who won fame in the old navy and who had commanded the defenses of Charleston for the Confederacy. She met Hall during the war while he was serving in Charleston in her father's command. Though a member of a navy family, she had no liking for adventure and left Charleston reluctantly. She was to travel to Cairo with Colonel Graves. They met in New York, where she clung to him helplessly as she faced the unnamed perils of an ocean voyage. She was dark—swarthy even—not in good health, and, Graves thought, "painfully ugly." She was, however, both sprightly and intelligent. With her was her school-age son Ingraham. Hall, waiting in Cairo, was nervous, worried over her health and comfort, and he wired New York to learn if she had arrived safely. He wired again at Liverpool and once more at Naples—spending over $200 on telegrams. Mrs. Hall was impressed by the size of London, pleased with the sights of Europe, but en route she confided to Graves that she had no intention of liking anything in Cairo. In Alexandria the anxious husband came aboard the boat and guided his wife and Graves to the Cairo train through the clamoring swarm of porters, donkey-boys, and beggars. Hall took his wife and child to his room and helped Graves to get settled nearby. In gratitude for his services on the journey, Mrs. Hall undertook Graves's darning and mending. Soon the Halls found it necessary to rent three unfurnished rooms for $20 a month. They had their meals sent in from a restaurant. No living arrangements in Cairo would please Mrs. Hall—and it was evident, too, that her husband, for all of his competence, was incapable of handling money. Mrs. Hall took charge of their finances and tried to free them of debt, but she spent much of her energies trying to persuade her husband to resign and return home. Hall was reluctant; he knew, he told his fellow officers, that back in the States they would starve. After a year, worn down by worry, Hall was ordered to Europe by his doctor. In Paris, Mrs. Hall prevailed on him to continue the journey home. Hall sent in his resignation, alleging bad health. He was suffering from a liver ailment, said Graves—an ailment he had had for twenty years.

Two other women joined their husbands briefly in Cairo but quickly found Egyptian life distasteful. Mrs. Charles W. Field with her two teen-age sons accompanied the Confederate general as far as Switzerland; he went on to Egypt to spy out the land. Soon he found a place for them in Cairo and sent her reassuring messages. She did not like the apartment, found Egyptian society dreary, and determined to leave. Her sons, moreover, promised to be a problem, and she concluded that they should be put in school in Virginia. After three months she left, though for the next two years, equally unhappy in Virginia, she planned to return when Field was able to send money for the trip.

Mrs. Charles Loshe, too, had but a brief period in Egypt. Loshe, born in Germany, had migrated to the United States in the decade before the war. Unable to find a place in society, he entered the army. When the Civil War began, he received a commission as a lieutenant in the Thirty-Fourth Iowa Volunteers, the sickliest regiment in the war, which lost more men from disease than other outfits lost in battle. Colonel William McE. Dye put trust in him as a soldier and got him promotions, but at war's end Loshe returned to the regular army as a lieutenant. When Colonel Dye went to Egypt, he recommended Loshe to Stone and used his influence to persuade his protégé to ask for release from the army. At the time of his discharge, which Sherman granted willingly, Loshe was in Arizona, where he had been for almost nine months. Six weeks before going to Arizona he had married; his bride stayed behind in New York. Upon discharge, Loshe hurried to New York and arrived the day after his son was born. Less than five weeks later he sailed for Egypt. After a year, Loshe sent for his wife. She arrived with the baby, took over Hall's quarters—and stayed five months. Her sudden departure started tongues wagging. "I think," said Graves sagely, "she wants to be with her mother at the occurrence of an event which will probably happen before the expiration of the next nine months."

The disordered menages of the Locketts, the Halls, the Fields, and the Loshes were the exceptions. Most of the Americans in Cairo lived happily enough with one another—though not by any means always happily with the Egyptians. Fortunately, the principal American family was a well-adjusted group. Both General and Mrs. Stone made strenuous efforts to maintain harmony among the American officers and their families. From time to time there was friction between the chief of staff and his officers, and there was invariably much criticism of the general's official conduct, but the criticism seldom extended to his person or to Mrs. Stone.

"Madame" was indeed a cultured and accomplished lady who presided graciously over her household. Stone's oldest daughter Hettie—"Miss Stone," in the manner of the age— was a companion and a constant help to her stepmother. There were three younger children, a boy, John, and two girls, Fanny and Todas Santos. The youngest child was born in Egypt.

Early in his Egyptian career, Graves dropped by the Stones' and later wrote his wife Chichi of an evening at the general's home. He found Miss Stone, ". . . hat on, just in from a ride," among the flower beds at the side of the house. Around at the back he found General Stone and Madame sitting on the veranda, with the children playing in the yard. After a little, the children went in to sing their evening songs, with Mrs. Stone accompanying them on the piano. "I never saw children nicer than the little Stones," said Graves, who longed for the sight of his own youngsters. Todas was just the age of his

Willie, and soon Graves had encouraged a correspondence between the children—with the parents turning pedagogues to shepherd the commas and discipline the grammar of the letters. Once Mrs. Stone aided Graves in the purchase of dolls for his children, and she and Hettie dressed them in appropriate Egyptian costumes. As a rule, the American officers dropped by the Stones' in the evening, sometimes sitting late in the general's study, fighting the battles of the Civil War or listening to Stone reminisce about his campaigns and surveys in Mexico. At Christmas Mrs. Stone gave a party for the Americans, with toys for all the children. On September 30, 1875, during the noon hour at the Citadel, General Stone remarked that he had never had to wear glasses, ". . . and here I am fifty-one years old today." The officers seized upon the casual remark and sent a basket of champagne to the general's home. That evening they gathered with their wives at the Locketts' and went to toast their commander on his anniversary.

Not all the Americans, of course, were fond of the Stones, and one of them carried his personal enmity to the edge of paranoia. Dr. Edward Warren had been surgeon general of North Carolina during the Civil War and had a record as a superb administrator. He had organized the medical corps and obtained drugs, supplies, and hospitals to make North Carolina troops the best cared for in the Confederate armies. In addition, Dr. Warren was a physician of high competence. But he was totally unable to get along with his fellow man. He was discontented, of an irascible disposition, and given to contention and controversy. After the war he went to Baltimore, won a good practice by his medical skill, and founded a medical school in opposition to that of the University of Maryland. But his staff was soon divided by controversy. He founded another and was repeating the process of destroying it by quarrelsomeness when his participation as an expert witness in a murder trial hastened his collapse. In court Warren confounded the leading lawyers of Baltimore. His testimony saved a Mrs. Wharton from the gallows for allegedly poisoning her boarder, one General Ketchum. Since the public believed Mrs. Wharton to be guilty, Warren's testimony lost him the support of most of the citizens of Baltimore. One day as he was sitting in his abandoned office, he saw Colonel Walter H. Jenifer, of Maryland, clad in a strange uniform, passing the door. Warren called after him, brought him in, and heard about the opportunities in Egypt. He applied and was accepted. With his wife, his daughter, and a Negro servant, William Hughes, he arrived in Cairo in May, 1873—a propitious time, as it turned out, for the advancement of his career. It was a career marked by as much controversy as his Baltimore days. Warren was an inveterate gossip, with the manner of an old woman, and intensely jealous of all his associates. He had great facility in the making of enemies—a talent shared by his servant William and by his pet poodle. On one occasion William horsewhipped the sentry at the gate of the Citadel for failing to salute Dr. Warren, and when Ratib Pasha, commander in chief of the Egyptian army, rode up to interfere, William announced himself a free-born American citizen and threatened to whip the general too. A pasha, a guest of Warren, was set upon by the family poodle and forced to take refuge on the center table in the living room. Ever after, the pasha regarded Warren and his poodle as a menace to society.

For all his conflicts with the Egyptians, there was no question of Dr. Warren's high competence in his profession. With permission, he engaged in private practice and soon had as his patients all the Americans and many of the Europeans in Cairo. He won renown as well by his dramatic operation on the new minister of war. When Kassim Pasha fell gravely ill, the Arab physicians announced that he would die. Dr. Warren, called in, pronounced the abdominal disorder a strangulated hernia and declared that an operation was imperative. No Arab was willing to perform so serious an operation on so high-placed a personage, and Americans advised Warren that failure would reflect discredit on them all. But Warren persisted, persuaded the khedive's French physician to assist him, and operated—with the Arab physicians assembled in the garden and calling upon Allah and the women of the harem, screened by curtains, wailing in chorus over their master's distress. Kassim recovered, and thereafter Warren was in the good graces of the khedive. Soon high-ranking Egyptians were sitting in Dr. Warren's waiting rooms.

With Stone's consent the khedive made Warren provisional surgeon general in chief of the army, and Warren moved into offices in the Citadel originally occupied by a court functionary and—in contrast to the bleak offices of the general staff—lavishly furnished with silk-covered divans, damask curtains, elaborate wainscot, and marble floors. Warren promptly sent word of his new honor to friends in Maryland, hoping to confound the dire predictions of his enemies.

His enemies, real or imagined, were right. Dr. Warren's new rank did not alter his character as a gossip and intriguer. He soon developed an antipathy for Stone and particularly for Madame Stone. His office became the clearinghouse for all the discontent and malice of the American colony. Perhaps, indeed, his personal troubles augmented his basic disposition as a troublemaker. He had lost a son just before coming to Egypt. In Cairo, while Warren himself was laid up with eye trouble, his wife gave birth to a second son, who contracted smallpox and died. Certainly Warren believed that he and his wife had been badly treated by the Stones, and he managed to interpret every incident as evidence of Stone's conspiracy against him. His animosity to the Stones became an obsession.

Stone, in Warren's eyes, was the villain of the Egyptian service, and Loring, Purdy, Reynolds, and even his own good friend, the mild and gentle Raleigh Colston, were Stone's slavish supporters. So too was the American consul general, Richard Beardsley. He believed Stone and Loring, devoid of a sense of right and wrong, had set Mrs. Stone to conspire to prevent his appointment as surgeon general. When Warren received the appointment, Stone then claimed to have secured it for him. Stone, said Warren, was gambling with men's lives—sending explorers into Central Africa without regard for their health. When they returned, despite efforts to kill them, Stone claimed credit for their accomplishments. Above all, gossiped Warren, Stone must live in constant dread of Thaddeus P. Mott, shuttling between Constantinople and Paris, keeping in touch with his supporters in Egypt, preparing to return to oust Stone from the place he had usurped beside the khedive. Warren persisted in spreading misunderstanding, distrust, and recriminations among his countrymen. Some, after a falling-out with Stone, were persuaded to accept Warren's diatribes as truth.

One who questioned Warren's judgment and tried to untangle the weird webs he spun was Colonel Raleigh E. Colston. In May, 1874, Colston, who had come to Egypt with Warren and had spent many an enjoyable hour with him on shipboard, returned from a seven-month exploring expedition to stumble into a hornet's nest of animosities. According to custom, Colston visited the Stones, and a chance remark opened the floodgates. The Stones were hurt by Warren's conduct and were almost as full of gossip about Warren as the doctor was about them. Colston learned that Warren had prejudiced Loring against him. Then he found that Warren was explaining his own financial troubles by saying he had loaned all his money to Colston. He found that before he went on his expedition Warren had buttonholed his co-commander and filled him with stories against Colston. Eventually Colston—a gentleman and slow to believe evil about his fellow man—concluded that "the man must be a villain or a fool or both."

With animosity on all sides, Warren prepared to leave Cairo. Even in Baltimore Warren had suffered from eye trouble. In Egypt the glare and the sand had brought on severe attacks of ophthalmia. An eye specialist from Paris advised him that continual residence in Egypt would bring him to total blindness, and Warren asked for a leave of absence from the Egyptian service. He went to Paris and immediately resumed medical practice. As in Cairo, his competence soon brought him a thriving office. At the same time he tried to hold on to his Egyptian employment: he asked for extension of his leave. When he did not get it, he still determined to realize everything possible from the Egyptian government. For some time after his establishment in Paris he annoyed Stone by demanding the return of notebooks and furniture he claimed to have left in the Citadel. Stone made short work of the requests. He delivered the effects of Warren's office to the khedivial warehouse and bundled off Warren's personal belongings to the American consulate. But Warren claimed that much of his property was stolen in the process and continued to badger the chief of the Egyptian general staff. In Cairo the Americans suspected that Warren had made off with government property. "He was a great scamp," judged Graves, "and he certainly acted in a manner to lose the respect and confidence of everybody."

Yet, except for Warren's brief muddying of the waters, the Americans, for all their different personalities, lived in comparative harmony with one another and worked together without friction. It was not their relations with one another that harassed the days of General Stone. His gray hairs came, instead, from the conflicts that developed between the Egyptians and the Americans and from his efforts to see that the American corps made only a good impression on their hosts.

Had Charles Pomeroy Stone been able to confine himself solely to the management and administration of the Egyptian military system, he would have found ample outlet for his undoubted enthusiasm and devoted energy. But technical problems of the military were not allowed to consume all of his time and attention. As the ranking officer among the American contingent in Egypt, and the one American with constant access to the khedive and the court, he bore a peculiar responsibility for the conduct of the Americans. Frequently he found that problems of managing the various personalities who made up the American corps and the conflicts between the Americans and their Egyptian associates were more harassing than the pasha system which he hoped to abolish.

VI

Problems of a Pasha

Charles Pomeroy Stone's position in Cairo was ambivalent. He served two masters—the khedive and the American way of life, which he and his officers represented. It was his particular responsibility to understand and to interpret the Egyptians to his officers, to transmit the khedive's purposes and intentions, and to inspire these Americans with some of his own idealism and enthusiasm for the general reform of Egypt. At the same time, because of his access to the highest governmental circles, he became interpreter, defender, and apologist for his compatriots. Though for the most part his officers served faithfully, in the end Stone failed to increase the prestige of the Americans in Egypt. Perhaps, indeed, the problems he faced were insuperable.

Standing in the way of any real adjustment between the Americans and the Egyptians was an enormous cultural gap. The ways of life and the processes of thought of the Americans were far removed from Egyptian manners and mores. When cultural conflicts arose, the task of resolving them could fall only to General Stone, buffer between the Americans and the khedive. The Americans themselves varied greatly, and they showed varying degrees of willingness and ability to adapt themselves to Egyptian ways.

Early in his Egyptian experience Stone faced the problems created by brash young James Morris Morgan. The Louisianan had arrived in Egypt in swashbuckling manner and was elated over his initial success in browbeating the minor official who made difficulty about getting him transportation from Alexandria to Cairo. Thereafter, and perhaps inspired by the incident, he developed an uncontrollable capacity for personal clashes with Egyptians. He followed his initial success by a series of offenses that eventually led to his flight from the country.

Morgan had been in Cairo only a short time when he attended the opera with General Loring. During the intermission the prefect of police of Cairo, either in ignorance of the American's position in the khedive's service or in studied insult, turned suddenly to Morgan and demanded that he fetch him a glass of water. Morgan complied at once. High-spirited and impetuous, as he believed was fitting for a Louisiana gentleman, he quickly brought the glass of water and as quickly delivered it full in the prefect's face. Sputtering with rage, the prefect stormed to the khedive and received another cold dash. The American was justified, in Ismail's opinion. "I should have been disappointed had he not done so. I did not bring Americans here to wait on you or upon anybody else. You may consider yourself fortunate that he did not shoot you."

A person more mature than Morgan might have dismissed the incident and rested his case on the khedive's rebuke. But Morgan thereafter sought out incidents of personal slight and became obstreperous in his demands that his position as an officer and a gentleman be recognized. Some time later, in Alexandria, Morgan accompanied General Loring to a dinner given by a pasha. As other guests found their places at table and Loring took the seat of honor at his host's right, Morgan found there was no place for him. At Loring's insistence, Morgan explained that the general needed him at his side as interpreter, for Loring was unable to speak Arabic. Moreover, Loring had but one arm and needed Morgan beside him to help him cut his food. Both services, replied the Egyptian host, might very well be performed if Morgan stood behind his superior's chair. Morgan's fury was electric. Soothingly, Loring assured him that the pasha had not understood the nature of Morgan's position. Grudgingly and still indignant, Morgan accepted the chair placed beside Loring's. He was in fact angry with Loring, who had phrased the request as his need for Morgan's help rather than as Morgan's right as an officer. He would make Loring understand, he told himself as he sulked over the incident, that he was neither an interpreter nor a valet; a gentleman at home, he intended to be treated as one in Egypt. Who, he asked himself, were "these off-color beys" to snub him?

The next morning, resignation in hand, he swung off the train at Cairo and headed for the Citadel to see General Stone. The chief of staff listened patiently—a virtue he was learning as from day to day he groped for solutions to the seemingly endless problems posed by the presence of Americans in Egypt. He was properly shocked at the indignity Morgan had suffered but reminded him that circulation of the story would bring embarrassment to the chief of staff and great annoyance to the khedive. Then he sent him off for three days to reconsider his resignation and to meditate on his future in Egypt or elsewhere. When Morgan returned, he had no decision to make, thanks to Stone, for the general tore up his resignation and told him that his new rank as lieutenant colonel on the staff of the commander in chief, Ratib Pasha, would obviate the danger of future unpleasantness.

Then, as if Morgan needed help in getting into trouble, he acquired the most famous horse in Egypt. To the Empress Eugénie, guest of honor at the opening of the Suez Canal, Ismail had presented, among other gifts, a beautiful Arabian stallion. But when Eugénie returned to France, she did not choose to take the horse. Loring, the first of the khedive's new assistants, became its owner. Loring was a competent horseman, but he could not manage the spirited stallion with his one good arm. If Loring tried to hold the reins between his teeth, he risked breaking his jaw. The horse passed to Morgan, a lover of horses and an excellent rider.

Morgan, mounted on Napoleon, became familiar to Americans and Egyptians alike. He had learned his horsemanship in the ante-bellum South and was as willing to demonstrate his equestrian ability as he was to show off the superb animal's perfect response to his master's hand. His feats soon became a topic of small talk in Cairo, and Morgan won a reputation for recklessness. Even the khedive knew of the pair's performances.

Indeed, the khedive had firsthand knowledge. One day, as Morgan and Napoleon performed for carriageloads of spectators on the beautiful and busy Shubra Road, a stir and commotion just ahead signaled the approach of the khedive and his royal party. In obeisance to His Highness, spectators dropped to their knees or touched heart, lips, and forehead. Not so Morgan. While Ismail's escort glared, the American rode forward. As the royal carriage came abreast, he sent Napoleon rearing and came to rest, motionless as a statue, squarely beside the khedive's vehicle. Morgan himself executed a precise military salute. Ismail turned, leaned from the carriage, clapping vigorously, and called Morgan to him. Having received congratulations on his horsemanship, Morgan rode smugly on.

Morgan loved the attention Napoleon brought to him, but on one occasion the stallion disgraced him. Shortly after the Americans came to Egypt, the khedive's forces gathered in the capital for a great sham battle. General Stone and Lieutenant General Ratib were in command of the two armies. On the eve of maneuvers, Morgan, assigned to Stone's staff, attended the banquet given by the khedive. During dinner Ismail remarked that he looked forward to Napoleon's performance on the morrow and would be particularly interested to observe the horse's reaction to cannon and rifle fire. Morgan took this as a challenge, forgot his decision to ride a less spirited horse, and was determined to go into battle on Napoleon. The next day General Stone sent Morgan with a message to the pasha in charge of artillery. With speed and daring, Morgan spurred the horse into the presence of the pasha and executed his most dramatic salute. Then came disgrace. Napoleon, terrified by the sudden noise of heavy artillery, shivered and sank to his belly on the sand. The frightened horse ignored Morgan's spurs, and Morgan hastily sputtered embarrassed excuses to the amused pasha. When the firing ceased, Napoleon scrambled up and sped away. Morgan, mortified, gave him free rein as the horse carried them from the scene of humiliation.

In the long run it was Morgan's exhibitionism that brought about his departure from Egypt. It was one thing, he learned, to court attention on the public thoroughfares and even to devise his own unique form of salaam to the khedive, but it was something else again to defy the ancient traditions of the harem system. As he and the prancing Napoleon moved along the Shubra Road one day, a carriage bearing two Egyptian ladies approached. Other men in the vicinity quickly turned their backs or discreetly looked in another direction. Morgan reacted as he would have done at home. To impress them with his prowess, he put Napoleon through his jumping tricks. Morgan's boldness fired the ecstatic ladies to emulate his rash defiance of tradition. One tossed him a flower. As it fell beside the carriage, Morgan spurred Napoleon to a gallop, leaned from the saddle, and picked up the blossom without breaking the horse's stride or destroying the illusion that horse and rider were one. The enthralled lady then threw flower after flower, and as each fell to earth Morgan and Napoleon repeated their performance. Horses and vehicles surrounded the group. There was a rapidly growing traffic jam. At last Morgan guided Napoleon to the side of the carriage and rode in triumph beside the coquette. From the window she handed him one last flower, whose stem she had wrapped in a handkerchief. He had scarcely grasped it when the escort of eunuchs attempted to interfere. Clutching the memento of his romantic encounter, Morgan sent Napoleon into a gallop that shot him well ahead of his pursuers, and horse and rider flew along the road. Napoleon gracefully cleared the top of the protecting gates of a railroad crossing, catapulted over an old man on a donkey, and raced for home, where Morgan hastened to tell of the adventure. His friends listened aghast and solemnly informed him that he was in for serious trouble. Even as he stubbornly refused to heed those who advised him to leave Cairo at once or speed to the protection of the American consul, Ismail's foreign minister, Nubar Pasha, appeared. The khedive had heard of the episode, and his minister demanded the handkerchief. Morgan had overlooked the embroidered monogram on the dainty piece of cloth. PF, the daring flirt on the Shubra Road, was the Princess Fatma, the khedive's nineteen-year-old daughter. Her behavior had brought her notoriety and caused her father grave concern. It was rumored that a succession of her more daring admirers had disappeared. At once Morgan flung the telltale handkerchief into the fire. Bellowing that Morgan had not heard the last of it, Nubar left the room. All Cairo talked of the incident, and few men would risk association with the foolhardy American. At his regular eating place, and in the clubs Morgan entered, Moslem and Christian alike ignored him. Ismail, he knew, was furious. During the next days Morgan expected disciplinary action or a summary dismissal. Then he learned that the wife of Russia's consul general had used her considerable influence to save him. He was, she had insisted to the khedive, merely a high-spirited boy who meant no offense. Mollified, Ismail abandoned his wish to punish Morgan.

But continued clashes with Egyptian tradition soured Morgan on Egypt. After a leave of absence in France he could not recapture his early enthusiasm for life in the land of the Pharaohs. In early 1872 he announced that he saw no future for any American in Egypt: he was going home. He took a six months' leave of absence, returned to America, and sent back his resignation.

Men less flamboyant than Morgan created other problems for General Stone and added to the unfortunate impression Egyptians had of Americans. Fraud, property damage and destruction, and failure to meet bona fide financial obligations were constant sources of friction. Accused of fraud was Major Cornelius Hunt, instructor in Ismail's artillery school at Aboukir, a settlement on the bay between Alexandria and Rosetta.

The April following his marriage, Hunt took a six months' lease on a furnished house surrounded by a garden in Ramleh, a well-kept suburb of Alexandria. He refused to sign a contract guaranteeing good care of the property and had his own peculiar ideas about the payment of rent. He made a small down payment and prepared a receipt—in English. Thereafter, he met the owner's requests for full settlement with token payments. When, after six months, the owner brought in an attorney, Hunt denied agreeing to a contract, claimed the rent was but a third the amount named by the owner, and offered receipts showing that he had paid nine months' rent in advance. The landlord charged that Hunt had tampered with the rent receipts to make the partial payments appear full settlement and complained to the American consul at Alexandria. The attempt to untangle Hunt's confused dealings was still pending in 1873 when he was killed by a fall from a horse.

Other Americans had equally poor records in the conduct of business transactions. William W. Dunlap, a Kentuckian who had served in the Confederate forces in Missouri, ordered a uniform costing 690 francs and paid less than half that amount. He argued that it was a military expense and the Egyptian government should pay the bill. Only after the American consul moved to collect for the disgruntled tailor did Dunlap reluctantly pay up.

In Alexandria, Henry Hopkins Sibley had unpaid bills covering every phase of his expenses. His creditors, a landlord, a local merchant, and a bookdealer, took their complaints to the American consul. The landlord demanded some £22 to cover damage and destruction to the furnished house Sibley had rented. The American officer had broken the front-door bolt, ruined an armchair, stained and otherwise damaged a mattress, "left champagne glasses unwashed," and smashed tumblers, wine glasses, a jug, a decanter, numerous dishes, and other housewares. He had consumed a cheese the landlord had expected to have for his own use and had drunk dozens of bottles of the landlord's wines, ales, and other liquors. The merchant put in a bill for a long list of items, including gold-mounted coral studs, custom-made shoes, gold epaulettes mounted on blue silk velvet and decorated with Egypt's crescent and star in silver, a gold sword-knot with gold cord, postage stamps issued to Sibley over a three-year period, a dozen teaspoons, one copy of a London newspaper, and one telegram to Cairo. In addition, the bookdealer presented a bill for £52 for books and said he had loaned money to Sibley. He asked for interest on the total account. Sibley's creditors were still pressing for action in 1873 when the khedive, out of patience with Sibley's drunken incompetence, discharged him for "physical disability."

The Americans in Egypt had difficulty, almost from the beginning, when the government failed to pay salaries promptly and in full. No separate pay department existed, and from time to time an announcement directed the officers at the Citadel to apply to one or another government agency to sign the payroll and collect their salaries. Sometimes the money came from the khedive's privy purse, sometimes from the treasury, sometimes from the customhouse. Although the government's accountants computed wages on a monthly basis, the intervals between payments varied. After the first few months these intervals progressively lengthened. James Morris Morgan once collected his pay by swaggering into the customhouse and threatening the Egyptian agent with sword and pistol. Samuel H. Lockett declared that payless paydays in Louisiana during the Reconstruction had prepared him for Egypt. When he went off to Gura in 1876, his family survived only because he had been paid in advance and received extra compensation for field service.

Even the erratic pay schedule of the khedive's government, however, could not account for all of the tangled finances and overdue accounts of the Americans. Alexander W. Reynolds ran up a bill with Alexandria's Hotel d'Europe for well over £65 and owed more than twice that amount to the khedive's Grand New Hotel in Cairo. In addition, he left unpaid, at his death in 1876, bills for clothing, books, liquor, groceries, medicine, and even for his contribution to the monument fund for the deceased American consul, Richard Beardsley. E. Sparrow Purdy owed the khedive's hotel £385 for board and lodging before the manager brought suit. Purdy argued that he had incurred the expense during services for the khedive and was not liable, but the court ruled that the Egyptian government was not a party to his arrangements with the hotel. When Wilburn B. Hall went on leave in 1876, he left behind a bill for six months' rent. Even General Stone could not meet all of his obligations, and his financial problems followed him across the ocean. In June, 1875, the attorney for one of Stone's creditors in South Carolina—on the advice of Stone's enemy, Colonel Walter H. Jenifer—wrote the American consul at Cairo asking how to collect a long-standing debt.

Each case of financial incompetence, fraud, or debt-dodging contributed to the increase of hostility against the American officers. One claim against the Egyptian government was clearly an act of insanity. Colonel Thomas G. Rhett was among the first to arrive in Egypt. As former adjutant to Confederate General Joseph E. Johnston he had considerable experience in military administration and for a time worked well. But after two years under the Egyptian sun he began to nurse grievances and came to the conclusion that Stone was plotting to deny him his just rewards. He was ill and was given sick leave to go to Paris. There he asked for his discharge on grounds of health. Remembering the service he had rendered in the ordnance bureau, the khedive released him with an extra bonus of $7,000. But Rhett fulminated against Stone and claimed that he had been promised the rank of brigadier general, had been the victim of Stone's nefarious intrigues, and was entitled to back pay at the higher rank. Moreover, he wanted $25,000 compensation for his ruined health. The government rejected his allegations, but Rhett persisted. He went home and until his death in 1878 continued to press his claim. By the time of his death he had raised the amount of his demand to $45,000. Such a case might have brought the khedive to the same level of skepticism about

Americans that Egyptian landlords, wine dealers, and tailors had reached.

The extent to which the misconduct of Americans could embarrass the mission and cause Stone endless trouble was illustrated, soon after the first Americans arrived in Egypt, by the behavior of George H. Butler. Butler, appointed consul general at Alexandria, was a nephew of Benjamin F. Butler, the "beast" of New Orleans (and presently a violently Radical member of Congress). George Butler had his uncle's flair for headlines and drama but only a minimum of his Uncle Ben's shrewdness and political acumen. He was unable to stay out of trouble. He arrived in Egypt with the earliest group of Americans, and while they were making a good first impression Butler proceeded to make a bad one. He became involved in a series of blunders. First he tried to assume his duties without procuring from the sultan the exequatur of his office. When he presented his credentials, the khedive followed Egyptian custom and presented a horse to him. Butler knew the rule against American representatives' accepting gifts, but he took the present. Then he wired the U.S. State Department for permission to keep it. When permission was refused, Butler ignored the courtesy due the khedive and gave the animal to the American missionaries in Alexandria "for their untiring efforts to ameliorate and elevate the religious and social conditions of the poor of Egypt." Shortly Foreign Minister Nubar Pasha notified Butler of the khedive's displeasure and said that Butler would have to pay for the horse. Before this matter was cleared up a local merchant asked the U.S. State Department to collect from Butler a $400 debt. When two Americans in the Egyptian military service challenged a consular employee to a duel, Butler became a party to the farce. He complained to his friend Thaddeus P. Mott, then the khedive's personal adviser, that the American officers were showing gross disrespect for the American consulate and asked him to lay the whole story before Ismail.

Next, through the columns of the *New York Herald*, Butler battled American missionaries who accused him of improper conduct in office. He publicly whipped one of his detractors, then denied he had done so. He beat Cornelius Hunt with a cane. He fell out with the vice consul he himself had appointed, and each used New York newspapers to slander the other. When Butler learned that Ismail planned to award Vanderbilt Allen a distinguished service decoration, he notified the khedive that recognition for Allen would incur the consul's personal and political enmity. When Secretary of State Hamilton Fish, acting on Stone's complaint, warned Butler against such meddling, the consul wrote caustic messages to the khedive, to the foreign minister, and to the Ministry of War.

But before the State Department could complete a formal investigation of Butler's conduct in office, he was embroiled in another conflict. In July, 1872, he and his secretary met General Loring, one of the Reynoldses, and Major William P. A. Campbell in an Alexandria restaurant. Butler had heard that the major had said he should be whipped for his attack on the American missionary. When Campbell did not join the others in a salute as they passed the consul's table, Butler shouted, "Good evening, Major Campbell." Angered, Campbell strode over to him. In the ensuing fracas Butler's secretary shot Campbell in the leg. Butler dashed to the telegraph office and wired his congressman uncle that "rebel officers" had tried to assassinate him. He begged his relative to get him permission to leave Egypt, "if the emergency requires it." Next day Stone, Purdy, and a number of native officers met to consider the brawl. While they were meeting, Butler scurried aboard a mail packet and left Alexandria. Thaddeus Mott, now back in the United States, wrote a hasty note to Secretary Fish excusing Butler and blaming Stone, and Uncle Ben Butler joined in with an enumeration of the injustices done his nephew, demanding justice. "Only reason I ever had to think he lacked refinement," added the uncle, "was that he was a newspaper man." In Egypt the investigating committee dropped the Butler affair when Richard Beardsley took over the consular office and moved it to Cairo.

General Stone may not have been embarrassed by his "rebel officers' " forcing so undesirable a character as Butler to leave the country, but the conduct of another ex-Confederate on his staff brought shame to everyone. Major D. G. White, of Gifford, Georgia, was a graduate of West Point, but his military talents were limited and he achieved no distinction in the Southern army. After Appomattox, he tried to run plantations for his wife's father and brother but succeeded only in wasting his wife's fortune and almost bankrupting her relatives. Then, in 1870, he applied for a place in Egypt, and Mott accepted him without looking carefully into his record. He left behind his wife and two children, and their friends concluded that "she in Georgia and he in Egypt is a very good arrangement."

In Cairo, Stone attempted to find suitable tasks for the major and gave him various duties. Sent out with a detachment of soldiers and Arab surveyors on a minor exploring expedition toward Mt. Sinai, White stayed a month without sending back a message. Just as Stone was ready to send a search party after him, Major White turned up. He had nothing to report and so had not bothered to notify the office. For the most part, White gave the impression of being a carefree, genial person, but the general opinion was that he had "very little brains or capacity" and was "somewhat inclined to whiskey."

By the time his fellow Georgian, Lieutenant Colonel Graves, arrived in Cairo, White had come to be considered the drunkard of the Citadel. He went on one spree that lasted ten days, and his fellow officers were sure that he would drink himself to death and took turns watching him. In October the staff physician announced that if White continued to drink he would be dead in a week. But from a military standpoint, his "end" was more tragic.

"Poor Major White!" wrote Graves to his wife Chichi just two months after the combined efforts of the officers at the Citadel had saved the major from death by alcohol. "Poor Major White! His end is a sad one. Worse than death. Yes ten thousand times worse. He grew worse and worse, avoiding officers who tried to save him, abandoned himself to *lewd women*, drew $1,000 to send to his family in view of his departure on a little surveying trip up the Nile, and then *deserted!* Yes, *deserted!* He has run away and left the country and is branded as a liar and a coward and a thief! Can anything be more horrible?"

The absconding major was supposed to be on his way to the United States, but the officers nodded their heads knowingly and agreed that he had gone to Paris to "end it all" in debauchery. If White should manage to get back to Georgia, Graves wrote his wife, he would "abuse the Egyptian government, and the Khedive, and everybody in Egypt." It would be better for his wife and children, concluded Graves, if he never showed up. "He has been a common drunkard for years." But what finally became of White no one in Egypt ever learned.

The embarrassing conduct of Major White, the shooting affray in Alexandria, the aberrant financial conduct of some of the officers, and the juvenile behavior of James Morris Morgan all added to Stone's difficulties in defending the Americans to the khedive and to the Egyptian war department. Fortunately, there were some of his men to whom he could point with pride.

VII

Exploring the Sudan

It was well indeed for General Stone that both he and the Khedive Ismail had plans beyond the reorganization of the army and the establishment of a general staff. Stone Pasha was a geographer at heart, a surveyer by avocation, and a prospector interested in the earth's buried treasure. His passion for geography coincided with and complemented the viceroy's ambition to extend his domains and to exploit the riches of the African hinterland. Together the khedive and his chief of staff attempted to solve many of their problems, both economic and personal, by sending the Americans on exploring expeditions. The American army, after all, had spent most of its time in opening the American frontier, and its officers were more experienced in surveying than in preparing for battle. To General Stone, moreover, it must have seemed that the more men he could send away from Cairo, the fewer would be the problems with which he would have to deal in the Citadel.

From the beginning Ismail had used the Americans' talents for surveying. Charles Chaillé-Long, of Maryland, was sent into the desert to locate a site for a fort and came back eager for further adventures. Others went out to look for canal courses, railroad routes, and places that could be fortified in the event of war with Turkey. In a brief service of little more than a year, Eugene Fechet made a distinct contribution to Ismail's Egypt and presaged a twentieth-century controversy. A Michigan boy who had served in the ranks from Shiloh to the Atlanta campaign, Fechet was a veteran of many battles before he entered West Point in 1864. Upon graduation he served in

Alaska and Arizona before General Sherman released him for service in Egypt. His first assignment was to survey the region between Aswan and Khartoum. Fechet's able report designated Aswan as the proper place for a great dam which could control the floods of the Nile and be a future source of hydraulic power.

A fair number of Americans learned something of the topography of Lower Egypt, the management of Egyptian guides and soldiers, and the tactics of battling sandstorms and insects, finding water holes, and supervising the movement of supply trains of dromedaries. By the time General Stone had organized the section of the general staff devoted to maps, topography, and surveying, the men were prepared for more extensive expeditions. Behind Stone's eagerness to send men to the frontier lay a motive which he did not explain to the khedive. The chief of staff and his American colleagues were in rivalry with the British. The long-standing suspicion Americans had for perfidious Albion took on new manifestations beside the waters of the Nile. The Americans suspected—with ample justification it eventually seemed to them—that the Britons in the service of the khedive were not as singularly devoted as they to the interests of Egypt. The chief of staff watched with jealousy and suspicion the more dramatic role the British were playing in the khedive's domains.

For there were Britons in the service of Ismail. Almost a year before the khedive hired American officers to organize and supervise the Egyptian army, the viceroy commissioned Sir Samuel Baker as governor of the "equatorial provinces." No one was quite sure what the boundaries were, but Baker proceeded to explore what he believed to be his territory. He established military posts, brought native villages under "subjection," and collected taxes. He displayed more fervor than discretion in suppressing the slave trade, and eventually his efforts brought him into trouble. He ran afoul of the local slave-traders, unwisely interfered in intertribal controversies, and found himself opposed at every turn. An ambush sent him back to Gondokoro in hasty retreat, short of ammunition and fulminating against the fighting qualities of his Egyptian soldiery. He asked Cairo for help.

Stone immediately prepared to dispatch an expedition commanded by his old companion in Sonora and Baja California, E. Sparrow Purdy. The expedition was not to go directly up the Nile to Gondokoro. Stone planned (and Ismail agreed) that it should go down the Red Sea into the Indian Ocean, land at Zanzibar, and proceed westward until it reached the equatorial lakes and the headwaters of the Nile. Rumor placed the size of the force at from three thousand to five thousand men, but Cherif Pasha solemnly assured the American consul that only one hundred men would go. From November, 1872, until the following March, Purdy and his men were on the alert, momentarily expecting to leave. But there were untold complications: it was the rainy season; the sultan of Zanzibar, who profited from the slave trade, might not welcome an Egyptian military expedition; the British were in the region and international crises could result. As the months went by, observers in Cairo, as well as the beleaguered Baker in Gondokoro, began to suspect that the roundabout expedition by way of Zanzibar had purposes other than the relief of the governor. Eventually Baker received fresh ammunition and a handful of reinforcements through the regular trade route up the Nile. Stone, it appeared, was not especially interested in rushing to the aid of the Englishman; and the khedive, who had not reaped increased trade benefits from Baker's exploits, grew cold toward him.

But even though the "Baker relief expedition" proved abortive, Stone pointed out that the American officers' talents for surveying and exploration could be used in wider areas. In the summer of 1873, Stone suggested to Ismail that the equipment and personnel already gathered might well be used to explore and survey the area near the ruined city of Berenice on the Red Sea. In September the refurbished expedition, under the command of Colonel Purdy, set out from Suez. Stone instructed

Purdy to survey the ancient seaport and its harbor, to explore the surrounding country, and to await there the arrival of a second expedition.

The second expedition, leaving Lower Egypt on the same day, would survey the overland approaches to Berenice. It would go four hundred miles up the Nile to Kenneh, then strike southeast across the desert along an ancient Roman road. The two expeditions would unite in the coastal city, then together cross the desert southward to Berber on the Nile. On the way they would look for a route for a railroad.

The commander of the second expedition, only recently arrived in Egypt, was Colonel Raleigh Edward Colston, once a Confederate general. Repeatedly in his forty-eight years he had stood at the portal of the temple of success and an ill wind had slammed shut the doors before he could enter. He had been born—or so at least a rigidly pious Presbyterian uncle thought—under a shadow. Colston's father, a young Virginia physician studying medicine in Paris, had met and married the Duchess of Valmy, divorced wife of Napoleon's Marshal Georg Kellermann. She was of an aristocratic Italian family, but in Virginia the Colstons were scandalized to learn that their boy had married a Catholic and a divorcée. The opinions of his Virginia relatives mattered not at all to a lad in Paris in the 1830's, but when the young son of Colston was sent to Virginia and intrusted to his uncle's care, the uncle persistently demanded that Raleigh expiate the blot on the family escutcheon by entering the Presbyterian ministry. Raleigh did not agree, but his uncle's obsession harried his cadet days at the Virginia Military Institute. On graduation he remained as an instructor in French and, later, professor of military science. Unlike his colleague, Major Thomas J. Jackson, he was popular in the society of Lexington. He married Louise Boyer, daughter of a leading citizen of Rockbridge County. His future looked bright enough. But in the end, and through no fault of his own, most of the things he touched turned out badly. He should have been —and might have been—the man who stood "like a stone wall" at Bull Run. Colston and Major Jackson were in charge of the cadets who went off in April, 1861, to drill the recruits assembling in Richmond. They were commissioned colonels in the Virginia troops on the same day. Orders sent Colston down the James River, where he was too far away to be called to First Manassas, and sent Jackson to Harpers Ferry, whence he could march to fame. Ill health kept Colston from important campaigns for a year, and later in the war, as he was about to be given an important assignment, four North Carolina regiments protested so loudly against being commanded by a Virginian that army politicians in Richmond yielded and sent Colston off to an inconspicuous corner of the Confederacy. After the war fate still pursued him. He tried for a time to lecture on Stonewall Jackson's career but made no money at it. Then he ran a military preparatory school and failed. A second school was a success—at least he cleared $1,600 in its operation. But soon thereafter, personal tragedy overtook him. His wife lost her mind and was confined to an asylum. In desperation, hoping perhaps to break the jinx that had haunted his days, Colston went to Egypt.

In spite of his misfortunes, Colston was a charming gentleman, kindly, soft-spoken, thoughtful of others, and bearing no resentment against the men who had misused him. He arrived in Cairo in May, 1873, and waited until August for his formal appointment as colonel on the general staff and professor of geology in the military academy, but during his service in Egypt he never met a class or performed any but the most routine duties in the Citadel. He spent his first summer getting acquainted and making friends with his fellow officers. He was a favorite of the Stone family, a friend of Loring, an interested but noncommittal listener to Warren's gossip. He was fond of animals and filled his first letters home with descriptions of the little donkeys that were the universal mode of transportation in the capital. He acquired a kitten, which slept on the foot of his bed. He searched for a pup. He was frugal, watching his expenditures carefully, and sent home all he could save to care for his distraught wife and to aid a none-too-successful son-in-law. He welcomed the opportunity to go on an exploring mission because it would save him living expenses in Cairo.

Colonel Colston started out with enthusiasm and for the first four hundred miles of his journey enjoyed the leisurely trip up the Nile. They passed mud villages along the tree-lined banks, and sometimes he could see pyramids and ruins just beyond the shore line. The temptation to visit them overcame him, and the transports were halted while he examined relics of ancient dynasties. He commented of the people he saw that their complexions grew darker at every mile. After eight days of travel the expedition reached Kenneh, and, on September 27, mounted "horse-fashion" astride a camel, Colston set out toward the Red Sea. Behind him followed four officers and twenty-six soldiers, sixty-five camels and their drivers, and a number of Bedouin guides.

Second in command and piloting his own ship of the desert was Major William P. A. Campbell, who a few short years before had been a naval officer of the Confederate States of America. He had served in Savannah and in the defenses of Mobile, and he was sent later to England to take command of a condemned British sloop that a Confederate agent had purchased at auction and hoped to convert into a commerce-raider. In late November, 1863, Captain Campbell, clad in civilian clothes and accompanied by a young Scotsman, appeared with authority from the nominal owners to make a test run. Before the service crew aboard could protest, the new C. S. S. "Rappahannock" was beyond the marine league, but the steering gear and the propeller proved worthless and the ship drifted into the harbor of Calais. And there it remained. Without a command, Captain Campbell, accompanied by James Morris Morgan, strove to return to the Confederacy. They ran the blockade but not without unusual adventure. As they drew in sight of the Union squadron off the Carolina coast, the frightened captain of the runner proposed to surrender at the first burst of shellfire, but Campbell took over the ship, outmaneuvered the pursuing blockader, ran the batteries of Fort Fisher, and put the craft in at Wilmington. It was a skilful and daring stunt, and yet the plaudits of the watching Confederates were given mistakenly to the cowardly captain. With amusement Campbell watched the captain accept the praise. A few moments later, as he removed his gear from the ship, he witnessed an altercation between two men who ran out of expletives and began to shoot at one another. When one was hit and lay floundering on the planks, Campbell wryly exclaimed, "My own, my native land! Now I am sure that I am home again."

Colston was delighted to have Campbell as his second in command on the expedition to the Red Sea. "A genial and sterling gentleman," said Colston, as he did so unconsciously paying tribute to his own worthy qualities.

It was well that both Americans were genial gentlemen. They had much to learn, and men given to easy irritation would have broken under the frustrations which met them. It is true, they had few language difficulties. The highest Egyptian officer, a captain, spoke French well, and of course Colston spoke French from infancy. Campbell was an accomplished linguist, fluent in Arabic, and Colston had begun to study the language. The fourth officer was a good engineer with a smattering of several languages; when all else failed, Colston and Campbell could deal with him in the lingua franca of engineering. Their chief difficulties were not in formal communication but in the more difficult adjustments to new customs and cultures. Colston learned to ride sidesaddle like the Bedouins after one day's experience astride his camel. He learned much about camels—their evil disposition when young, their placid stubbornness when old, their inclination to lie down in protest when their loads were too heavy or badly balanced. He studied the camels and grew fond of Old Bull, which he rode across the eastern desert.

He learned something about Bedouins, too. One of the objectives of the first leg of the journey was the location and excavation of ancient reservoirs along the route. The reservoirs, built perhaps by the Romans, were easy enough to find, but excavation proved impossible. On reaching the first reservoir, Colston ordered the camel-drivers to fall to with shovels. But camel-drivers are specialists. They are Bedouins, not fellahin, and even the Austrian silver dollars with which Colston tempted them could not persuade them to a demeaning task. The reservoir remained choked with sand.

Thus, learning the ways of animals and men, surveying the land along the ancient route, after twenty-four days they left the great ranges of the eastern mountains and beheld the Red Sea and the Bay of Berenice. Out to meet them came Colonel Purdy with a welcoming squad.

At Berenice the two groups joined forces, but already orders were waiting for Campbell, sending him back to Cairo and thence to the equator with General Charles "Chinese" Gordon. The combined group, under the joint command of Colston and Purdy, had as second in command Alexander McComb Mason. Mason was a Virginian, descendant of the author of the Virginia Bill of Rights and grandson of Alexander McComb, who had once been the highest ranking officer in the American Army. Mason graduated from Annapolis and served in the Confederate Navy. After the war he became a soldier of fortune, fighting in Chile, sailing the China Seas, serving briefly in Cuba. A romantic at heart, he was taciturn by nature. He did not like Purdy, who was a meddler and constantly interfering with the organization and administration of the camps. In addition, Purdy was something of a braggart, both loquacious and boring. Had it not been for Colston there might well have been trouble between Purdy and Mason, but the Virginia general was genial, patient (as became a schoolteacher), and a gentleman by birth and long nurture. He did not like Purdy either, and his affection for Mason grew with their close association. He learned to calm Mason's smoldering anger, treated Purdy with civility and respect, and maintained harmony between them. The Americans, of course, saw eye to eye on matters of military discipline and where the ways of the Western world clashed with those of the Orient.

Before Colston arrived, Purdy and Mason had surveyed Berenice and its harbor. The combined groups spent the next two months examining the shore and the surrounding country. The town and harbor promised well for shipping and the railroad Ismail had in mind. They spent Christmas at Berenice and by the first of the year were ready to start on the next leg of their expedition. About New Year's, Colston's group moved from Berenice to a camp in a nearby wadi. A wadi, Colston learned, was any depression, from a gully to a valley, between hills. Colston made preparations in the Wadi Shanshef for the journey across the desert to the Nile at Berber. He and Purdy gathered fresh camels and fresh drivers. Part of the preparations involved entertaining, with excessive formality, the sheiks of the district. At last, having propitiated the local dignitaries and having obtained assurances of safe conduct, the explorers set out.

It was January 11, 1874. The horns sounded well before dawn and the rising sun broke on a scene of utter confusion. The camels were bellowing, balking, kicking, and biting. The drivers were fussing with the loads, burdening the beasts until they refused to move and lay down with stubborn determination. As the sun neared its zenith, the drivers urged and prodded the camels into line and the order to march was given. Plodding along at the slowest pace, the camels made few miles the first day, but after a week the drivers were leading them with speed and efficiency, and the orderly train moved ahead at a pace to satisfy even the impatient Americans.

Geology and geography were the primary interests of the expedition as it moved south from Berenice to Berber, and Colston and Purdy examined and wrote reports on a succession of wadies, streams, wells, and water holes. They did not, as Stone later explained to the khedive, make new discoveries in hitherto unknown territory, but they did make the first detailed, accurate, and complete report on the region. Above all, they showed that the route was completely feasible for a railroad.

On the twentieth day of the journey from Berenice they came upon two large wells—Bir Abral and Bir Sounta—and the remains of large and skilfully constructed fortifications. On the stones were Greek inscriptions, too broken to read, but the explorers concluded that this was the hunting lodge of Ptolemy mentioned in ancient writings. Two weeks later, at Derehib, they came to gold mines which the French had worked forty years before. They checked and found correct the surveys which the Frenchman Louis Linant had made. "It seemed like meeting an old acquaintance after reading Linant's book, and to find a memorial of civilized man in this desert which has never been visited since by such until we came," wrote Colston. They found the place on the cliff where in 1832 Linant had carved his name, and they lowered each other by ropes and carved their own names and the date. They took specimens of quartz for a gold assay.

But though geography and geology were of first importance to their mission, zoölogy was of equal interest to them. Sometimes they hunted, cutting loose from the caravan to bring in gazelles for food. One refractory camel resisted all civilizing influences and was butchered and the meat sold in camp. "It looks like fair beef," observed Colston. "It tastes like poor beef," he added, after taking a bite. Once two wild apes peeked at them from the top of a ridge, safely out of range. Occasionally they killed scorpions and snakes in the camps. Near the Nile they hunted for hippopotami and for geese.

The party acquired some domestic animals on the trip. Colonel Purdy, as Colston found, had many unpleasant characteristics but he shared Colston's love of animals. At one time the whole expedition was thrown into a furor when Tiggy, a pet cat, disappeared into the mountains. Search proved in vain, and the commanders left several men with Tiggy's mate Tom in the hope that she could be lured back. And there was "Miss Bessie," a baby gazelle, brought into camp with a milch goat for nurse.

Purdy immediately adopted her, but when the expedition moved on, he left the little animal and her nurse in a native village. He was highly irate to learn months later that she had disappeared. "Strayed off," reported the natives, who did not understand this odd concern for a pet. At Berber, Purdy was delighted when someone presented him with a monkey.

As the survey continued they met the sheiks of the villages and exchanged greetings with passing caravans. On entering Berber they heard women hidden in mud huts making a queer noise that sounded to Colston like "the mew of a cat and the note of a bird." But Linant's book had prepared them for this greeting. Linant called it the "glou-glou" and said it was "intended for welcome." Once there came into camp a visitor who said he had been Linant Bey's guide forty years before and claimed to be one hundred and twenty years old. He attributed his long life to diet; he ate no food but drank a *girbeh* of milk each day. Colston described him as active, possessed of all his faculties, and with a good head of hair and very good teeth. All this was recorded without skepticism, and Colston added that the old man was said to have eighteen children and a hundred camels.

The visitors and the passing strangers were no problem to the expedition, but there were personnel problems within the camp. After a time the Americans learned to ignore the constant bickering among the drivers. More serious was the negligence of an Arab officer who failed to keep the water bags filled with clean water. They placed him under arrest. There were complaints against the doctor, one Hassan Fahmi, who interfered with discipline and was the cause of insubordination. The Americans held a hearing, found the charges accurate, and sent him back to Cairo for punishment.

In early March, after three months of wandering, they came to the Nile at a point several days' march above the Fifth Cataract. The trip down the river to Berber was easy enough, and there were new sights to see, fine hunting, and local officials to receive or meet with dignity and graciousness. They arrived in

Berber in the midst of a dust and windstorm, and when the air cleared the city itself rose like a phantom from the desert. Its setting was superb, its majestic palms and tall acacias with broad-leafed tops cast welcome shade on cool gardens, but for all its setting the city was a disappointment—a collection of squat mud huts, with an occasional house of European style. On closer inspection, Berber was a depressing place. Its people were equally unattractive. The three Americans went to the bazaar and found the inhabitants "strange and hideous specimens of humanity." Men and women alike were nearly naked, and unmarried women customarily wore only a scanty loin cloth. They were, all of them, thought Colston, "blackened corpses." The Negro population—and most of the population were Negro—were the "blackest and ugliest" he had seen.

Yet, for contrast, the Americans were delighted to visit Sitta Maria Laforge, the widow of a former French consul at Berber. She was an Abyssinian Christian—"not darker than a Cuban," remarked Colston—and wore a thick veil over the lower half of her face. Her brow, eyes, and nose were beautiful to the men, who for months had not seen even the women of desert villages. She was tall and graceful; her dress was silk, European in style. She was forty, but the Americans thought her no more than thirty. Madame Laforge received them graciously and served them lemonade and coffee. She told them—she spoke only Arabic—that she had made two trips in her lifetime. During her husband's life she had been once to Gondokoro and once to Cairo. She carried on an extensive trade in aromatic gums and ivory. Her house, set in a handsome garden adorned with peacocks, confirmed the local legend that she was fabulously wealthy. The Americans were much impressed, and when in the evening she sent food—including wheat bread—to their camp, they loudly sang her praises.

Berber's commercial importance was considerable, but slaves were its most profitable merchandise. Although Ismail had prohibited the slave trade in his domains, his authority was weak in Berber and the slavers openly carried on their business.

To the west and south lay the uncharted regions of Darfur and Kordofan, and from their unknown recesses came an unending stream of slaves. The Negroes were, at least in the opinion of the Virginians Colston and Mason, "fit for nothing else in fact," and neither made any objections when members of their entourage struck bargains in the slave market. Colston's personal servant bought a Negro boy from the far interior of Africa, and one of the soldiers, a Coptic Christian, created a stir among his fellows when he paid $80 for a girl whom he proposed to marry when he got back to Cairo. Colston confined his own purchases to specimens of silver filigree work for friends, Stone among them, in Cairo.

The expedition remained in Berber for nearly a month. During most of that time Colston was ill. He had had an irritation of the bladder when he was in Berenice, and it had continued to trouble him along the route to Berber. In Berber he suffered from lumbago, or so he diagnosed it, and his back and loins pained him constantly. He remained in bed much of the time, and Purdy and Mason made all the preparations for the return journey. On April 12, the caravan, including the slaves bought in Berber, started for Cairo. Colston, still in pain, traveled only with difficulty. He bought a native saddle but found he could not use it comfortably. His dromedary was easy to ride but, like its rider, feeble.

Their route lay almost directly north. Between Berber and Korosko the Nile made a great bend to the west, and the route across the desert was both shorter and simpler than the river route. But it was not to be an easy trip. The new desert was unlike those the Americans had previously crossed, the kind of desert the Arabs call *el jebel, el berriyeh*, the mountain and the wilderness. In such they had found wadies, watercourses, and water holes. In the wadies were flowers, and often the plants contained so much moisture that for days at a time neither camels nor sheep needed to be watered. Trees fringed the valleys, and the land abounded in grouse, "capricorns," hares, and wild asses, as well as scorpions, locusts, serpents, and the scavengers, the vulture and hyena. There was deadwood for fires, and the Americans enjoyed hearty cooking. Nothing, they thought, was better than a roast of lamb from the Sudan sheep that grazed on the aromatic grasses of the desert. The buzz of the camp, the music of a viol, endless chatter and laughter, and fragrant Mocha coffee were welcome at the end of the day's journey.

But the desert they were about to cross was different. It was an *atmoor* (Colston said, ". . . the superlative desert, the desert *par excellence*")—a plain of hard gravel, diversified only by zones of deep sand, rocky belts, and rugged defiles. It was barren of vegetation, apparently devoid of all life, and the sun's glare on the yellow sands could cause blindness. Half the rare wells on the *atmoor* were exhausted; the remainder had a scant supply of brackish water. The marches were terrible; yet it was better to keep moving than to stop. And as they marched, the sun beat down on the sands, making gun barrels and the leather of the saddles blistering to the touch. Even the vulture and the hyena wandered only at night. Soldiers and camel-drivers covered their heads with blankets and turbans. Along the route lay the bleached skeletons of camels —Colston counted forty in a mile. There was no fuel except dried camel dung. At night there were only small fires. There was no music, and tongues were too parched for talk.

On the third day there was excitement in the camp. During the night the slave girl had run away. She was afraid, so the rumor ran, because her purchaser was a Christian. Immediately the commanding officers sent out a search party, knowing that under the fierce sun and without water she would die. For a day she was lost on the desert. When she was found, the American officers summoned her before them, and the impromptu court discovered the reason for her flight. She had fled to escape the beatings her master gave her. The caravan moved on.

After nine days of the desert they reached Korosko. Here they took leave of their camel-drivers, loaded soldiers, equipment, and collections of specimens on a steamer, and started down the Nile. Tourists once more, they stopped to visit ruins along the banks until they came to the railhead at Assiout. The Arab officers were put in charge of the men and equipment, and the Americans boarded the train for Cairo. They arrived on May 7, almost exactly eight months from the day of their departure.

Immediately the khedive summoned the explorers for a first-hand account of their experiences. In particular, Ismail asked for information about Colston's route from Kenneh to Berenice, but to their mutual annoyance Purdy persisted in interrupting to answer all the questions. He was eager, Colston observed, to claim all credit. The khedive had to await a formal report, and through the summer and fall of 1874 Colston, Purdy, and Mason worked at the Citadel, classifying the specimens they had brought back, making fair copies of maps from hasty sketches, and writing their reports. When they were done, General Stone and the khedive had complete information upon which to base their plans for Egypt's development.

For the explorers life in Cairo seemed far more hectic than the days in the desert had been. Colston tried to resume his former living arrangements in the capital: he got a room, retrieved his pet cat, and took in a puppy so young that he had to sit up nights feeding it with a spoon. He bought, as well, a beautiful sorrel horse of animated spirit and pure pedigree. But the horse turned out to be a "stumbler" that threatened to throw him, his dog did not thrive, and his new room was infested with fleas. Then, too, his lumbago continued to trouble him. The minor exasperations of Cairo seemed more irksome than the travail of the *atmoor*.

The explorers had returned at the height of Warren's quarrelsome career, and Colston discovered that Warren had turned Loring against him, that the Stones and the Warrens were not speaking, and that there was an air of uneasy tension in the American colony. In the hotels, the cafés, at dinner parties, in the Citadel, Purdy played the braggart. Colston avoided him whenever possible, as did most of the Americans. In such an atmosphere Mason grew morose and less companionable. The only relief for Colston, Mason, and Purdy was the arrival of accounts of the exploits of Chaillé-Long, far up the Nile in Uganda. All three of the explorers would have welcomed an opportunity to resume their travels.

The opportunity was in the making. For months there had been troubles in the Sudan, in Kordofan, and in the vast unknown region of Darfur, which lay to the west of Kordofan. When Sir Samuel Baker asserted the khedive's authority over Kordofan, he had announced that the slave trade was forbidden. But his efforts to stop the trade had cut off the trade in ivory and ostrich plumes and, instead of enriching the Egyptian empire, brought distress. His lack of discretion dismayed Ismail as much as it angered the slave-dealers of distant Darfur. Early in 1874, as Chinese Gordon was taking command of the equatorial provinces, the sultan of Darfur attacked Egyptian outposts. The Egyptians moved into Darfur, occupied El Fasher, the capital, and began a policy of conciliation. Clearly, Ismail intended to proclaim Egyptian suzerainty over Darfur. In fact, as English observers in India and in London solemnly warned, this move had less to do with exterminating the slave trade than it had with Ismail's ambitions to expand his imperial domains. The skeptics said he planned to take all the Sudan and Abyssinia and the lands beyond the equatorial lakes. The skeptics, as usual, were right. Ismail wanted to extend the railroad up the Nile and into the Sudan, and he was making ready the formal annexation of Darfur. In the Citadel, Stone Pasha immediately turned his attention to schemes for exploring the new domain. The opportunity for which Colston and Purdy and Mason were waiting was at hand.

By December, 1874, the chief of staff had ready a sheaf of instructions, careful and detailed, for the exploration of both Kordofan and Darfur. Two expeditions were equipped in readiness for a long tour in the deserts. Officers were selected and briefed. One expedition would go into submissive Darfur, which in another month would be formally annexed to Egypt. The other would go to Kordofan, a more accessible region. For the Darfur expedition he chose Purdy as chief and Mason as second in command. The other group, ordered to make the most minute survey of Kordofan, had Colston at its head. Assistant to Colston was Horatio B. Reed, a New Yorker who had served in the Civil War as a lieutenant in the Fifth United States Artillery and had won brevet promotions for daring and gallantry. As a lieutenant colonel of the Twenty-Second New York Cavalry, he fought under Sheridan and at the end of the war was colonel of his regiment. He remained in the army until 1870. In the spring of 1874 he arrived in Cairo with his bride. Unlike the experienced hands on the expedition, Reed did not take kindly to the Kordofan assignment, and young Mrs. Reed, who accepted the substance of Warren's diatribes against Stone, was distressed at the prospect of separation from her husband. The expedition was expected to be gone two and a half years.

Stone's instructions were that the two groups under the command of Colston and Purdy were to set out together up the Nile to Aswan and take the railway around the cataract and then go on to Wadi Halfa, where Colston would pick up his camels. From Debbe on the Nile, Colston was to explore seventy-five (and not more than one hundred) miles to the south on the route from Debbe to El Obeid, capital of Kordofan. He was not to spend more than fifteen days at this. He was to note water and pasturage, dig wells, and then proceed to El Obeid. He was expected to make maps and note fuel supplies and spend no more than forty-five days on this part of his trip. He was to collect specimens, and specimens, maps, and reports were to be packed in tin tubes. . . . The instructions went on and on, giving details, demonstrating Stone Pasha's attention to minutiae, but allowing for none of the exigencies that might be met in an unknown territory. Stone provided a time schedule for everything (even the camels were to be rested only at stated times). During the rainy season the commanders were to make their reports. Eventually—just when was clearly set forth in the schedule—Colston would survey and explore as far as the western boundary of Kordofan, and there his group would meet Purdy, exploring eastern Darfur. Together they would continue, exploring the south of Darfur and then striking off toward the region of the equatorial lakes, there dividing again to extend the boundaries of geographical knowledge east and west of the mountains. Of course, as Stone Pasha explained to Purdy Bey and Colston Bey, there would be additional and more detailed instructions forwarded to them at various points on their routes.

On December 5, 1874, with suitable fanfare, the officers and soldiers boarded a Nile steamer. The khedive had received the commanders, conferred upon them his august blessing, and impressed upon them the importance of their work. All Cairo came to the boats—the general staff in full uniform—to see them off, and the farewells delayed the start until afternoon. Only young Mrs. Reed was tearful, and her sobs were alternately those of sorrow and of anger.

The trip up the Nile was uneventful, but it gave evidence that General Stone, for all the elaborateness of his instructions, had not been able to take everything into account. Lieutenant Colonel Reed was sick. The barges loaded with men and equipment, including howitzers and ammunition, did not tow smoothly. When they reached Aswan on Christmas Eve, they were off schedule and thereafter never did return to the time-table Stone had so carefully prepared. It was January 4 when the expeditions reached Korosko, January 9 before they came to Wadi Halfa, and there the feast of Bairam held them up for another ten days.

Here the expedition was to divide, Purdy continuing along the Nile until he struck the caravan route into Darfur. Here Colston got his camels—five hundred of them—and two hundred drivers to care for them. But no one had thought to specify the age and general physical condition of the animals. They were clearly in no condition to strike out across the *atmoor.* The usual confusion of organizing a caravan delayed the start until the afternoon of January 18. They traveled four hours that day and, exhausted, made camp in the dark. The second day was better. They traveled seven hours and made camp at four in the afternoon. But some of the camels were so slow that they were still straggling into camp at seven o'clock. The next day four were dead and fifty or sixty were too weak to be loaded. Colston stopped a day to rest the animals. The following day the group marched for three hours and four camels fell by the wayside. Before a week was up five more were dead and forty-one were missing. Some twenty of these belonged to a Bedouin who, having been paid in advance, deserted and took his camels with him. Colston began to send frantic messages to the governor of Dongola, pleading for more camels.

At the same time that Colston was finding that his animals were in no condition to stand the hardships of the march, his second in command was failing him. On the day of the three-hour march Lieutenant Colonel Reed had chills and fever. Day after day he was too ill to attend to his duties and so ill that he could not keep pace with the exhausted camels.

Worried by Reed's condition, Colston consulted another member of the party, Dr. Pfund, a great, bearded German who had long been in the employ of the khedive. He had been educated as a surgeon but long since had turned naturalist and had begun to go on desert expeditions. He was a man in his sixties, wise in the ways of the desert and wise enough in the ways of men. On the trip he gathered, mounted, bottled, and classified specimens of various kinds, preparing an unusually complete collection of rocks, birds, plants, insects, and reptiles. He had neither authority nor responsibility for the conduct of the expedition, but he was the only available medical man.

Perhaps Dr. Pfund, whose medical knowledge had slipped away from him in the years he had been a naturalist, needed no great amount of medical lore to diagnose Reed's illness. The old doctor rightly surmised that the man could not be cured in the desert. He advised Colston to send Reed back to Cairo and ask Stone for a replacement.

Despite the weakness of animals and men, the work got done. Colston made his surveys, prepared the data for his maps, noted the contour of the land, the vegetation, the rock formations. He cleaned out water holes, dug wells, and located reservoirs. With all their labors and in spite of handicaps, Colston's group made progress.

Just before they reached Dongola, Colston heard from Purdy. So far as the animals were concerned, it was the same story. In the first two days on the old caravan route Purdy's group lost fifty-three camels. But Purdy did not share Colston's bad luck with subordinates. McComb Mason was made of sterner stuff—or perhaps he was not homesick for a wailing wife in Cairo—and he performed his duties sturdily.

Two months to the day after their departure from Cairo, Colston's men came to Dongola—an "insignificant town," he said, but the capital of the region. On the outskirts they stopped while the officers and soldiers put on full dress and the men unpacked the cannon from the backs of camels and mounted them on carriages. By the time they were ready, an escort had appeared. Into the town they went, the horses of their Arab escorts pirouetting and raising a glorious cloud of dust. The local troops were out with a band, and more voluntary escorts mounted on donkeys guided them into the very presence of the governor of Dongola. Colston gave alms to the beggars, exchanged presents with the governor, and heard him promise that in a week everything would be ready—even fresh camels.

On February 17, Reed left Dongola with an escort. Late in March he arrived in Cairo—confirming his wife's prediction that he would not stay long on the expedition—and the night after his return Colonel and Mrs. Reed appeared at the opera.

On February 20, Purdy, Mason, and several Egyptian officers arrived in Dongola—that far on the road to Darfur.

Twelve days later their slow-moving expedition came in, camped for five days, and set out again on its journey.

In Cairo, General Stone was disgusted when Reed appeared, though he returned with the first consignment of Dr. Pfund's specimens. "His return here causes much unfavorable comment upon himself as well as the American officers," the chief of staff complained. He should have stayed at Dongola until he was well enough to go on with the expedition. Of course the service was hard, but "when one wishes to do hard service he can do it. . . . A bad example," said Stone.

In place of Reed, Stone determined to send Major Henry G. Prout as assistant to Colston. But recognizing no immediate need and not wanting to pass up a chance for further explorations of the Sudan, he ordered Prout to proceed down the Red Sea to Suakin and then cross to Berber on the Nile, exploring as he went. There he was to go up the river to Khartoum and prepare to join Colston. A few days after Reed's return, Prout was on his way, exploring carefully and reporting that most of the route was highly suitable for a railroad.

Prout, too, took no medical officer with him, although Reed's illness emphasized the need for a doctor on an exploring expedition. In fact, Stone had planned to send Dr. Warren with Prout. He made all arrangements to rid himself of this thorn in his flesh and needed only the signature of Ismail's son Hussein, the prince minister of war, to exile the annoying doctor. But the evening before the order was to be signed, someone—Dr. Warren thought it might even have been the minister of war himself—came in darkness to Dr. Warren to reveal what was afoot. The doctor had been suffering from a severe attack of ophthalmia but at the moment was well on his way to recovery; at the news of Stone's "plot," he feigned a relapse. He sent for his assistant, an Arab doctor, and ordered him to take over the duties of the office. The next morning Dr. Warren's name was at the head of the sick list. The assistant solemnly assured the minister of war that the doctor was too ill to move and would be unfit for duty for many weeks. Stone was chagrined, Prout went off without a medical officer, and Warren silently blessed the luck that had enabled him to evade an assignment which he was convinced would have led to his death.

Long before Prout reached Kordofan, Colonel Colston himself gave proof that exploratory groups entering primitive country must anticipate illness and disease. For a month Colston's party remained in Dongola waiting for the dilatory governor to furnish camels. Late in March the group proceeded to Debbe, a "small and insignificant" village on the banks of the Nile. They lost another week waiting for camels, then spent a week surveying a valley called the Wadi Massoul. For seventy-two miles the wadi appeared waterless and unpromising. On the expedition Colston was exposed to the sun and returned ill to Debbe. In two weeks he had developed a "liver complaint" and began to lose control of his legs. Dr. Pfund examined him and recommended that he abandon the expedition and return to Cairo. But Colston had a soldier's pride. Because Stone and the khedive had intrusted the expedition to his care, he would not quit. "I prefer dying on the desert to abandoning this work." Although he was suffering severely and could mount a horse only with the help of two men, he started for El Obeid on April 20. Almost immediately the expedition entered a desert where water holes were from ten to twenty-five miles apart. For twenty days Colston surveyed, took barometric readings, gathered specimens, and supervised the cleaning and enlarging of water holes and wells. Progress was slow; time and again the suffering commander was forced to halt the expedition while he rested. After a week he was unable to mount a horse or a camel and was carried on a litter. When he admitted to himself that he could not continue, he lay on the ground and sobbed. "This is harder to bear than the physical pain," he wrote in his diary. Again Dr. Pfund urged him to turn back.

But there were still other problems to be faced. The adjutant who would succeed him was an errant rascal, and Colston swore he would not turn over his command to such a villain. "Every day discloses more instances of oppression and exaction," moaned the commander. And there were the soldiers—equally untrustworthy. Several came before him, charged with stealing the food of the dromedaries. Another soldier insisted that his dromedary had died on the road and showed a piece of hide to prove it, expecting to be paid a high price for the missing camel. It was an ancient trick, as Colston recognized. Often drivers cut a piece of skin from a living camel, turned the beast loose in the desert, and produced the bloody swatch as evidence of loss. Colston sent some of his men to hunt the suffering animals and often was able to save them. On another day a captain of infantry and the adjutant filed charges against each other. Colston sighed, "If Prout were only here to take command, I'd die easier."

Meanwhile he suffered. "Oh, Night of Hell!" Colston was heard to cry. A storm blew away his tent, and his servant and a soldier fought to hold a blanket over their stricken commander. The paralysis crept to his back, and he could not turn over without aid. He asked Dr. Pfund to tell him when he had but three or four days to live. The good doctor advised him to make his will. With that, Colston stopped the expedition to set his house in order. He wrote to General Stone, to the khedive, and to his family. He named Ward, Purdy, and Mason as his executors. "I can look on death calmly," he wrote in his diary. "Hard as it is to see all my hopes blasted and to die in such torments in this god-forsaken country!"

Yet after ten days he felt well enough to continue. He broke the march for hours, even days; but still the expedition went on. Finally, on June 3, seven weeks out of Debbe, Prout arrived in answer to Colston's plea to Khartoum. For another five days Colston remained in charge, instructing Prout. Then, still four days short of El Obeid, Colston relinquished the command.

For six months Colonel Colston remained in El Obeid. To his surprise he began to recover. Late in June he discovered that he could move one leg, and not long after he regained some control over the other. Slowly the swelling went down. There was a Catholic mission in El Obeid, and the priest and the nuns looked after him. The Mother Superior urged him to make a pilgrimage to Lourdes, but Colston believed a miracle had happened in Kordofan: he was well enough to walk. With the help of two soldiers he got about the town. Stone was proud of him. The khedive was pleased. Purdy never knew a "more plucky man." "Fortunate for the rest of us," wrote the commander of the Darfur expedition, "there was a *man* among us."

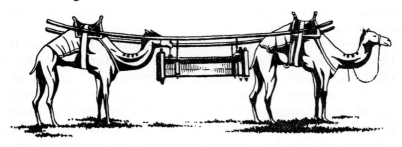

Late in November Colston left El Obeid. Unable to mount a horse, he rode in a litter slung between two camels, "one before and one behind." With him went a squad of soldiers— and among them a "black angel" whom Colston had come to value highly. Often he blessed the day when he had yielded to a soldier who begged permission to take his wife a short distance to stay with relatives. Colston was not surprised when the soldier later asked if his wife might continue with the expedition. In El Obeid she nursed Colston, and on the trip to the hospital at Khartoum she cooked for the men who carried him. Colston came to believe that without her he could not have survived. By the spring of 1876 he had recovered sufficiently to withstand the journey to Cairo.

In the meantime, Prout had taken over the expedition. Twenty years younger than Colston, he was better able to endure the hardships of desert exploration. His preparation, too, was better than that of his predecessor. A native of Fairfax County, Virginia, he joined the Federal army in 1863 and served as a private in the Army of the Potomac. In 1871 he graduated in civil engineering at the University of Michigan. While still in college he led an exploring expedition into southwestern Colorado. His work brought him to the attention of General Sherman, who recommended him to the khedive as a highly competent engineer. In Kordofan Sherman's judgment was confirmed. Prout's energy was great, his explorations thorough, and his observations penetrating. He had wisdom beyond his years. If he were perhaps less genial than Colston, the expedition lost nothing in efficiency by the change in command.

When Prout joined Colston in the desert, he brought with him a detachment of soldiers and a caravan of forty-four camels. In Khartoum he discovered and enlisted the services of an Arab surgeon, and for a time it seemed that the doctor would be the most useful member of the expedition. While Colston lay paralyzed in El Obeid, the rainy season—the *kherif*—began, and sickness spread among the men. Deaths from fever ran as high as seven or eight a day, and there were times when all the soldiers in the camp were stricken. The camels and horses suffered as much as the men. Prout reported: "I am almost without assistance. . . . Adjutant-Major Hamdi has been very ill for a week. The daily sick report shows from twenty-seven to thirty men sick. . . . Our servants are all sick. The Arab surgeon of the expedition, although quite ill, displays an unlooked-for energy in attending the sick. . . . The people here say that this is an unusually healthy *kherif!*"

Despite the *kherif*, Prout pushed his explorations. He sent out a detachment under Dr. Pfund and another under Major Hamdi. He himself led a third. He planned to make a huge map of Kordofan, gather the statistics of the country, and present everything in a single report. He ordered fresh quinine from Cairo, fresh camels and fresh men from the mudiriyeh of Kordofan. The detachment led by Prout swung in a great circle of seven hundred miles to the southern boundary of the province, covering in six weeks the least-known part of Kordofan and penetrating still hostile territory. For nine months he probed into every part of the land and at length prepared a report that won the unqualified praise of the chief of staff. The report, the maps, and the "conscientious appendices," said Stone, "evidence how much can be done by an able, instructed and honest-minded officer . . . when that officer thinks less of the risks and discomforts around him than of the accomplishment of duty for duty's sake."

Major Prout merited indeed the words of Stone Pasha. He had covered the geography and the topography of Kordofan. The soil, he reported, was sandy, with some clay, and cultivable if it had an adequate water supply. There were only three small lakes, and the rainfall averaged about 32 centimeters a year. Prout saw little hope for improving the water supply for the area as a whole: the scant rainfall, the porous soil, the heat, and the long dry period would make irrigation a tremendous task. But there were districts where improvements might be made. He thought that one hundred thousand cattle might be grazed in the province, although crops of *dokhn* (corn), beans, and onions—the main foods of the people— could scarcely be increased to support a larger population. He found hematite in the mountains but no wood or coal nearby to process it. He thought that the gum forests might be exploited and that ostriches could be raised if they were protected from the rapacity of the people—but this, he added skeptically, depended on the state of the feather market.

As well as making a map, gathering statistics, and reporting on the soil, climate, water supply, mineral resources, and economic potentialities of Kordofan, Prout studied the people and took note of their living conditions, their customs, and the way they dressed. They were, he found, a mixture of many African races—the natives of the region, their conquerers from Darfur, and the Turks and fellahin of Egypt who had in turn conquered the Furs. There were Greeks and

Levantines and Abyssinian slaves and a constant influx of Negroes from the south. Among them was every variety of face, form, and figure. One group stood out. They were people of a dark complexion with a reddish tinge, of good height, slender, oval-faced, with narrow brows, straight noses, full lips, and a "large and coarse mouth." They were often good-looking and, wrote Prout, sometimes handsome. He added, with what may have been a touch of humor or a flicker of Anglophobia, "The profile is more like the reigning family in England than the true Negro profile."

The population included villagers "scattered pretty uniformly" over the area north of the thirteenth parallel, nomads who wandered with their herds, and mountain people. Major Prout had seen little of the mountain people, but he carefully observed the villagers and the nomads. The villagers dwelt in *tokels*, cylindrical structures fifteen to twenty feet in diameter and three to five feet high, surmounted by a high conical roof, the whole built of weeds and stalks of corn lashed to a frame. The nomads lived in tortoise-shaped huts of mats thrown over frames. In camp the huts were grouped in a circle and inclosed by a thorn hedge.

The native dress of Kordofan was simple: a single piece of white cotton wound around the body and thrown over the shoulders. Children under ten went naked. Both men and women braided their hair, greased it with mutton fat, and decorated themselves with trinkets. Some of the women wore a huge gilt ring in one nostril—"an arrangement," thought Prout, "probably invented by some tyrannical husband who placed wives and dromedaries in the same class." They seemed to him an unhappy people. "Even the children seem weighed down with the gravity of life." In El Obeid there were amusements—and Prout noted carefully the gyrations of a belly dancer—but they provoked no gaiety in the people.

As for customs, Prout noted those matters pertaining to sex, family relations, and burials. Both boys and girls were circumcised. For the most part, marriage customs were similar to those in Egypt. But in some areas a wife shared her husband's bed for three nights and on the fourth night could entertain her friends. In one tribe a girl had to present her brother with a child as his bondman—the father of her own choosing—before she could marry. Burial among the lower classes was simple. The body was placed in a shallow trench, covered with a little dirt, and left to be unearthed by the hyenas.

Major Prout found little religion among the Kordofans. A Roman Catholic mission in El Obeid had accomplished little more than to relieve some of the sickness and suffering. Except in El Obeid he saw no one at prayer; everywhere he found superstition and the wearing of talismans. The people of the villages and the nomads were nominally Moslems, but their knowledge of the faith was rudimentary. The mountain tribes were heathen. "Moreover," he wrote, "such a people can hardly be said to have any morals." Murders were so frequent that he seldom rode out of El Obeid without seeing the body of a victim. Cattle-stealing was common. Adultery was rife. "Few girls are chaste, and the men don't seem to care whether their brides are virgin or not." It was not a pretty picture, and Prout thought little of the land or the people. The inhabitants were lazy and "abject cowards." "They are a mean-spirited, incontinent, rascally race in whom I see the material for very good slaves, but who will disappear from the earth before they are sensibly elevated above their present condition."

"In the philanthropist, and in the missionary, they may excite an intense interest," Prout decided. "It is not, however, as sufferers to be relieved, or as sinners to be saved, that we are to consider them here; but as subjects of the Egyptian Government. As such, they will never add, I am convinced, to the wealth, to the strength, or to the glory of the state!"

So saying, Prout left Kordofan and set forth to join Purdy in Darfur. He had the usual difficulties on the long trip which, by his own choice, lay across an unexplored desert, and he lost fifty-five of his three hundred camels. This time he had carefully selected his camel train and was determined to take more than a month for the trip from El Obeid. Thereupon he added one footnote to his adverse commentary on Kordofan. "I determined to try thoroughly," he told Stone, "the effect of easy marching and good care." The experiment convinced him that the camels as well as the people of Kordofan were not much good. "The camels bred in the villages of Kordofan," he reported in disgust, "are inferior in strength and endurance to any that I have seen elsewhere."

Late in April, 1876, Major Prout reached El Fasher, capital of Darfur. For more than a year Purdy had been exploring the far stretches of the khedive's newest province, much as Prout had been doing in Kordofan. He had come by an easier road, following the caravan route, and had established headquarters at El Fasher. Perhaps Darfur was more pleasant than Kordofan, or perhaps Purdy was a less critical observer than Prout. At any rate, his first reports were of a countryside that was healthy and fertile, with a climate dry and cool. Abundant cattle throve on lush grasses. But further investigation revealed that such oases as El Fasher were scarce enough, and by the time Prout arrived to compare notes the two men were agreed that Darfur was probably even less promising than Kordofan. Prout checked Purdy's observations, and Purdy began to prepare a final map of Darfur and a report on his expedition. They concluded that Darfur would not repay Egypt the cost of conquest, and certainly was not worth the cost of military occupation.

A few months in the summer of 1876 were sufficient to complete their labors in the Sudan. They had succeeded, despite the desert climate and the failures of body and spirit, in fulfilling their mission. They had surveyed, measured, and assessed the Sudan to the satisfaction of the chief of staff, Stone Pasha, and to the delight of their royal master Ismail, khedive of Egypt. Whatever might have occurred—and much indeed had happened—to dim the luster of the Americans in the Egyptian service, only honor and praise came to Colston, Prout, Mason, and Purdy for their work in Darfur and Kordofan.

VIII

‿‿‿‿‿‿‿‿‿

Chaillé-Long in Central Africa

The explorers of the Sudan were not the only Americans to push outward the vague frontiers of the khedive's empire or to make distinct contributions to geographical knowledge. At the same time that these veterans of the Civil War and surveyors of the American West were making their observations of desert terrain and native tribes in Kordofan and Darfur, Lieutenant Colonel Charles Chaillé-Long, formerly a Union soldier from Maryland, was penetrating Equatorial Africa and seeing sights that had never before met the eye of civilized man. In fact, it was while Colston and Purdy were just beginning their first trip from Berenice to Berber on the Nile that Chaillé-Long set off for the equatorial provinces with Chinese Gordon. Before the Sudan explorers left for their major journeys into Darfur and Kordofan, all Cairo was buzzing with the news of Chaillé-Long's intrepid adventures in Central Africa.

There was a fundamental difference between Chaillé-Long's work on the upper waters of the Nile and the duties of Purdy, Colston, and Prout in the Sudan. The region from Suakin to Berber and even to far-off El Obeid and El Fasher was known territory, its limits vaguely defined, its routes known at least to traders—Arabs and sometimes even Europeans—who led their caravans in the ancient commerce in slaves and ivory. The American officers who explored the land were not making new discoveries. Instead, with chronometers and barometers and telescopes and slide rules, they were making a scientific survey. But Chaillé-Long, in Uganda, the Nyanza country, and in the land of the Makraka Niam-Niam, led expeditions of exploration and discovery. His contributions were military and political; the only instrument of modern science he carried was an elephant gun.

The difference in their work reflected differences in their previous experience and in their personalities. Purdy had been a surveyor; Colston had received the rudiments of an engineering education at the Virginia Military Institute; Prout had graduated in engineering and had been surveying in Colorado. Chaillé-Long was only an ill-educated and inexperienced youth when he wangled recommendations from Montgomery Blair and persuaded Thaddeus Mott to take him into the Egyptian army. He had had no battle experience in the Civil War, but he thought of himself as a fighting man and dreamed of storming Turkish redoubts in behalf of Egyptian liberty. He was slightly built, his features were almost delicate, and his health was never good; yet he had the compulsive drive for physical achievement that often forces frail men to feats of endurance that would dismay more robust associates.

Chaillé-Long arrived in Cairo in 1870 with an early contingent of Americans and was an old Egyptian hand by 1874 when he went off to his adventures in Central Africa. He had been something of a problem to the khedive and to Stone, who had tried to use him in various jobs. Shortly after his arrival, Ismail sent him riding to the east to find the spots where earthworks might be built to resist a Turkish invasion. But as war never came, his talents as a scout were not exercised. He had, it appeared, few other gifts. He did speak French and was diligently studying Arabic, so Ismail assigned him to teach French in the military school at Abbasiyeh. At the same time the khedive put him on the staff of Ratib Pasha, commanding general of the Egyptian army. The position rated a dress uniform glittering with gold embroidery and carried the impressive title of "Chief of the Sections of Military Correspondence, Law and Inspection." Chaillé-Long quickly got himself suitably caparisoned, but Ratib did not want even so resplendent a staff officer. Next, General Stone sent Chaillé-Long off to Alexandria to help General Halid Pasha organize a staff in Loring's bailiwick. Halid had no more use for Chaillé-Long than had Ratib, but he was not so skilful as his chief in ridding himself of the American. He insulted him frequently, and at last, since Chaillé-Long bore the insults patiently, withheld his pay for several months. Thereupon Chaillé-Long filed charges with the khedive and had the satisfaction of seeing Halid banished to an assignment in the Sudan.

Although the Egyptian officers did not take kindly to Chaillé-Long, the Marylander got along well enough with his fellow Americans. In Alexandria he lived in the palace where Loring and the two Reynolds families maintained their crowded menage. Old Gauley, the senior Reynolds, took such a liking to Chaillé-Long, calling him "Son" in affectionate condescension, that the Egyptians believed they were related. In Cairo, as well as in Alexandria, Chaillé-Long hung about the coffeehouses and the cafés, went to the opera, and loafed conspicuously. He was congenial, had good taste in wine and food, and was more than a little vain about his dress.

Above all, Chaillé-Long was ambitious for fame. Perhaps because he had no special talent or special training he had a greater variety of assignments than any of the American officers. Stone even tried him for a time on the general staff in the Citadel. None of the posts that he filled ever quite suited him, and none gave him the recognition that he craved. He thought of himself as a fighting man, and the routine tasks of a peacetime army only increased his restlessness. In the spring of 1872 he went to Paris to recuperate from an attack of typhoid and improved his time by visiting Napoleon's battlefields and daydreaming of bygone times when men of valor could prove their worth.

Because he had learned to speak Arabic fluently and had wide acquaintance with the khedive's operations, Chaillé-Long was an ideal man to send off to Central Africa with Chinese Gordon. Stone and the khedive, both of whom had tried to place Chaillé-Long, realized that his abilities fitted him for Gordon's staff. There was, however, another motive for sending the American with the Englishman: the khedive never quite trusted Gordon, and he knew Chaillé-Long shared the general suspicion of British designs held by other American officers.

The Americans were convinced that British imperialism in Africa boded no good for Egypt, for the khedive, and, ultimately, for them. The British were interfering in the administration of Lower Egypt and poking an inquisitorial nose into tax-collecting and public finance. British adventurers were worming their way into the confidence of the king of Abyssinia; others were influencing the sultan of Zanzibar, who held sway over lands at the equator far below the Gulf of Aden. In Central Africa Henry M. Stanley, whom Chaillé-Long called a pseudo-American, was wandering in the jungles, where he had once found Dr. David Livingstone, to advance the "dubious aims" of England. British influence had led the khedive to intrust to Sir Samuel Baker the extension of his domain into Equatorial Africa, and after Baker's failure it was the Prince of Wales himself who urged that Chinese Gordon take Baker's place. The Americans could find ample evidence to bolster their suspicions of England.

So, too, could the khedive. When Ismail's representatives approached Charles George Gordon, the British soldier of fortune presented the terms under which he would accept this mission. By virtue of long experience he had considerable bargaining power. As a military engineer he had fought in the Crimean War. Later he went to China and rose in the service of the emperor. In 1864 he commanded the "Ever-Victorious Army" which, in thirty-three engagements, suppressed the Taiping Rebellion. Before he would agree to enter the Egyptian service, he demanded almost independent sovereignty over his territory—demanded that his relations with the khedive be on a par with those between the viceroy and the sultan. Under pressure Ismail yielded power over governmental administration and permitted Gordon to have his own system of finance. The army was to be Egyptian, and Gordon was to take Colonel Chaillé-Long on his staff.

Gordon agreed, and sent for Chaillé-Long, who sat with a group of Americans who were speculating, as was all Egypt, about what manner of man Gordon would be. Chaillé-Long unfolded the note which read, "Will you come with me to Central Africa? Come and see me at once. Gordon."

Chaillé-Long found Gordon at the hotel. The Britisher was seated at a table with both a Bible and a bottle of brandy open before him. He poured a drink for Chaillé-Long and immediately told him that he himself had insisted that Chaillé-Long accompany him. The British consul general, Edward Stanton, and even the foreign minister, Lord Derby, said Gordon, had fought against Chaillé-Long's appointment and insisted upon Gordon's choosing a Briton for his chief of staff. Gordon advised him to be wary of Stanton and Derby. In return Chaillé-Long thanked him for his solicitude. Gordon was impressed. "A good American, a sharp fellow," he reported, confident that Chaillé-Long had appreciated his choice of him.

Whatever favorable impression resulted from the first interview did not last. The two men, the American and his British commander, were really much alike. Each was ambitious, each romantic, each dreamed of exciting adventure and of a heroic role. Each was jealous of fame, an egoist, and each envious of the other. To the end of their lives—and Chaillé-Long survived Gordon by more than three decades—each belittled the other's accomplishments.

On the day following their first meeting Chaillé-Long received a different version of his appointment. The khedive summoned him to the palace to give him instructions in secret. Some time before, Ismail told him, emissaries from M'Tesa, king of Uganda, had appeared at Sir Samuel Baker's headquarters. This Central African kingdom was a region in which the British were interested. Several years earlier, the English explorer John H. Speke, who discovered Lake Victoria, had visited Uganda. Now Henry M. Stanley was preparing to visit M'Tesa, and the khedive wanted Chaillé-Long to arrive before Stanley and forestall efforts to extend British influence and control over the land. "Go to Gondokoro," ordered Ismail, "but lose no time in making your way to Uganda . . . and Egypt will owe you a debt of gratitude."

Whether Gordon knew of these instructions—and Chaillé-Long thought he did not—he said nothing. "An American, named Long, a colonel in the Egyptian army," he reported to a correspondent, "has asked to come with me, and if I can I shall take him." He ignored William P. A. Campbell, whom Stone had called back from Colston's expedition to accompany Chaillé-Long.

On February 21, 1874, Gordon's party, which included Chaillé-Long, Campbell, and a handful of Arab officers, departed ceremoniously from Cairo. They went to Suez and down the Red Sea to Suakin. There the staff, mounted on camels (with Chaillé-Long on a pony) and accompanied by a detachment of soldiers, rode for days across miles of desert to Berber on the Nile. Gordon prided himself on this demonstration of physical endurance and concluded that Chaillé-Long and Campbell, who showed signs of exhaustion, were weaklings.

From Berber, continuing his efforts to impress both his staff and the natives of his domains, Gordon hurried up the Nile to Khartoum. The governor of Khartoum and the local dignitaries hardly had time to prepare to receive their new commander, but a salvo of guns and a parade of troops were readied to welcome him. And there was a banquet and entertainment by a dozen Abyssinian dancing girls in clanking bracelets and girdles of leather strips. Gordon was properly impressed and determined to give a dinner to surpass the native performance.

By this time he had concluded that Chaillé-Long was a weakling and incompetent. "Self is the best officer to do anything for you," he reminded himself sententiously. But when he came to give his dinner, he found he had no equipment for serving his guests. It was Chaillé-Long who scouted out the crockery, cutlery, and linens abandoned by Baker.

Thanks to Chaillé-Long the dinner went off well enough, but the next morning Gordon made an announcement that would make his arrival long remembered in Khartoum. He had come, he said, to advance Egyptian trade; hereafter all trade in ivory would be a government monopoly. He gave the merchants who had been his guests the night before exactly three months to give up the ivory business and to turn over all their stores to the government. The astounded merchants protested. They carried their grievance to Chaillé-Long and pleaded with him to intercede with Gordon. The American, who was as astonished as the merchants, advised Gordon to rescind his order or at least to postpone it for five years. But Gordon was adamant and ignored Chaillé-Long's prophecy of disaster. Years later, when revolt surged through the area, Gordon admitted that Chaillé-Long was right, rue-fully confessing, "I laid the egg which hatched the Mahdi."

Having laid his egg in Khartoum, Gordon took off for Gondokoro, a thousand miles farther up the Nile. The journey, which took almost a month, Chaillé-Long found "terribly tedious and uninteresting," with roaring hippopotami to disturb their sleep and clouds of mosquitoes to make both day and night hideous. Gondokoro was a village of a thousand conical straw huts inclosed by a palisade. The inhabitants of the surrounding villages seemed hostile, but one chieftain, Lono by name, a splendid giant six and a half feet tall, was friendly. When Chaillé-Long visited him, Lono proudly displayed his four hundred wives and generously offered several to his visitors. But Chaillé-Long refused the honor. He was not much impressed by the native Africans. He watched the dances put on for his entertainment and concluded that they resembled the frenzied performances of the Negro in America. "Civilization," he pronounced, "has done little for the Negro." He viewed with distaste the squalor, the nakedness, the native custom of smearing themselves with cow dung as a protection against mosquitoes. He suffered, as well, from the heat. "Africa is a country accursed of God," he wrote his father. Chinese Gordon needed but four days to agree that Gondokoro, at least, was no place to stay. He announced that on the fifth day they would return to Khartoum.

To Chaillé-Long, who had a mission to perform, Gordon's announcement offered an opportunity to escape surveillance. He managed to miss the boat, and Gordon, believing his indolent chief of staff had overslept, put off down the Nile without him. When, after a day or two, it was clear that Chaillé-Long was not hurrying to catch up, Gordon concluded the American had gone on to Uganda. Eventually he gave it out that he had sent Chaillé-Long to M'Tesa in order to be rid of him.

In Gondokoro Chaillé-Long hastily prepared to carry out the khedive's secret instructions. He picked five men to accompany him. Two were Sudanese soldiers who had served in Mexico; the others, a groom, a cook, and an interpreter. With them traveled a Ugandan returning to his own country. Chaillé-Long carried a few pounds of sugar and coffee, a few packages of rations. He took along only a change of clothing and a "gorgeous uniform" concocted for ceremonial occasions. In addition he chose gifts for M'Tesa from the storehouse in Gondokoro—red cloth, tarbooshes, a large mirror, a music box that played "Dixie," and a hand-cranked electric battery. Then Chaillé-Long heard that horses were unknown in Central Africa. He determined to ride—and the horse he chose to take he named "Uganda."

On April 24, 1874, equipped and accoutered, Chaillé-Long and his party set off. For the first part of the journey, to Egypt's southernmost outpost at Foweira on the White Nile, they accompanied three hundred porters returning to the interior for a load of ivory. The trek was not without its adventures. Several times, when the company had to cross swollen streams, Chaillé-Long stripped off his uniform and led the way. His successful ministrations during recurrent illnesses among the men gave him stature as a medicine man. When some of the company looted a Mogi village and the Mogi raided the camp and followed the column with menacing yells, Chaillé-Long led the attack that drove them off. His horse Uganda struggled through swamps and fell into elephant holes. At Foweira, where the Nile was alive with hippopotami and crocodiles, Chaillé-Long ferried the horse across the river in a dugout. From porters in the camp he knew that hardships would increase when they left Foweira. But he endowed himself with an appropriate title—*M'Bugaru,* the White Prince—and sent to M'Tesa a formal request for permission to visit his capital.

On a rainy May 25—a hard month from Gondokoro—Chaillé-Long led his party out of Foweira. Dissatisfaction had grown. The interpreter proved to be intemperate and insubordinate, and a new, untried man replaced the faithful groom, who had taken sick. That morning Chaillé-Long was racked with fever and his mind was filled with doubts. The whole adventure seemed foolhardy.

But Chaillé-Long did not have the temperament to dwell in the valley of despair. He had ambition, a lust for glory, and an unbounded egotism. His very physical weakness challenged his spirit and compelled him to feats of endurance. His spirits revived when Rionga, the native king of a nearby tribe, received him with honors and arranged a reception. Chaillé-Long welcomed the tents, the bananas, milk, sweet potatoes, and *merissa* (compressed banana milk) that Rionga presented to him. He was less pleased by the delay as Rionga arranged two nights of native dancing. But the visit gave him an opportunity to test his preparations for M'Tesa. He gave Rionga gifts similar to those he was carrying to Uganda, and the king responded with unrestrained delight. The horse, too, entranced the natives, and Chaillé-Long's marksmanship won him the title of *Great,* making him Great White Prince. He was pleased at the consternation and delight produced by shocks from his battery. His spirits and his confidence were never long submerged.

Chaillé-Long planned to return from the capital of Uganda by way of Lake Victoria and the Nile, through a region where Rionga's rival and enemy Keba Rega held sway. Rionga predicted that Keba Rega would kill them. With the warning in his ears, Chaillé-Long and his companions plunged into the jungle. For a dozen fever-racked days they fought their way through swamps and brush to the borders of Uganda. En route Chaillé-Long touched a poisonous weed which caused his feverish lips to swell and bleed. As Chaillé-Long approached a border village in a banana grove, the terrified natives fled. The visitors appropriated the huts and spent the night. Early the next day messengers arrived with the impressive news that the Grand Kahotah, M'Tesa's "minister of foreign affairs," was on his way. Then drums and horns combined in a deafening din, and the Grand Kahotah appeared and established himself in a neighboring hut. Over came gifts of bananas and tobacco and word that the foreign minister would receive Chaillé-Long.

Chaillé-Long made a bold stroke—"Central African diplomacy," he called it. He replied that he had not come all the way to Uganda to be greeted by an underling but to see King M'Tesa himself. It worked. The foreign minister invited him to proceed to the capital over roads swept clean before him. But would he delay a day or two to give the king his host time to prepare a suitable village for the honored guests?

The delay brought an additional problem. The interpreter who had accompanied Chaillé-Long from Gondokoro slyly told the Grand Kahotah that they had come to conquer Uganda. By the time the traitorous interpreter had been sent back to Foweira under a guard of M'Tesa's soldiers, the Ugandan capital was ready to receive the visiting dignitaries and the escort for the Great White Prince had arrived.

There were four thousand of them—huge black men, naked, shining with grease and plastered with cow dung and

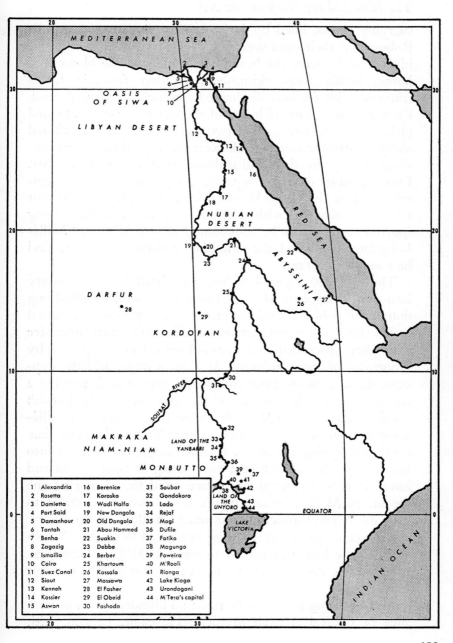

MEDITERRANEAN SEA

OASIS
OF SIWA

LIBYAN DESERT

NUBIAN
DESERT

RED SEA

DARFUR

KORDOFAN

ABYSSINIA

SOUBAT RIVER

MAKRAKA
NIAM-NIAM

LAND OF THE
YANBARRI

MONBUTTO

LAND OF
THE
UNYORO

LAKE
VICTORIA

EQUATOR

INDIAN OCEAN

1	Alexandria	16	Berenice	31	Soubat
2	Rosetta	17	Korosko	32	Gondokoro
3	Damietta	18	Wadi Halfa	33	Lado
4	Port Said	19	New Dongola	34	Rejaf
5	Damanhour	20	Old Dongola	35	Mogi
6	Tantah	21	Abou Hammed	36	Dufile
7	Benha	22	Suakin	37	Fatiko
8	Zagazig	23	Debbe	38	Magungo
9	Ismailia	24	Berber	39	Foweira
10	Cairo	25	Khartoum	40	M'Rooli
11	Suez Canal	26	Kassala	41	Rionga
12	Siout	27	Massawa	42	Lake Kioga
13	Kenneh	28	El Fasher	43	Urondogani
14	Kossier	29	El Obeid	44	M'Tesa's capital
15	Aswan	30	Fashoda		

carrying lances, lined up forty to fifty abreast to march to Ruboga. At their head went the flags of Uganda and Egypt; in their midst were the beaters of drums and the blowers of horns; beside them skirmishers wearing fantastic fezzes trimmed with feathers discharged flintlocks as they danced. From behind the broad leaves of the banana grove frightened girls peered curiously. For two days the parade continued along the freshly swept road. Near the capital messengers arrived bearing greetings and welcome from the queen mother. From the outer gates to the palace, thousands prostrated themselves before the Great White Prince. The king himself sent a message that he wished to see the horse. Chaillé-Long spurred forward. As he dismounted before M'Tesa, Chaillé-Long later recounted, the astonished multitude gasped to find he was not a centaur.

The next day a guard of honor escorted Ismail's emissary into the presence of M'Tesa. For the occasion Chaillé-Long donned his gold-trimmed uniform, and his two soldiers dressed in red shirts and white pantaloons. Through seven successive gates they proceeded to a pyramid-shaped hut supported by a corridor of inner columns. M'Tesa, a large, athletic, copper-colored man of about thirty-five, approached, wearing a white turban, gold-trimmed cloak, gold belt with Turkish scimitar attached, and Moorish sandals from Zanzibar. Chaillé-Long dismounted, and M'Tesa saluted him, at the same time cautiously eyeing the horse. Chaillé-Long gave Uganda into the care of his soldier Selim, now acting as both groom and interpreter, and entered the palace amid the clamor of the spectators. M'Tesa backed before him down the corridor to his gold-draped throne. He motioned Chaillé-Long to a seat—and the court gasped at his being permitted to sit. The British agent Speke had been forced to stand in M'Tesa's presence. Chaillé-Long concluded that his own mission was off to a fair start.

In the ensuing interview he made no blunders in his observance of Central African protocol. He came, he said, with greetings from the great sultan at Cairo. The king smiled, and the crowd screamed ecstatically that their king had brought so powerful a prince to Uganda. Then M'Tesa rose and blinked his eyes—and it was Chaillé-Long's turn to be amazed. Thirty executioners, one stationed at each of the columns, jerked from their hats their ceremonial cords of office. In a flash each seized and dexterously garroted a writhing spectator. It was more honor than Chaillé-Long had bargained for.

From the palace, so suddenly become a charnel house, M'Tesa led Chaillé-Long and his soldiers to the garden to view the king's hundred wives. The wives were delighted. "They surrounded me," said Chaillé-Long, "examined carefully the gilt trimmings of my uniform, and laughed in astonishment at my hair, as I doffed my tarboosh from my heated head." Then M'Tesa presented him with an albino boy and with one of his own daughters, a child of eight. When the visitors returned to their own specially built hut, messengers arrived with more gifts—fifty-six bunches of bananas, three packets of sugar cane, twenty goats, and fifty cows. His goggle-eyed interpreter assured Chaillé-Long that he, the Great White Prince, was, next to M'Tesa, the greatest man in all Uganda.

The next day Chaillé-Long returned to court. The king and his attendants buzzed with pleasure over gifts of cloth, tarbooshes, beads, mirrors, and a music box. To the king he presented an elephant gun with ammunition. And, as at Rionga's court, it was the electric battery that commanded the most delighted attention. M'Tesa called Chaillé-Long "brother" and promised to grant his every wish.

Chaillé-Long had two wishes. The first was for a treaty—an agreement, rather—by which M'Tesa should acknowledge himself a vassal of the khedive. This M'Tesa readily gave. In return he begged for the means to construct the houses and the palace Chaillé-Long had sketched for him. But Chaillé-Long's other wish brought royal hesitation: he asked permission to visit Lake Victoria and to return to Foweira by way of the Nile. The king's ministers demurred, and M'Tesa himself spawned arguments to dissuade his guest. When M'Tesa argued that Keba Rega would surely kill him and the great sultan at Cairo then would kill M'Tesa, Chaillé-Long countered by swearing that he would surely die in Uganda if he could not return by the river. If he died, Keba Rega would blame M'Tesa and eventually would monopolize the luxuries that came to the king who controlled the river route. Other chieftains, Chaillé-Long pointed out, were rich—"Whilst you, M'Tesa, with all your ivory, are little better off than the poorest of your people. . . . You have nothing that goes to make up the life of the great king you are." In the end, Chaillé-Long won.

He won after almost a month of daily visits. It was for Chaillé-Long a fever-racked month, his pleas interrupted by bouts of dysentery and spells of delirium. Once, so weak that his two soldiers had to carry him, Chaillé-Long saw M'Tesa become jealous over the attention his wives paid the Great White Prince. His hopes sank. Again, when he punished the disloyalty of the Ugandan servant who had come with him from Foweira, he feared that M'Tesa might take offense. At last, on June 6, he listened hazily, almost too ill to follow the king's words, as M'Tesa ordered the execution of seven men to propitiate the river spirits and gave his consent to the journey.

On July 14 Chaillé-Long started for Lake Victoria. He still did not have permission to go down the river from the lake to Urondogani; once they were started, he hoped to persuade his Ugandan escort to accompany him. But his powers of persuasion proved inadequate. After three hours of marching they came to the lake at a point near Murchison Creek, where his guides and escorts refused to go on the water. The next morning forty canoes, each with a complement of "musicians" bearing drums and horns, arrived. After an hour of furious contention over who should have the honor of carrying the Great White Prince, they rushed upon Chaillé-Long and escorted him to the victor's canoe. For four hours, as guest of the "Ugandan navy," Chaillé-Long traveled on the Victoria Nyanza. He took soundings, noted the absence of tides and sea shells, and concluded that the lake, a dozen or so miles in diameter, was not so extensive as Speke and Baker had alleged. The navy had received strict orders from M'Tesa and flatly refused to take Chaillé-Long across the lake, and his escort returned him to Murchison Creek. It had not been a wholly successful expedition, but Chaillé-Long consoled himself with the belief that he was the first white man to venture on the waters of Lake Victoria.

At Murchison Creek he extricated his reluctant groom-interpreter from a bevy of Ugandan girls and returned to the capital. Thence, on July 19, he left once more, this time to the northeast for Urondogani on the White Nile. He was not greatly disappointed that he had not been able to go from Victoria to Urondogani, since Speke had earlier traveled that stretch, but beyond Urondogani no one was certain that the river led to Lake Albert. Chaillé-Long was determined to establish the connection.

It took nine days to reach Urondogani. Once there, Chaillé-Long found that M'Tesa had sent more presents—this time eight nude young girls and his eight-year-old daughter, whom Chaillé-Long had deliberately left in the capital. In addition, there were a twelve-year-old boy and two toddlers. Chaillé-Long ruefully accepted this offering—he could not offend M'Tesa and, as the guides explained, M'Tesa would kill the children if they proved unacceptable as gifts. Chaillé-Long distributed the girls among his escorts as a reward for faithfulness. The boy and the "Princess M'Tesa" he kept. Looking forward, down the course of empire, he planned to have her educated in Cairo and married to an Egyptian officer who would return as the khedive's minister to Uganda.

For the moment, high plans of empire gave way to the painful realities of exploration and discovery. The children were a burden and so was the horse, which had served its purpose so well. A few miles below Urondogani, Chaillé-Long met M'Tesa's "fleet admiral," who turned over to him four canoes. The princess, the boy, and two of his men were to travel with him; the groom leading the horse was to proceed overland under guard. With guides and oarsmen Chaillé-Long started down-river toward unknown regions.

The next few days were filled with hardships and crowned with high achievement. The hardships began when the guides were threatened by a boatload of Keba Rega's men. The guides mutinied, refusing to go further. Chaillé-Long quelled them at pistol point. The party ran short of food and were run off when they attempted to steal bananas from groves along the river. On August 11, they lost the river channel and moved back and forth through weedy growth in search of the current. It was a fortunate mishap. It dawned upon Chaillé-Long that he had come upon a new and unknown lake. It was, he thought in the exuberance of new discovery, larger than Lake Albert was reported to be, larger even than Victoria, whose waters he had seen. As he realized the importance of this discovery, he explored its reaches—searching for the river that would carry them onward to M'rooli and the stretches of water which other explorers had traveled. After two days they set their course by the North Star and found an outlet.

Four days from the newly discovered lake (which Chaillé-Long named Hussein, Ismail changed to Ibrahim, and British geographers renamed Kioga), they drew near M'rooli, where they were to meet the groom with the horse. Chaillé-Long fired a shot in signal, and suddenly the sedge of papyrus lining the shore came alive with shrieking savages. Canoeloads of them pushed out from cover, hurling lances as they came. The attackers were Keba Rega's men. The huge sheik in the leading canoe shouted, "You can't escape—you die here." Crouched in the bottom of Chaillé-Long's canoe, Princess M'Tesa reported what was threatened. Chaillé-Long needed no translation; the leader's purpose was unmistakable. Quickly Chaillé-Long lashed together the four canoes, piled the metal cases loaded with his clothing and M'Tesa's gifts in the stern, and prepared to give battle. The White Prince who had astonished Rionga and M'Tesa with his marksmanship stood in need of his skill. Just as the enemy leader came alongside, Chaillé-Long's bullet hit him full in the chest. His fall capsized the attacking canoe, and Chaillé-Long's men picked off the swimmers. From a papyrus island a savage leaned forward to plunge his lance into Chaillé-Long. A soldier fired quickly, felling at one shot both Chaillé-Long and his assailant. The bullet grazed Chaillé-Long's nose and broke it, but it had saved his life.

Luck, courage, and speed were with the embattled flotilla. Their leader gone, the attackers hesitated, got in each other's way, and came upon Chaillé-Long in a single file of canoes. Chaillé-Long's men paddled desperately while Chaillé-Long and others fought off the enemy. Before nightfall they had killed eighty, and those that remained abandoned their canoes to race for vantage points along the banks. Paddling vigorously throughout the night, Chaillé-Long outdistanced them.

On August 20, three days after the battle, Chaillé-Long and his party met a detachment out of Foweira. At the post the garrison greeted them warmly, and the admiring King Rionga sent in gifts of milk and eggs. Finally Chaillé-Long's groom arrived with the horse. After a month Chaillé-Long, with the military escort provided by Rionga, went overland to Karuma Falls. By October 17 he was back in Gondokoro.

Gordon, too, was at Gondokoro, and he greeted Chaillé-Long warmly. "Long," he said, "you have done a great work —more than any man here." In his journal Gordon recorded that Chaillé-Long had "greatly improved, and is worth a good deal to me, if he will stay." Yet it was not in Gordon's nature to be wholeheartedly generous, and soon a patronizing note crept in. To his brother he wrote about Chaillé-Long's increased value, but added ". . . nothing like suffering to give a man experience." By the time he made his formal report to General Stone, Chaillé-Long's stature had diminished and

Gordon's had grown. Gordon asserted that he had received emissaries from M'Tesa, that he had sent Chaillé-Long to Uganda, and that he had given him his own horse for the trip. Eventually he was to assert that Chaillé-Long had seen M'Tesa only once, and he would suggest disparagingly that Chaillé-Long's lake was no more than flooded lowlands.

But if Gordon minimized Chaillé-Long's achievements, Chaillé-Long maximized them; if Gordon despised Chaillé-Long's physical weakness, Chaillé-Long emphasized his fevered illnesses to glorify his indomitable spirit. He was the first white man upon the waters of Lake Victoria, and in his accounts he "navigated" the lake. He had brought Uganda and the powerful M'Tesa under Egyptian suzerainty and to enrich Cairo had diverted the fabulous ivory trade from Zanzibar. He had established the course of the Nile from Lake Victoria to Lake Albert, and the lake he had come upon was the "true" source of the mighy river. Months later, far out in the deserts of Darfur, Raleigh Colston chuckled over a story he picked up from a visitor. Chaillé-Long, so the tale went, had asked the official cartographer to "make Baker's lake as small as possible and make mine as large as possible."

The minimizing and the maximizing would go on for decades, stretching into the twentieth century, and with more than a few overtones of nationalistic rivalry in the controversy. But at the moment the khedive was impressed, and his judgment cast Chaillé-Long's achievement in historical perspective. "There is a young officer," said Ismail, "who, with two soldiers, has done in a few days more for Egypt, than Sir Samuel Baker, with an army, accomplished in four years, with an expenditure of two and a half million dollars."

In Cairo the immediate effect of Chaillé-Long's exploits was to raise "American stock" in the popular market. It encouraged Stone the geographer and Ismail the imperialist in their plan to send Colston and Purdy into Kordofan and Darfur. The khedive promoted Chaillé-Long to colonel with the title of bey and conferred on him the medal of a commander in the Order of Medjidie.

While Cairo chattered and Americans in Egypt preened themselves on Chaillé-Long's achievements, the new colonel awaited his next task. Still in the future were further adventures, battles, discoveries, and conquests to be made for Egypt's empire. Central Africa would see much of Colonel Chaillé-Long.

The adventures began almost immediately. A few days after he arrived in Gondokoro, Chaillé-Long set out for Khartoum by steamer. Hardly had they passed Lado, fourteen miles below Gondokoro, when a great mass of sudd—the floating vegetable matter which often makes the White Nile unnavigable—stopped the vessel. The captain called on Chaillé-Long to save them. The "navigator" of Lake Victoria took a stand on the bridge until he brought the steamer safely through. Beyond Fashoda, the pilot, drunk and violently abusive, ran the steamer upon a sand bar. "Weak and ill I was," Chaillé-Long was to recount, "but the captain was utterly powerless to maintain order." Chaillé-Long seized the pilot, dangled him over the rail above the waiting crocodiles, and restored him to meekness if not sobriety. Thus, victor again over the multiple hazards of the Nile, Chaillé-Long came to Khartoum.

He arrived to find that during his journey down the river Major William P. A. Campbell had died of typhus. The disease had struck down four members of Gordon's staff. For one of their number, and for Campbell, Gordon had developed an intense dislike. "Campbell and [Auguste] Linant are intensely selfish and have not the slightest consideration for me or anyone." They were, he thought, "perfect brigands," and before Campbell died Gordon thought him an "imposter," not half so ill as he made out. "If you put *your* finger down *your* throat *you* [too] will be sick." Gordon had them taken to a hut and reported that they were "only partially

attended by one of the best doctors (me) that I know of."
Assuming Campbell to be well enough to work, Gordon left
him in charge of stores in Khartoum. After Gordon left for
Gondokoro, the sisters of a convent nursed the officers, but it
was already too late. When Chaillé-Long arrived, he found
that Campbell, who had served the Confederacy on the high
seas and the khedive on the Mediterranean and crossed the
desert with Colston, had been buried in the Catholic cemetery.

Chaillé-Long himself was sick, his body so swollen that he
could not get into his clothes. His new honors and the admiring visits and messages from friends and dignitaries helped to
keep him going, and between spells of high fever he busied
himself with preparations for return to the south. He enlisted
four hundred and fifty soldiers and sent them with supplies to
the mouth of the River Soubat. On Christmas Eve, 1874,
Chaillé-Long arrived at the Soubat and found to his disgust
that the supplies had been distributed to those Africans who
had fled to the Egyptian camp in fear that local chieftains
would sell them into slavery. It was expensive, he sighed, and
it would be more so when other tribesmen learned of the
"Freedman's Bureau" maintained by the Egyptian government. He left some men at the Soubat and went on up the
river to Gordon's new headquarters at Lado.

Gordon was disappointed when he learned that four hundred of the soldiers brought by Chaillé-Long were Arabs. He
decided that Chaillé-Long could learn for himself that as soldiers Arabs were far inferior to blacks. Moreover, he soon
began to find fault with Chaillé-Long's behavior. Undoubtedly, Chaillé-Long, now a bey and a commander of the Medjidie
and with a substantial record of achievement behind him, was
reluctant to fall back into a subordinate role. But Chaillé-
Long's new-won fame made it impossible to dismiss him. So
Gordon took occasion—"when we were both in good tem-
pers"—to explain to Chaillé-Long that "we should never be
able to get along with one another when near." For this
reason he had decided to send Chaillé-Long to Makraka. "It is

a good thing to get Long off," he congratulated himself, "for he is a trial to me."

The land of the Makraka Niam-Niam lay southwest of Gondokoro. It extended to Darfur in the north, and on the east its borders came near Lake Albert. Within this region were slave-trading sheiks, and there were rumors that the Niam-Niam were cannibals—though only adults were allowed to eat human flesh. Chaillé-Long doubted these stories and was prepared to disregard them.

In the Makraka area dwelt a pygmy race, the Akka—according to legend as old as Herodotus—whom the Niam-Niam called "Ticki-Ticki," fierce warriors no taller than a child of six or seven but of great strength and endurance. These, whom few white men had seen, Chaillé-Long planned to recruit for the khedive's army. But across the route which ivory caravans must take there lay the land of the hostile Yanbarri whose poison arrows carried terror and death to travelers. It was to this region, potentially rich, that Chaillé-Long turned his eyes.

In the last days of January, 1875, Long started southwest from Lado. With him went his two soldiers who had suffered in Uganda and fought off the river hordes of Keba Rega. They, too, bore commendations and promotions from the khedive. The Great White Prince of the Ugandan expedition rode a new horse, for, alone of Chaillé-Long's earlier companions, Uganda had succumbed to the hardships that beset them. But on this expedition Chaillé-Long and his two faithful soldiers were not alone. With them were seven hundred troops whom Long would establish in frontier posts in the Niam-Niam country. They were mostly Arabs, and Chaillé-Long—who shared some of Gordon's suspicion of the fighting qualities of Egyptian soldiers—placed more confidence in the twenty Sudanese who made up his personal bodyguard. There were also one hundred and fifty native porters, each to be paid one cow, who bore supplies and equipment for the posts and who might be called upon to balance tusks of ivory on the return journey.

Unlike the Uganda trip, the journey to Makraka proved easy. Instead of jungles and tangled swamps to cross, there were verdant, parklike clearings and stretches of parched desert. The expedition made good time. Within a week they traveled one hundred and fifty miles and reached the country of the terrible Yanbarri. Here Chaillé-Long posted a strong rear guard, marched his men in double file, and sent ahead skirmishers along the rocky road hemmed in by mountains. Tall canelike grass hid from view Yanbarri villages only occasionally glimpsed. Yet with all these precautions, the Yanbarri fatally wounded a straggling Sudanese, hovered about the camp each night, and shot arrows through the sides of their tents.

Beyond the Yanbarri country, at the border of Makraka, they came to the station of a veteran ivory trader, one Latroche, who had worked for Egypt ever since Ismail had made ivory a government monopoly. Near Latroche's camp Chaillé-Long came upon some three or four hundred young girls whom visiting sheiks had presented to the trader. These, with Latroche's ready consent, Chaillé-Long distributed among his Arab soldiers, who until then had been far from happy at the prospect of spending two years in this region.

With Latroche as guide and mentor, Chaillé-Long marched his men into the land of the Niam-Niam and stationed them in strategic posts. The "conquest" of Makraka was simple. Sheik after sheik came in and pledged himself to keep the peace, to send his ivory to Cairo, and to abandon trade in slaves. Each visiting sheik brought presents. Some brought women whom Chaillé-Long distributed among the soldiers. Most brought ivory. Eventually there were six hundred tusks—and six hundred porters to carry them back to Lado.

But the most interesting of Chaillé-Long's acquisitions was Ticki-Ticki. He did not penetrate the hiding place of the Akka pygmies, but he did receive tangible proof that they were not mythical creatures. Far out in Makraka he met a sheik who owned a pygmy woman. Chaillé-Long was delighted and paid a yard of red cotton cloth for her. She was an adult, possibly twenty-five years old, three feet nine inches tall, and as broad as she was tall. She wore only some bangles on ankles, arms, and neck. Asked if she would go with him, she replied, in Arabic, "Yes, if you won't eat me." Chaillé-Long bound the bargain by giving her a cloth to cover her nakedness. Quickly Ticki-Ticki wrapped it about her neck and dutifully trotted after her new master.

Another sheik gave Chaillé-Long a Monbutto or Goorah-Goorah girl, said to be the daughter of the king of Monbutto. This tribe, too, so story had it, was of man-eating propensities. She joined Chaillé-Long's growing collection of "anthropological specimens" to be presented to the khedive.

The conquest of Makraka took less than two weeks, and within a month of the departure from Lado Chaillé-Long was ready to return. His entourage was much larger than it had been. He left most of his soldiers at strategic posts, but his new porters were Niam-Niams, eager to fight, and his Sudanese guard had been augmented by fighting men who had been a part of Latroche's establishment. Chaillé-Long hoped they were impressive enough to deter the Yanbarri, but, even so, he planned forced marches across the hostile territory.

His fears of Yanbarri attack were justified. In a narrow mountain pass the Yanbarri fell upon the column. Eight or nine thousand, or so it seemed, charged upon the intruders, shooting poisoned arrows and hurling lances, but to the surprise of the attackers Chaillé-Long's porters suddenly turned into trained soldiers with Remingtons. The Yanbarri leader fell at the first shot, and Chaillé-Long led a detachment to drive the main party of savages from their strategic position on a cliff overhanging the pass. Once the party gained the plateau, the porters piled up their ivory in a barricade and plunged into the jungle after the fleeing Yanbarri. The next day they returned to the ivory fort to announce that they had burned twenty villages and captured forty goats. That night Colonel Chaillé-Long smelled meat cooking over the camp-fires of his victorious host. He made a tour of inspection to confirm the rumor he had heard long before: the Niam-Niam were eating the slaughtered enemy.

The expedition returned to Lado without further adventure —except for the giant python that attacked Chaillé-Long in his tent and which his soldiers killed and ate. Chaillé-Long received his formal promotion to colonel and a medal bestowed upon him by the khedive of Egypt and the sultan of Turkey. He then went to Rejaf, south of Gondokoro, where Gordon now had his headquarters.

Gordon greeted him warmly. He was seated before his hut cleaning an elephant gun, a bottle of cognac beside him, a meerschaum pipe in his mouth. "Dear old fellow," he called out as Chaillé-Long approached, "how are the man-eaters?" Then, waving his hand to the bottle: "Now take a drink, do, and don't forget the quinine."

Chaillé-Long poured himself a drink and settled down to discuss the future. Already the two men, so much alike in their egotism and ambition, had agreed that they could not live together. Central Africa, however, had room enough for both. "What do you care to do now?" asked Gordon. "Perhaps," he suggested, "you had better remain here. We will divide the provinces. You may take the lakes from your old friend M'Tesa, from Uganda to Fatiko. I will make you viceroy."

"And what will you be?" Chaillé-Long asked.

Gordon said, "Oh, I will take the rest and reside in Khartoum."

The prospect pleased Chaillé-Long very little. At the moment his mind was on Cairo, Paris, perhaps even far-off Baltimore. Besides, exploration, adventure, conquests, and "Central African diplomacy" were his forte, not the daily routine of administration. He advised Gordon to establish Rionga as king at M'rooli, cement the union with M'Tesa, and let the two drive Keba Rega from the country. For himself, he would prefer to go back into the Niam-Niam country with cavalry, strike westward through Monbutto and the land of the Akka pygmies, and conquer even to the Atlantic Ocean, for Egypt.

But Gordon's ideas and plans ran east, to the Indian Ocean. As the two men sat drinking cognac and playing games with half a continent, Gordon outlined his scheme. He proposed that Chaillé-Long go to Cairo and persuade the khedive to send an expedition down the Red Sea and the Indian Ocean to Zanzibar. Gordon, building a road to Uganda and Lake Victoria, would strike east along the route of the slave caravans to join Chaillé-Long marching west from the coast. The plan was grandiose and captured Chaillé-Long's imagination. Since the first stage would take him back to Cairo, he agreed. The men parted amicably.

It took Chaillé-Long two months to reach Cairo. On March 20, 1875, he left Lado, taking with him two Niam-Niam warriors, the Goorah-Goorah girl, and the amusing Ticki-Ticki— "almost a rhomboid," he said, chuckling every time he saw her. At Khartoum he collected the Ugandan boy and the Princess M'Tesa. In charge of his "ethnologic menagerie" went the two soldiers who had shared his adventures. En route the members of the party were both exhibits and sightseers. Sheiks, governors, post commanders, local dignitaries, and travelers gathered to admire the heroes. At Berber, Chaillé-Long, an honored guest in a sheik's fruit grove, was approached by a bronzed and bearded man. "Colonel Long, I believe," he said. It was Henry Prout on his way to join Colston's expedition in Kordofan. At other stops the party went ashore, guidebook in hand, to view temples, visit ruins, and climb pyramids. They crossed the Korosko desert on camels, journeyed down the Nile by steamer, and, finishing the journey by rail, on May 22 arrived in Cairo.

Still in his desert costume, ragged and dirty as any beggar, Chaillé-Long hurried to the Grand New Hotel. As he expected, there he found a group of American officers. Up to old

General Reynolds he went, his hand extended and the whine of the beggar in his voice: "O Pasha, give me backsheesh. I am poor," he pleaded. "Get out, devil take you," said the old general. "Why, Gauley," said Chaillé-Long, "what a reception for an old friend!"

In days to come all Cairo would embrace the hero as Gauley had done. Early the next morning the khedive listened entranced as Chaillé-Long told of his exploits. The next day Ismail held a public reception—and Ticki-Ticki danced. Later, Chaillé-Long, clad in the full splendor that had impressed M'Tesa's court, related his discoveries to the Khedivial Geographical Society. It was Ismail himself who summed up Chaillé-Long's achievements: he had extended to the equator the boundaries of Egypt, conquered the Niam-Niam country, suppressed hostile tribes, explored rivers, discovered a lake, and found new and unknown tribes in the desert. He might well have mentioned, too, that Chaillé-Long had brought out enough ivory to pay the cost of many such expeditions and opened the routes for a continuing stream of ivory into the khedivial coffers.

For the Americans, Chaillé-Long's triumphal return was the high watermark of their sojourn in the delta of the Nile. In the excitement over Chaillé-Long, Egyptians momentarily forgot their mistrust of the Americans. From the midst of this harmony, Chaillé-Long departed to Paris on furlough.

IX

wwwwwwwww

The Rocky Path of Empire

Followed by the echoes of Cairo's plaudits, Colonel Charles Chaillé-Long arrived in Paris. Even without the "ethnological specimens" who had so delighted the khedive, he expected to repeat the triumph he had made in the Egyptian capital. For the moment Paris received him well enough: he met the French pretender, the Count de Chambord, visited with the sultan of Zanzibar, and spoke of his adventures before a special session of the Societé de Geographie de Paris. Yet the harmony of general acclaim was marred by a sour note. The British press was less enthusiastic than Cairo and Paris about Colonel Chaillé-Long's achievements.

British newspapers had been sniping at Chaillé-Long since his return from Uganda. A correspondent of the *London Times* wrote from the Soubat that the lake discovered by Chaillé-Long was not important, that he had no instruments with which to measure the lake or even to define its location, and that because he was unwell at the time his observations were unreliable. In the United States the *New York Times*, which had hailed Chaillé-Long's first reports, took its cue from the *London Times* and threw doubt on Long's achievements. With no regard for accuracy—and with no reliable sources of information—the American papers reiterated the British attack. Sir Samuel Baker, said the press, had opened the country above Gondokoro, overthrown Keba Rega, and established friendship with M'Tesa. The waters over which Chaillé-Long traveled were friendly, and Chaillé-Long's stories of M'Tesa's executing his subjects were doubtless apocryphal. For proof, the press cited Baker and Livingstone, who made no mention of such customs. To Chaillé-Long this attack seemed a deliberate plot to deprive him of the credit he merited, and he planned to combat the British canard.

Before he could arrange an extension of his leave, General Stone ordered his return to Cairo. In Europe, said Stone Pasha, he was to obtain suitable clothing for a year and a half in Central Africa. But Stone did not indicate where he was to be sent. He said only that Chaillé-Long would have ten days in Cairo to prepare a new expedition. Reluctantly Chaillé-Long left Paris—informing the newspapers that he was off, under orders, to conquer new worlds. For quotation he added, "A good soldier never asks 'Why?' . . . The great consolation," he intoned, "is that one must be of some use and importance in the world." This sentiment delivered, he set out for Egypt.

On September 9, 1875, a palace officer met him at the railway station in Cairo, helped him through the clamoring hordes of beggars, porters, and would-be guides, and hurried him off to a conference with General Stone and Cherif Pasha, the minister of justice. They told him that on the morrow he would lead an expedition into Abyssinia to assert Egyptian claims to the provinces that lay along Abyssinia's northern border. Chaillé-Long hurriedly bade farewell to his fellow Americans in the hotels and cafés. But new orders arrived, this time from the khedive, instructing him to remain in Cairo. A week later he left to take command of a party exploring the Juba River, which flows into the Indian Ocean almost exactly at the equator.

In actual fact, Chaillé-Long's expedition to the Juba River and Colonel Arrendrup's expedition to Massawa—a mission which Chaillé-Long might have commanded—were cognate parts of the khedive's grandiose plans for imperial expansion. Massawa lies on the Red Sea, four hundred miles due east of Khartoum on the Nile. The Juba River lies five hundred or more miles due east of Lake Victoria and the southernmost reaches of Uganda. With control of sorts along the Nile,

Ismail dreamed of dominating the caravan routes, of building railroads eastward from his Central African domain to the Red Sea and the Indian Ocean. Chaillé-Long could explore the equatorial river. Colonel Arrendrup, a thousand or more miles to the north, would brush aside Abyssinian opposition and conquer the route west to Khartoum. Whatever trade from Central Africa—gold, ivory, gum, and ostrich plumes— did not move north along the Nile might go east, as before, along the caravan routes. But hereafter all trade would pass through Egyptian territory and pay fees into the khedivial coffers in Cairo.

Both parts of the imperialist scheme turned out badly, one very nearly a complete fiasco, the other a near-tragedy. In each was a basic failure of judgment by the agents. In each were indications of British rivalry. In each, too, there were costly errors that contributed to eventual disaster for Egypt.

Chaillé-Long's assignment resulted in failure, but not because its agent was unprepared for his job. Months before, upon return from the land of the Niam-Niam, Chaillé-Long had laid the groundwork for his part in the khedive's plans. In Rejaf he and Gordon planned an expedition through Uganda and along the equator to the Indian Ocean. The khedive approved of the scheme, and now Gordon was ordered to carry it out. Gordon was to cross Uganda, strike out to the east, and meet Chaillé-Long pushing west from the mouth of the Juba.

It was a dramatic project whose fulfillment depended on the energy, the imagination, and the discretion of those intrusted with it. Unfortunately for Ismail's dreams, Gordon had no intention of executing his part. He did not share Chaillé-Long's enthusiasm for adventurous exploration in dangerous lands, and to lead an army to Uganda and from Uganda to the sea was, he knew, both laborious and costly. Moreover, he knew, if only from the newspapers, that England would not approve. Already British agents were in Uganda trying to undo Chaillé-Long's work with M'Tesa, and British influences in Zanzibar, south of the Juba, could be expected to object to any disturbance of the established trade routes. Moreover, Gordon had no wish to add more laurels to Chaillé-Long's crown. Having rid his bailiwick of Chaillé-Long, he did not intend to have him back. When Gordon got orders from the khedive to march to the Juba, he quietly determined to ignore them. Chaillé-Long had orders, said the khedive, to wait with his expedition until Gordon arrived. "They will wait a long time, I expect," Gordon responded privately.

But if Gordon refused to exert himself, Chaillé-Long showed excessive energy. On September 16, 1875, he left Cairo, went to Suez, and loaded on two vessels munitions and supplies and three companies of men. Commanding the vessels and the naval part of the expedition was McKillop Pasha, a Scot who had served in the British navy. In a month the party arrived at the Juba. They found it impossible to enter the mouth of the river and, instead, went a little farther south to the village of Kismayu, a collection of huts with some importance as a slave-trading center. The village was clearly in the domain of the sultan of Zanzibar, and soldiers in the stone fort guarding the harbor waved them away. An Egyptian officer went ashore with a flag of truce and came back with four local officials who ordered them to depart. McKillop held the officials as hostages, and Chaillé-Long landed his troops and captured the fortress and the town. Included in his booty were four hundred slaves, whom he ordered to "scuttle away." Then Chaillé-Long marched overland to the Juba and on a bluff high above the river built a fort of his own.

Chaillé-Long's judgment was bad. He had mistaken Zanzibar for Uganda and had given a display of force which, however effective it may have been as Central African diplomacy, was out of place on the Indian Ocean. Here he was no Great White Prince mounted upon a mythical beast and shocking inland natives with a hand-turned battery. Instead, he had invaded the territory of a friendly state, destroyed property, and abused a flag of truce. The sultan of Zanzibar was weak and sorely tried by internal dissensions, but he knew his rights. He protested to his "brother," the Khedive Ismail, against this unfraternal conduct and, more importantly, he appealed to the British consul general in Zanzibar. The consul general hurried to Aden and sent a message from the sultan to Lord Derby, the British foreign secretary: "The Egyptian pirates are in the land: have taken away my army, cannon and country. Come to my aid."

While the Sultan's exaggerated appeal was making its way to London, and the slow processes of diplomacy were moving to destroy him, Chaillé-Long sat in his fort in blissful ignorance of the furor he had aroused. In the meantime, Colonel William H. Ward, once of the Confederate Navy, arrived to make a survey of the harbor and the shore of Kismayu. While he worked, Chaillé-Long set out up the Juba in a steam launch. He traveled one hundred and fifty miles, gathered information on the peoples and products along the banks, and returned convinced that the river could serve as the base for his westward march to the lakes. He awaited orders from Gordon.

While he waited, he received a visitor. The brother of the prince of the Comoro Islands came to offer him the crown of the islands—"so unworthily worn by my brother." Chaillé-Long hurried him off to Cairo, half-hopeful that Ismail would order him to proceed to the island kingdom in the Mozambique Channel.

He heard no more from the prince who would betray his brother, and he got no orders from Gordon in the interior. Instead, on Christmas Day, Chaillé-Long and McKillop received a peremptory order from their sovereign, the Khedive Ismail: "Withdraw your command and return to Egypt." Early in January McKillop carried Chaillé-Long, prostrate and delirious with fever, aboard his ship, and a month later Chaillé-Long stumbled ashore at Suez. He was certainly ill— and more than a little sick from humiliation. Ismail, unable to resist the pressure of the British, had let it be known that Chaillé-Long had exceeded his authority and had acted without discretion. But he remained a popular hero, and he consoled himself by recalling past achievements and buoyed up his spirits by preparing for a furlough in the United States.

Ismail's inability to resist British pressure for the recall of Chaillé-Long and McKillop stemmed largely from the disastrous failure of the Arrendrup expedition. This was the expedition that Chaillé-Long had expected to command and for which Stone had called him back from France. It was logical enough to transfer Chaillé-Long to the Juba, since Chaillé-Long and Gordon had plotted the equatorial scheme, but there was little logic in intrusting the Abyssinian forces to untried hands. Arrendrup, who replaced Chaillé-Long just before the expedition left Cairo, was a Dane with little military experience. He had appeared in Cairo a few years before as a civilian employee of the Egyptian war department. Stone liked him, found him trustworthy and competent, and took him on the general staff as a lieutenant colonel. His talents were administrative and clerical, and he lacked Chaillé-Long's experience. Rumor had it that on the night before the expedition was to leave Arrendrup's wife had prevailed on Nubar Pasha to give her husband the command.

On September 10 Colonel Arrendrup left Cairo with three battalions of infantry, three batteries of mountain artillery, and a troop of cavalry. His destination was Massawa, far down the Red Sea, but the Americans on the general staff, who thought it their business to plan and arrange such things, were completely in the dark about the objectives of the mission. Only Ismail and his privy council—and Stone Pasha—knew Arrendrup's intended destination and purposes.

The background for the expedition lay, as the khedive and his pashas knew, in a long-standing conflict between Egypt and Abyssinia. As early as 1866 Ismail, for increased tribute to the sultan, had obtained title to Massawa and other parts of the Red Sea coast. He laid claim as well to lands in the interior which were claimed also by Abyssinia.

The Rocky Path of Empire

In 1872 Ismail sent Werner Munzinger, a Swiss adventurer who had been consul at Massawa for both Britain and France, into the disputed province of Bogos to claim the land. Abyssinian King John countered by appointing a Scot, John Charles Kirkham, as governor of his northern territories. For several years Munzinger and Kirkham, in the names of their respective sovereigns, engaged in intrigues and negotiations with local tribal chieftains, governors, and religious leaders. Finally, hoping to establish orderly government along a proposed rail route from Massawa to Khartoum, Ismail ordered Arrendrup to Massawa to consolidate Egypt's claims.

Arrendrup began his brief campaign by informing King John that he had come to restore order on the frontier and invited him to meet to decide upon a boundary between Egypt and Abyssinia. On Kirkham's advice, John made no reply but hurried about his domain enlisting tribal chieftains and their warriors to help drive out the invader. Meanwhile, Arrendrup advanced into the interior toward Asmara and Godofalassie and had, or so it appeared to him, an open road to Adowa, the capital of Abyssinia.

In Cairo the news of Arrendrup's rapid advance brought consternation to some Americans. General Stone called Lockett into consultation and on a map pointed out that Arrendrup was one hundred miles from his base at Massawa. Lockett was horrified at the hazardous adventure. Arrendrup had at best three thousand men. But Stone was more sanguine and argued that the Abyssinians were semibarbarous and their forces inferior to the Egyptians in organization and equipment. "But," countered Lockett, they were "warlike, lovers of liberty, and possessed of great courage." He advised Stone to have Arrendrup stop where he was, fortify, and wait for reinforcements. Half-convinced by Lockett's outspoken advice, Stone reassured him that all this "will be attended to."

But whether or not Stone intended to follow Lockett's advice, it was too late to send reinforcements. He did send Major James A. Dennison, five years out of West Point, who had been in Egypt since the first of the year, to help Arrendrup with engineering problems. Dennison had served in the Civil War before going to the academy and had been on the frontier after his graduation. He was practicing law in upper New York when General Sherman induced him to go to Egypt. Despite his few years, he was a soldier of experience and a man of courage and judgment. Stone hoped that Dennison would bring balance to Arrendrup's intrepid advance. Once in Abyssinia, Dennison urged Arrendrup to pay some attention to his lines of communication and supply, and Arrendrup permitted him to establish a fortified camp some fifty miles in his own rear and one hundred and fifteen miles from Massawa.

Before other aid could reach him, Arrendrup marched into a trap. At Gundet, a mountain pass, the Abyssinians attacked and destroyed an advance party. Against Dennison's advice, Arrendrup rushed almost two thousand soldiers into the same spot. Rumor placed the number of Abyssinians at forty thousand. It was sufficient to surround the Egyptians, who made no effort to fight their way out or to hold off the attackers. They huddled together, fired into the air, and waited for death. It took the Abyssinians less than an hour to destroy them—Arrendrup among them.

The men in the outposts and the wounded who were able to crawl away from Gundet reached the comparative safety of Dennison's camp. Quickly the American strengthened the wall about his position as the Abyssinians began to assemble before him. In desperation, Dennison determined to drive them away before they concentrated, but his officers told him that the men, demoralized by the sight of the wounded dragging into camp, would refuse to venture beyond the wall. King John sent a demand for immediate surrender. Dennison answered that he would have to consult his superiors. This ruse gave him time for a night march into the mountain passes. By pushing steadily for thirty-two hours, he brought back to Massawa this remnant of the Arrendrup expedition.

In Cairo, the war office first attempted to suppress all news of the disaster at Gundet. Then, as rumor spread the story of a defeat, it gave out an official, glory-tinted story of how uncounted hordes of Abyssinian barbarians had surrounded Arrendrup's men, how Arrendrup and his gallant troops had fought all day, how with breechloaders and artillery they had cut down the Abyssinians like wheat, how they had run out of ammunition and fought with bayonets and muskets used as clubs until every hero was slain. But the Cairo populace, having a more realistic opinion of the fighting qualities of the fellahin, rejected the official propaganda for a more credible version which a telegraph operator in Massawa privately tapped out to a fellow telegrapher in Suez. The populace of Cairo, and even the American officers, had reasonably accurate information about the debacle before news of it reached Stone and the inner circles of the palace.

In the meantime, Stone began feverish preparations in the Citadel for a new invasion of Abyssinia. He called Lockett and set him to work making maps. Other officers he sent hurrying about to get information, and they searched Gordon's reports from the equatorial provinces and those of Purdy, Colston, Mason, and Prout from the Sudan for incidental light on Abyssinia. By the grapevine, word traveled that certain of the Americans—Colonel Charles Field, Colonel Henry C. Derrick, Major Charles Loshe, Captains David Porter and Henry Irgins, and Doctors William Wilson and Thomas D. Johnson, all recent arrivals who had experience in battle—should prepare to leave for a campaign.

In the palace of the khedive there was no question about sending a new expedition to Abyssinia. The prestige of Egypt and the credit of the khedive demanded that the defeat be avenged, but there was no unity of opinion in the councils. Nubar Pasha, the foreign minister, headed one group, which General Stone supported. It was internationalist in outlook and in favor of the reforms Ismail was making. Opposed, lacking interest in expansion or internal changes, was a nativist faction headed by Cherif Pasha and supported by Ratib Pasha, general of the armies. The Nubar-Stone faction favored the conquest—even the annexation—of Abyssinia. Cherif and Ratib, with perhaps a glimmering suspicion of the qualities of Egyptian soldiery, proposed a punitive expedition to settle the turmoil in the border provinces. Nubar favored the sending of a strong force. Stone, hoping to prove the merits of his American officers, supported him and advocated that the command be intrusted to an experienced veteran of the Civil War. Under pressure Ismail yielded to Cherif, agreeing that the expedition should be punitive only and that it should be commanded by an Egyptian. As it turned out, perhaps it would have been better had Stone surrendered gracefully, restricted his Americans to their familiar work in the Citadel, and furnished no more than expert advice to the invading army; yet in his eagerness to prove the worth of his command he insisted that the Egyptians be guided by American advice. The khedive agreed, and the Cherif-Ratib faction yielded. Perhaps, indeed, they saw an opportunity to prepare an alibi in case of failure.

Stone's initial choice for the American second in command was William McEntyre Dye. In November, while the secret conferences were going on at the palace, Stone called in Dye and, pledging him to secrecy, broke the news of Arrendrup's defeat, telling him that he had been selected as chief of staff for the proposed expedition. Dye's reply amazed him. The colonel informed him that he and all of Cairo knew the outcome of the affair at Gundet. Moreover, Dye had a mind of his own. He refused the assignment. He would, he said, gladly serve in any capacity under General Stone or Loring, but he had little confidence in native officers and none at all in the general in chief, Ratib Pasha.

Stone's next choice was General Loring. For years Old Blizzards had been enjoying a sybaritic existence in his palace in Alexandria while minding the coastal defenses and reminiscing about his long years as an active soldier. On Stone's summons, he came to Cairo and sat in the conferences. He was willing enough to accept the assignment as chief of staff and second in command to Ratib Pasha. He believed that he would be in charge, with Ratib but a figurehead. Loring was pleased when the khedive, on the eve of their departure, called in Ratib and his second, joined their hands in symbolic unity, and instructed Ratib that he was to follow Loring's advice in all things.

However much Ismail may have hoped that his commanders would be "of one mind," the differences between the two were insuperable. Each was, in his own way, personally loyal to the khedive. Ratib, a Circassian, had been a slave of Said, Ismail's predecessor as viceroy. Said sent him to Paris for military training; on his return he was made a lieutenant. A short time later Said took offense at something, and Ratib, humiliated, put a pistol in his mouth and pulled the trigger. The bullet left him badly disfigured, but the scar was looked upon as a badge of honor, and Said promoted him. By the time Ismail became viceroy, Ratib was nominal head of the army.

General Loring made no attempt to express his loyalty in so violent and dramatic a manner, but he was an ardent admirer of the khedive and a sincere believer in Ismail's progressivism. Other Americans, finding inconsistencies in Ismail's conduct, were skeptical about the intent and the efficacy of a number of reforms, but Loring defended him against all critics. Once, on the way to Gura, Colonel Dye urged Loring not to make a contemplated move. "By God," exclaimed Loring as he yielded, "I will not put in unnecessary jeopardy the soldiers of the great and good man who has given me an asylum in my old age."

Aside from loyalty to the khedive, the American and the Egyptian had nothing in common. Ratib was a small man, about five feet four inches in height, and weighed about one hundred pounds. He was wrinkled, wizened of feature, with—so Loring thought—a crafty look in his eye. He did not look like a fighting man, and he was not. Loring had fought since childhood; Ratib had never seen a battle. Ratib was mild, almost reticent, in manner; Loring was excitable, given to violent outbursts of temper under strain, as suddenly calming and attempting to make amends for any offense he had given. He admitted ruefully that he could not punish subordinates consistently; he told a story of once striking a servant and then giving him a dollar. "And ever after," he recalled, "the rascal tried to make me strike him again."

Ratib and Loring made an ill-assorted pair. Differences in personality, even without the wide differences in culture, would have led to conflict, and a student of Loring's career might have concluded that he was a poor choice for second in command. He had questioned Stonewall Jackson's decision at Romney, and he had struck off on his own line of retreat after Pemberton's defeat at Baker's Creek. Loring Pasha had a mind —and a temper—of his own. If he and Ratib were to be of one mind, it would have to be Loring's.

In the councils that planned the campaign into Abyssinia, the Egyptians had an opportunity to see the fundamental differences not only between Ratib and Loring but between Egyptian and American concepts of war. Conferring with Nubar, Cherif, Ratib, and Prince Hussein, the minister of war, sat Colonel Field, who had commanded a corps in Lee's army, and Colonel Dye, who had led an Iowa regiment at Vicksburg, on the Red River, and before Mobile. Stone bustled in and out of the meetings, displaying a huge map of Abyssinia which Lockett had made, explaining the intricacies of staff work, emphasizing the necessity of supplies and transportation, and educating the conferees on the logistics of the coming campaign. To the Egyptians it must have been apparent the Americans were planning a war of conquest. But the Egyptians had no intention of waging such a war. They would make a demonstration, convince King John of their might, and, with an exchange of presents, negotiate peace on the frontier. The difference in approach did not become explicit, and as the campaign progressed the Americans were sure that the Egyptians were errant cowards.

It began, nonetheless, with the outward appearance of harmony. At Suez, before embarking, General Ratib entertained all the officers at dinner at an English hotel, and good fellowship prevailed. Stone saw them aboard their steamer, tossed them a code as his farewell gesture, and stood waving as their vessel put out to sea. With them in transports went four regiments of infantry, one of cavalry, two field batteries, and units of mountain batteries, rocket batteries, and sappers and miners. Altogether there were eleven thousand men, eleven hundred horses, and twelve hundred mules. The Americans were amazed and a bit nonplused when they heard Ratib complain that only one of the regiments was composed of blacks from the Sudan. The Egyptian officers apparently placed no confidence in their fellow countrymen.

The Americans first assigned to the expedition numbered eleven. Only Loring and Dye had been long in Egypt; the others had arrived within the year, and at least one of them, Captain David Essex Porter, son of a Union naval commander, had been sent at once to Massawa on arrival. Dye's duties were those of adjutant general, and his assistant, Robert S. Lamson, had just completed his education as a mining engineer before coming to Egypt. Colonel Field, recently arrived, was inspector general. No more familiar with Egypt was Henry C. Derrick, chief engineer. James A. Dennison's brief experience had included his exploit in extricating the survivors of the Arrendrup disaster. Captain Henry Irgins, equally new to Egypt, was also assigned to the engineers. Major Charles F. Loshe, who until the last moment had been busy in Stone's office gathering supplies, accompanied the expedition as quartermaster. The doctors, William Wilson and Thomas D. Johnson, were staff surgeons. A like number of Egyptians, a German, and an Italian, made up the headquarters staff. Somewhat later Colonel Charles I. Graves was sent to take charge of harbor transportation in Massawa; in January, Colonel

Lockett, who desperately needed the extra pay and had energetically intrigued to be taken along, arrived in response to Loring's request for an expert on fortifications. This roster almost exhausted the list of Americans available for service. Colston was ill; Prout, Purdy, and Mason were exploring the Sudan; Chaillé-Long and Ward were on the Juba. Only Stone, Hall, and Martin in Cairo, and Old Gauley Reynolds in Alexandria, were left in Lower Egypt.

On December 14 the expedition arrived at Massawa and began the confusing task of debarking. The harbor was good, but the town, built on a small coral island connected to the mainland by a causeway, possessed no facilities for a military establishment. A Catholic convent, two or three government buildings, and a few private residences were alone respectable. The natives lived in conical thatched huts infested with insects and reptiles. The streets were so narrow that the inhabitants walked in single file (Loring called it Indian file). The people smelled strongly of the grease with which they dressed their hair. Although the governor welcomed the officers to his residence, the nights were so hot that even there they could not sleep. After a few nights Loring thought he knew why the people looked so miserable and exhausted.

In a crowded area and suffering from the climate and the inevitable confusion of organizing an army camp, the men grew irritable. From the beginning all kinds of mistakes and minor annoyances beset them. Loring spent hours getting Ratib to order needed engineering instruments from Cairo, hours more straightening out the muddle caused by Ratib's confused telegram. In Cairo, Derrick, unfamiliar with Egyptian ways, had directed one Egyptian to pack an odometer for him, only to open the box in Massawa and find a small gimlet. He would have been less annoyed, he commented dryly, had it been a harem and no more surprised had it been a medieval catapult.

Paper work was especially annoying to the Americans. Dye's division handled all orders and communications, but he had no clerks on his staff who could write English or French. If an officer dropped into his office, he found himself drafted to copy some desperately needed material. Withal, it was necessary to translate orders into at least three languages. "Send a clerk who writes English and French; English at least," Dye begged in a message to Stone. "If you can, one who is lame and halt, if not blind; one who knows nothing beyond clerical duties; one, if you please, who stinks, or has some other repulsive quality which will protect him in my employ." Without such a clerk, said Dye, there would be no reports—"although we may stumble through the multifarious duties."

The duties were indeed multifarious, and the Americans believed they had to attend to them all. Dye counted the confusion of one day: couriers arriving in the night; messengers starting off at three in the morning; camels arriving; vessels bringing field telegraphs—and no place to put anything. There was no water—the pumps had struck rock. No tents. Not even trees for shelter. And Lutfi Effendi, the only translator and clerk, forever saying his prayers!

"Tell him to cut them damned short," cried Loring, waving the stump of his arm and striding—steps a full yard—about the room. His face was red, his eyes flashing, his vocabulary profane. The scene at headquarters was one of constant confusion.

Part of the confusion sprang from conflicts with the Egyptians. Ratib knew and understood only the pasha system of running an army, a system by which each commanding pasha assumed responsibility for supplying his unit, maintaining its internal order and discipline, moving it toward an objective, and leading it in battle. It was a system in which responsibility was fixed and clear, and to Egyptians the mountainous paper work of the Americans seemed unnecessary, the division of labor among a headquarters staff confused and irresponsible. To Americans the pasha system seemed fraught with possibilities of corruption. When Ratib canceled a beef contract the Americans had made with a foreigner in Massawa and gave it to a native whom he knew, the Americans were sure his act was evidence of his lust for graft. They were dismayed by a system in which each battalion, company, and detachment made its own arrangements for a commissary and quartermaster stores. Everywhere they saw the scheming, crafty, guilt-stained hands of the clerks—mostly Copts, who might secretly favor the Abyssinians—who exercised undue influence over the native officers. They considered Ratib's chief clerk a personal enemy.

The confusion was confounded and the dismay of the Americans increased when, without warning, Prince Hassan, Ismail's third son, arrived in Massawa. He was a youth of twenty-three who had gone to school in Germany and held an honorary commission in a Prussian regiment. He came to get a taste of campaigning and brought with him fifty retainers, a huge striped tent, innumerable animals, and baggage and equipment suitable for a princely establishment. Ratib was delighted. He was personally devoted to the royal family, and he welcomed the prince to the staff and deferred to him in councils of war. Ratib enjoyed, too, a permanent place at Hassan's rich and overflowing table. Loring refused an invitation to join the royal mess, but he accepted frequent, almost daily, invitations to partake of epicurean viands. The other Americans, forgetting that Abraham Lincoln's son had once had an honored place on Grant's staff, resented the prince and his prerogatives.

The Americans resented discipline as well, and they filled their letters to their families in Cairo with details of their discontent. They complained bitterly when Ratib imposed censorship upon the foreigners and ordered them to send all their letters unsealed to his office for transmission. Families and friends in Cairo suffered from long delays of news. The censorship applied even to official communications to General Stone. Loring protested and eventually got a modification of the order for official letters, but personal mail continued to be censored.

Long days of preparation in Massawa served only to aggravate the conflicts between the Americans and the Egyptians. The impossibility of reconciling the established pasha system and the superimposed staff organization, the contrast between Egyptian methods and the American drive for efficiency, were clashes of disparate cultures. Newly arrived Americans were, perhaps, more prone to quick criticism than older hands might have been, but even Dye and Loring, who had been in Egypt long enough to have some understanding of Egyptian ways, were full of complaints and made no effort to explain one group to the other or to act as liaison officers between them.

But if the Americans were bewildered by the preparations in Massawa, they were made distraught by further problems as the expedition moved against Abyssinia. In Cairo, at the palace conferences, Stone had outlined his plans. "What do you think of them?" he had asked Dye, surely confident that the answer would be complimentary. "General," replied Dye, "our great difficulty will be transportation." Events confirmed his prediction. There were no camels in Massawa, and it was weeks before the governor was able to provide sufficient to allow the first section to move into the interior. The beasts they got were scrawny and sickly animals and the drivers a scurrilous lot. Loring urged Ratib to put Major Loshe in charge of transportation, with full authority to discipline—with beatings if necessary—both officers and men. Loshe tried to determine what baggage and equipment each man and unit should carry and to assign animals to units. No one obeyed his orders; in the packs loaded upon the camels delicacies replaced necessities and personal belongings replaced ammunition. Loshe found it impossible to be everywhere at once.

No small part of his problem came from Prince Hassan's retinue. Loring and Loshe persuaded the prince to leave his great tent behind, but his personal servants loaded the camels with luxuries for his table. Loshe thought he had assigned the proper number of animals for the prince—and he reserved some for the staff. The prince's men, concluding that they needed more camels, simply appropriated those for the staff. Loring spotted them and rushed up, waving his stump of an arm and crying, "Where in hell and damnation are you taking that camel? It belongs to the doctor!" Calmly came the bland reply: "His Highness sent me for it." "Great God," shrieked Loring, "this is a pretty kettle of fish. Every cook, sais, or whatnot is a prince, and a major general's order is but a puff against a squall. We are going to the devil sure enough."

These scenes, repeated every morning on the march, were a bedlam of shrieking camels, yelling drivers, and cursing officers. Harmony found no place. Crates of crockery, boxes of wine, tables, even stoves filled with hot coals, were loaded upon the camels and mules. Along the trail the animals kicked off their loads, scattering property and creating minor stampedes.

It was not the transportation system alone that remained in confusion. Equally snarled were the lines of authority and the multiplicity of conflicting orders. Ratib introduced Loring to the line officers as his second in command, but the gesture meant nothing to them. The Americans, for all their work in organizing a general staff, their map making, their staff school, and their influence in teaching sergeants to read and write, had not instructed the Egyptian officers in American concepts of the proper relations of line and staff. The officers obeyed orders only when they came from Egyptians—an attitude certainly encouraged by the clerks and, so the Americans thought, by Ratib. In the opinion of the soldiers the foreigners were merely ornaments to the commander. Moreover, in their minds the prince was the true head of the expedition.

Yet, despite the confusion, the expedition got under way. Late in January, 1876, the soldiers struck their tents, the officers bade farewell to the hospitable governor, and the army moved off to the south and west on the way to Abyssinia. Along the route they glimpsed gazelles, hares, dog-faced baboons, guinea fowl, grouse, and partridges, all sent fleeing from their path. "Every night we hear the resounding roar of the lion, free in his native wilds," exulted Derrick, who was happy to be away from the fetid heat of Massawa. But through the ranks ran a shiver of apprehension at the thought of a lion lurking to seize stragglers and deserters. Before long the transportation system fell into a hopeless snarl. The prince's baggage dotted the road all the way from Massawa, camels wandered off in the wilderness, mules dragging gun carriages strayed from the ranks and went charging up gullies on expeditions of their own.

At last they reached Bahr Reza. Here they built a fortified depot. After a day's march they came to Addi Rasso. Here again the officers reorganized the transportation, and they built a garrisoned depot to guard the route and to dispatch men and supplies to the advancing army. Thereupon the officers fell into a dispute over the proposed direction, and even the nature, of the advance.

Beyond Addi Rasso lay the route to Adowa, capital of Abyssinia, over rugged terrain; immediately ahead lay the mountain and pass of Khaya Khor; and beyond, the plains of Gura and Haala. During the Cairo conferences, all the officers had agreed that Egyptian prestige demanded they wage a successful battle against King John and even pursue him to his capital, if necessary. But at Addi Rasso neither Egyptians nor Americans showed enthusiasm for a quick descent on Adowa. They agreed that they should advance only a short distance and there build another fort.

X

Gura

Choosing a location for the fort brought on a new dispute among members of the expedition. The American engineers, Dennison and Irgins, with the strong support of Dye, wanted to strengthen the small fort already erected at Khaya Khor Pass. Ratib thought the main fort should be well out in the Gura Valley. Loring agreed but favored a location nearer to the hills on the far side of the valley. As the dispute went on, Colonel Lockett, builder of the defenses of Vicksburg, arrived to throw the weight of his prestige into the balance.

While the expedition was forming in Cairo, Lockett had been eager to join it and appealed for support to his old friend Loring, who insisted on having Lockett with him. Stone refused to let him go, but Lockett continued to plead for assignment in the field. From Massawa Loring repeated his requests, and finally Stone yielded. Late in January Lockett arrived in Massawa as head of a special expedition for scientific exploration. When dispute over the fort arose, Loring summoned him to Gura. Lockett cast his vote for Loring's location and returned to Massawa.

The site selected was a poor choice. It lay in the valley where ridges and hills commanded it and gullies ran within a few hundred yards. Here, to Dye's disgust, the soldiers erected a rectangular blockhouse. Loring, said Dye, had "blockhouse on the brain," and he argued that "an obstreperous mule" could easily kick it over. About the fort ran a line of breastworks.

The establishment of the fort, which held about five thousand men, brought no end to the confusion and conflict among the officers. The army in camp was as great a problem as the army on the march. Nearby was the village of Gura, whose Abyssinian inhabitants were disposed to be friendly. The soldiers descended on the market, stole produce, and beat the villagers. They abused the women. They plundered houses. When the Americans proposed disciplinary measures they only got into more disputes with their Egyptian colleagues over sentries, guards, and punishments. At Addi Rasso, Colonel Dye had lost his temper, accused Lieutenant Lutfi Effendi of leaving a valuable box in the road, and struck him. Lutfi was a popular officer, more than usually efficient and widely admired for his piety, and his smoldering resentment spread among the officers of the line. Everywhere the Americans met surly faces and obstructionist tactics.

Loring stormed. During the two and a half days of Lockett's visit to Gura, Loring poured out his grievances to him. He wanted, he explained, to hurry forward to Gura provisions and ammunition sufficient to make a campaign against the Abyssinian king before the rains began. It was impossible to get his orders obeyed. Although he had given the most positive commands that nothing but ammunition, hard bread, and salt be brought to Gura, train after train arrived with soldiers' baggage and "rubbish." The army was eating up rations, he complained, as fast as they arrived. Lockett listened, then had an interview with Ratib and the prince. Unlike Loring, they did not unburden themselves to the visiting officer, but everywhere Lockett sensed the antagonism between the Egyptians and the Americans. He found, he was to report, no harmony, no concert of action, no confidence.

Lockett traveled back to Massawa in two days over roads which the battalion of engineers had made, and he was much "impressed by the working power of our soldiers." Yet, though the roads were better, the caravans moved neither faster nor more efficiently. Loshe was at Massawa sending out trains as fast as he could load them. Colonel Field was sent back along the route to Addi Rasso and Bahr Reza to hurry things along. On March 2 Loshe thought he was ready to send one last big caravan with the last of the stores to Gura. But the Arab officer in Bahr Reza seized over seven hundred pack animals on which Loshe had counted and sent them off to Gura carelessly loaded. It was Ratib's order, he explained. As Loshe scoured the country for more animals, the Arab officer commandeered a camel train returning to Massawa and promptly exchanged the healthy camels for the worst of his caravan and sent the culls to Loshe. Moreover, Loshe found that the Arab had taken the entire labor force, and it was only after he had impressed some sick soldiers, Massawa civilians, and even fugitive Abyssinians that he was able to get his caravan started. It was then March 4, far too late to help the doomed army at Gura.

In the month that the Egyptian army had taken to make its two-day march and to begin its token invasion of Abyssinia, King John had been scurrying about his country raising an army. His was a feudal land with provincial governors presiding over chieftains of tribal villages. To the governors and chiefs King John made his appeal, and quickly the tribes began to assemble. Warriors gathered with muzzle-loading muskets, swords that resembled scythes, war clubs, and strange weapons. With them came women and children. Since the army had no commissary, no quartermaster, and not even a headquarters staff, it lived off the land. Each village through which the army passed joined in. It was less an army than a rising en masse, and the gathering tribesmen were more moved by the hope of plunder than by the wish to drive off the invader. At their head was John, a large handsome man in his early thirties who had fought his way to the kingship and who went into battle accompanied by two lions as pets.

As the Abyssinian monarch rallied his followers, the Americans found additional reasons to complain of Ratib. They thought indeed that he failed to take advantage of opportunities to undermine the enemy. Before they left Massawa, King John sent his British adviser Kirkham with one hundred and fifty mutilated prisoners from the Arrendrup disaster. The prisoners, he hoped, would deter and frighten the Egyptian soldiers, and Kirkham had instructions to negotiate. He asked permission to pass through the lines to solicit Queen Victoria's good offices as mediator between the belligerents. Instead, Ratib put Kirkham under arrest and contemplated retaliation. The Americans thought Kirkham should be treated with respect and opposed Ratib's violation of the flag of truce. Dye, for one, refused to get Kirkham drunk in order to extort secrets from him. Eventually, still a prisoner, Kirkham died of natural causes in Massawa. The Americans thought the treatment accorded him a grave error and held Ratib to blame.

Equally serious, in their opinion, was Ratib's misuse of the aid proffered by Abyssinian chieftains who had defected. One who came into camp to offer his services was Liege Barrou—tall, "magnificently formed," Loring noted, and "much the finest specimen" of an Abyssinian the Americans had seen. He could rally thousands against King John, he told Loring. Ratib rejected the offer, gave him a field glass and an umbrella as symbols of authority, and sent him off with his men into the hills. Nor was Ratib willing to use the services of Welda Mikael, who came in with three hundred followers. Mikael, who had claim to the Abyssinian throne, arrived with the air of a prince. On either side of him stood his officers of state, one busy picking vermin from his master's body. The prince had a bearer to carry his scimitar, and when he sat a servant held his bare feet. Ratib served him coffee and drank the native *tedge* with him. He was given the title of ras, the equivalent of a pasha, and was sent away into the mountains. In Loring's opinion Ratib did not intend to fight and did not want allies who might insist on battle.

Even if Ratib sought to avoid battle, it was Loring's conviction that he should find out what the enemy was doing. Loring tried to persuade the Egyptian to use the services of the Abbé

Duflot, who controlled a Catholic province of Abyssinia. The abbé came on Loring's invitation and brought experienced scouts with him. Ratib rejected his aid, and it was only after Prince Hassan had criticized the commander for "making old women" of his soldiers by keeping them huddled in camp that Ratib sent for Duflot and asked him to help in scouting operations. The Americans, Derrick, Irgins, and Dr. Wilson, left on missions of reconnaissance.

One such mission brought information that King John's army was ready to move. The Abbé Duflot and Captain Irgins —the latter also clad in priestly garb—set out to ride completely around John's army. It was a dangerous mission, and Irgins jokingly pointed out that it was far more dangerous for him than for the abbé: if they were captured they would be castrated, a fate worse for a layman than for one who had already taken a vow of celibacy. The two scouts, accompanied by an Abyssinian guide, were gone for four days, traveling through villages swarming with enemy warriors. They reached a point only thirty miles from Adowa and observed strategic roads, watercourses, and mountain passes. They escaped capture on one occasion by killing a chicken and scattering blood and feathers on the path. The superstitious Abyssinians would not venture on a road which sorcery protected.

They returned to report that King John's army—perhaps fifty thousand warriors—was concentrated in the next valley. It was the kind of army that could be held together only by moving. Deserting Abyssinians brought in the news that the force was short of water and must make for the Mareb River. The valley of Gura lay between the Abyssinian army and the river, and the only roads across the valley ran between Fort Gura and the smaller Egyptian fort at Khaya Khor.

It took no prescience to know that King John's motley army would soon be upon them. At the moment the bulk of the Egyptian army was in the Gura Valley behind good entrenchments. A second part was divided—one body in the Khaya Khor Valley under Osman Bey, another, with most of the artillery, in the fort at Khaya Khor Pass under Osman Pasha. Still a third part, with supplies, was moving up from Bahr Reza under Colonel Field. In the Gura fort Ratib consulted with Dye, Loring, and Derrick. Ratib wanted to call all forces into the fort. Dye thought the forces in Gura should be transferred to the pass at Khaya Khor, where, with artillery protection, they could attack the Abyssinians as they tried to cross the valley. Loring favored Dye's plan but despaired of convincing Ratib. The Americans favored aggressive action—to attack the enemy and perhaps pursue him to Adowa. Ratib preferred to fight, if fight he must, on the defensive. But, argued the Americans, King John and his men might cross the valley between the units of the Egyptian army without offering battle. "Let him pass and go to hell," answered Ratib.

On March 6, Ratib, Loring, Dye, and Derrick rode the five miles to Khaya Khor for consultation with Osman Pasha and Osman Bey. Derrick and Dye, with Loring nodding assent, urged that messengers be sent to beg Field to bring his men to the pass. They advised that Osman Bey move to Khaya Khor, that the troops at Gura, except for a small detachment, join them there, and that cavalry scouts go out to report on John's movements. If, said the Americans, John attacked Khaya Khor, they could defeat him; if he tried to cross the valley, the Egyptians could attack him on his flank. Ratib spoke briefly with the native officers—too briefly to have conveyed the plan, Loring thought—and said he agreed. At Gura, Loring urged that the troops move out at once. Ratib stared at him incredulously. His whole manner, reported Loring, was "masked by insincerity and cunning." He had no intention of moving.

By this time the Americans had concluded that the Egyptians were errant cowards. A group of monkeys silhouetted on a hilltop had thrown consternation into the ranks on the way from Massawa until the soldiers were convinced that the monkeys were not ferocious Abyssinians in wait. Again, one night a sentry accidentally discharged his gun while pacing the northern battlements of Fort Gura, and panic so struck the soldiers that their officers could not get them into position to defend the fort. The Americans believed that Ratib and his officers were as terrified as the men. They expected nothing from the Arab commander—neither concentration of troops, nor defense of position, nor attack.

Expecting nothing, the Americans were surprised when Ratib began to move. Early on the morning of March 7, Osman Pasha sent word that Osman Bey had brought his men into Khaya Khor and that the Abyssinians were near him. Suddenly Ratib ordered five thousand men to march out, leaving twenty-five hundred and some artillery in the fort. For a moment the Americans believed that Ratib would try to reach Khaya Khor. But only for a moment. He led his army outside the fort a few hundred rods and stopped.

Before the long line was a wooded area cut by deep gullies that could conceal and protect an advancing force. Back of the line and cutting across the route from Fort Gura was a large gully. Still farther back were the hills and ridges that formed the boundary of the Gura Valley. On the right of the line, nearest to Khaya Khor and almost reaching to the roads which King John's army must use to cross, was a battery of artillery. Here Dye took his stand and assumed command of the guns.

Through the morning, clouds of dust and signs of skirmishes kept the Egyptian forces informed of the Abyssinian advance. For a moment it looked as if they would attack the force at Khaya Khor—making it possible for Ratib's troops to close in. But King John's forces veered away from the mountain and began to come down the valley. Early in the afternoon Ratib shifted his line, but the only effect of his move was to place the gully at his rear more squarely between his troops and the fort.

By that time skirmishers were attacking all along the line and firing became general. Small groups of Abyssinians darted out of the brush at the Egyptian line, and the Americans began to move rapidly. Loring rushed troops from one point to another; on his reddened face the sweat of excitement glistened; he was again on the parapets of Yazoo, on the firing line at Baker's Creek.

Against the Egyptians, the Abyssinian line began to take shape a mile and a half away. There were fifty thousand arrayed—if not organized—in full barbarian splendor. Into battle each Abyssinian warrior carried a shield; the massed shields glittered in the sun. Banners appeared, and tribal chieftains rallied their warriors about them. In the rear were the women and children, scarcely less fierce than their bloodthirsty menfolk.

Probably King John had not intended to give battle at this place. He had planned only to make quick thrusts at Khaya Khor and at Fort Gura—attacks that would serve to keep the Egyptians occupied while the Abyssinians hurried across the valley to the water beyond—but finding the Egyptians outside the forts and threatening his progress, John attacked.

The first attack fell on the Egyptians' right. Here Dye had his artillery concentrated, but the protecting battalion had been withdrawn. Toward his position came five columns of yelling, screaming tribesmen. Dye opened with his mountain batteries and with rockets. He drove back the first attack, but a second, rallying in the woods, was more difficult to meet. This time the sheer mass of attackers made even artillery fire ineffective. Dye's men took up their carbines. Dye sent frantic messages to Loring, to Ratib, to anyone who could send him reinforcements. Captain Porter, then Irgins, then the doctors, Johnson and Wilson, went rushing to Ratib to demand support. Some of the Abyssinians got past Dye's position, turned his flank, and launched a new assault from the protecting hills at his rear. He hurried Derrick off with the message that his right was being turned and he could not hold out. He thought that fifteen or twenty thousand warriors were concentrated against him.

Derrick found Loring and Ratib incapable of action. Loring, wild with excitement, was issuing orders in a torrent of words that no one understood or obeyed. Ratib seemed calm, but it was the calmness of despair, of a fatalism which seemed to recognize that the stars in their courses had taken matters from his hands. Ratib, at the moment almost stupefied, was concerned only for the safety of his prince. Without a word to Loring or Derrick, he turned his horse and rode off in search of Prince Hassan. Soon the prince and his bodyguard were hustled off to the fort. The haste was Ratib's; the prince left slowly, reluctantly, and his withdrawal was almost a ceremonial procession.

For all the vagaries they had witnessed in the Civil War, the effect of the prince's retirement was something that the Americans could not have anticipated. Until that time, the Egyptian soldiers had been firing, relatively ineffectively, in the general direction of the Abyssinian hordes. Often they loaded their breechloaders and simply pulled the triggers without aiming. In the penny-pinching extravagance of the khedive's finances, there had been money enough for modern rifles but none for ammunition to waste on target practice. The Americans had trained a staff in map making, bookkeeping, and the elements of logistics, but they had not supervised instruction in the aiming and firing of a gun. Nor had the Americans ever considered that bad eyesight—a problem they had recognized and dealt with in the artillery—prevailed in the ranks of the infantry and that large numbers of their soldiers could not see the enemy. On the firing line they fired—but over the heads of the enemy. Though they could not see, the soldiers knew that their firing was ineffective. When the prince withdrew, the troops—supposing they were ordered to retreat—simply followed him.

It was not a panicked flight from the field of battle; it was almost orderly. The soldiers dropped out of the line and followed their prince to the rear. Prince Hassan and his bodyguard went toward the fort, passing around a small hill. The troops, following, did not see Hassan turn again toward the

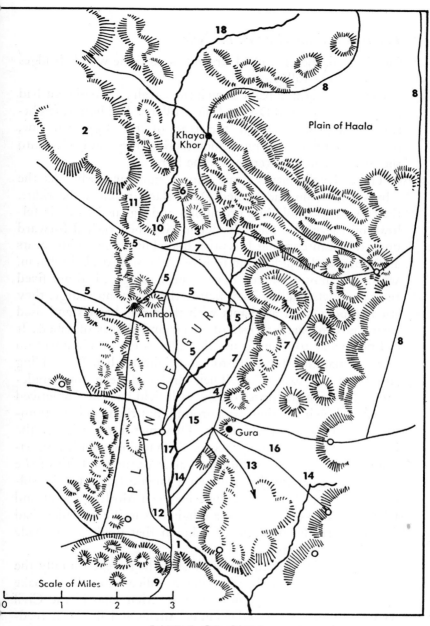

BATTLE OF GURA

1. Intrenched camp
2. High plateau
3. Osman Pasha's camp
4. Egyptians slaughtered
5. Abyssinian troops
6. Khaya Khor Pass
7. Egyptian troops
8. To Addi Rasso
9. To Godofalassie
10. Fort Hassan Pasha
11. Mount Zuban
12. Fort Gura
13. Line of retreat
14. Water holes
15. Wells
16. First encampment
17. Line of advance
18. Torrent bed

fort; instead, they marched straight toward the wooded ridges
that edged the valley.

Far to the right, a panic struck the cavalry. A regiment had
been placed to guard Dye and the artillery. The horses, frightened, stampeded toward the rear of the Egyptian line,
trampled soldiers, overran a mountain battery, and piled into
the slowly marching retreat on the left.

These developments came almost simultaneously. As the
Abyssinians who had turned Dye's flank reached the ridge,
they saw the whole line crumbling and signaled to their fellows on the plain. The advancing tribesmen rushed forward
upon the disintegrating Egyptian line. They came with spears
and sabers and fought hand to hand. The well-drilled fellahin,
who knew how to march but not how to fight, had not fixed
their bayonets. Falling back before the barbarian charge, they
tried to poke their assailants with their rifle barrels and used
their guns to parry thrusts of spears and slashes of sabers. It
did not occur to them to use the rifles as clubs. They had no
more preparation for hand-to-hand fighting than for holding
steady on the firing line. Their drill had been for parade-
ground maneuvers; never on the drill field had they practiced
a charge. Their religious background, not their military training, served them in their plight. They met death stolidly: the
hour had come, and they accepted their doom with resignation. In a religious war, fighting valiantly for the faith of the
Prophet, they might have shown a fanatic fury. To the soldiers, this, for all the difference between Moslem Egypt and
Christian Abyssinia, was not a religious war. Their leaders had
failed to use the weapons of religion that might have made
warriors of fellahin.

The Americans tried in vain to stay the retreat—to rally the
men, to get regimental and company officers to halt, to make
a stand, to organize a countercharge. Men who in the Civil
War had reorganized soldiers in cornfields and along the reed-
grown banks of rivers, and had seen those men retake a field,
cried out for a rally that would save the day. Thirteen years

before, at Prairie Grove, Arkansas, Dye had gathered the Twentieth Iowa along an orchard fence and poured out such a flame of musketry that the enemy was halted, enabling the artillery to reach a position to wreak havoc on the Confederate lines. Almost a dozen years before, at Petersburg, Virginia, Derrick had seen a section of the Confederate line explode and thousands of Union troops rush into the gap in an effort to break through to victory. But the Confederates had rallied, poured into the breach, and repulsed the charging Federals. There was none of that spirit on the battlefield of Gura; the Egyptian soldiers had been enlisted against their will for a war in which they did not believe.

One part of the battle was yet to come—a part which was tragically reminiscent of the crater before Petersburg. Between the Egyptian lines and Fort Gura lay a deep, perpendicular-sided stream bed at a point where the left of the Egyptian line had rested. The first troops to leave the battle crossed the ravine safely enough, but as the panicked cavalry piled after and the charging Abyssinians pressed, men began to stagger and fall and other troops tumbled over them. In a few minutes hundreds of men, officers of staff and line, and, in Dye's words, "surgeons and sheiks, infantry, cavalry and artillery, riderless horses and transport animals, struggling camels and floundering mules" struggled in inextricable confusion. They raised clouds of dust that choked and suffocated the men and animals. Nothing could save them, for the Abyssinians were upon them, slashing with cruel weapons, shrieking in their thirst for blood. A thousand men died there, and only the eagerness of the Abyssinians to loot the bodies of their victims stayed further slaughter.

Prince Hassan saw what was happening and tried to rally the cavalry to ride out of the fort against the Abyssinians. But the men who had followed him into the fort would not venture out again. With no resistance, Abyssinian horsemen rode down and slaughtered soldiers struggling out of the ravine.

Some fugitives turned to the hills behind the fort, but warriors were waiting there to cut them down.

The battle lasted more than two hours and a half, from the first shots until the remnants of the Egyptian army were huddled inside the fort. Most of the staff officers, riding through the Abyssinian cavalry and skirting the death-heaped ravine, reached the fort and safety. Dye had a wound in the foot which was bleeding badly. Dr. Wilson had a broken leg. Others were unhurt, but a quick count showed that Dr. Johnson was missing. He had been wounded and was a captive of the Abyssinians. One Egyptian division commander who had tried to rally his men at the beginning of the retreat had been killed. Several beys who had commanded regiments were dead and one was a captive. One surgeon, chief of the medical men, who had remained in the fort during the battle, rode out on the field during the retreat and was captured and murdered by the Abyssinians.

Outside the fort, stretching from the ravine to the roads that crossed the valley, lay the bodies of the dead and wounded. During the night the wounded crawled to the fort. Their ghastly wounds were far worse than anything the Americans had seen on Civil War battlefields. Abyssinian lances, spears, and sabers had cut great gashes and severed hands, arms, and legs. The cries of the wounded mingled with the festive shouts of the Abyssinians celebrating their victory. It was three days before the army physicians, some of them severely injured, could attend to all who needed aid.

During the night the officers, American and Egyptian, took counsel. What, they asked themselves, had happened to Osman Pasha and the strong artillery position at Khaya Khor? Why had no shot come from the fort while the Abyssinians had been within range of the guns? He had not opened fire, Osman Pasha explained, because he feared the Abyssinians might be angered and attack him.

Beyond the pass of Khaya Khor, in the plain of Haala, Colonel Field had heard the sounds of battle. After the conference at Khaya Khor he had been warned that the enemy would attack, and he was hurrying his troops and supplies to the pass but was still too far away. During the night Field and his men reached the fort, but Osman Pasha refused to allow them to enter the dangerous valley.

In the American view, the situation was not hopeless. During the Civil War, after defeats of only slightly less moment, armies had rallied and snatched victory from the jaws of disaster. As Dye and Loring saw it, the troops at Khaya Khor, including those that Field had brought up, should be ordered to Gura. The Abyssinians, as the information brought in by escaping prisoners proved, were not invincible. They spent half the night in an orgy of celebration and slept without posting sentinels. They tied prisoners back to back and left them unguarded. With three battalions at Gura, three at Khaya Khor, and two brought by Colonel Field, the Egyptians could muster five thousand men. The Americans wanted to attack at dawn. But Ratib could not understand their reckless plan. Instead, he ordered several hundred soldiers to go from Gura to Khaya Khor.

In the morning the Abyssinians appeared on the hills, and sharpshooters kept up an annoying fire throughout the day. Some of the warriors, bent on loot, came down on the plain and captured mules and camels wandering outside the fort. They scavenged the battlefield, picking up guns, parts of uniforms, abandoned tents. Sporadic firing from the fort prevented them from coming too near, but one Abyssinian crawled to the very walls and was making off with a tent before the Egyptians sighted him. He fell at the first shot and lay as if dead, waited, grabbed his loot, and sprinted away. A second shot brought another deathlike fall, and once again he ran. Twice more the scene was played, and at last he was safely beyond range of the guns.

Emboldened by the paralysis of the Egyptians, the Abyssinians came in force the following day, March 9. This time they made a concerted assault. They came along the ravine that had become a charnel house on the first day of battle and under its protection drew close to the fort. They sallied forth to occupy the breastworks that the army had abandoned. Within sixty or seventy yards of the fort, their sharpshooters hid behind bushes and picked off the soldiers.

Inside the fort was pandemonium. Some of the Sudanese fought well, and the artillery stubbornly resisted the assault, but the Egyptians cowered in fear until their officers drove them to the walls with whips. Loring, so he claimed, found Ratib hiding behind a stack of hard bread. By the time he ventured out of his bread fort, the Egyptians had beaten off the assault.

The Abyssinians abandoned the field and their wounded. When they had gone, the Egyptians went out to kill the wounded, slashing and mutilating some, burning others alive by throwing flaming branches on them. That night the Abyssinians took a terrible vengeance: they murdered almost a thousand of their prisoners.

Having failed to take Fort Gura, King John's army began to disintegrate. The Abyssinian soldiers who had answered the call to arms had hoped for loot. In the battle they seized camels and mules and fought over the spoils. Fifty men, an Abyssinian told Loring, would rush upon one camel and fight over it. The victor took his prize and rode for home. The scavengers of the battlefield went off with their trophies. The resistance of the fort convinced the Abyssinian warriors that booty would be purchased dearly. The warriors left, taking with them their prisoners to hold for ransom. Each prisoner belonged to the man who had captured him.

One such prisoner was Dr. Thomas Johnson, who had a severe wound in the leg. His captors stripped him, tied his arms behind his back, and drove him before them. Given no food or drink, no clothing, no shelter from the burning sun or the chill of the night, he lived for several weeks in terror. He saw other prisoners killed and several times expected to be killed himself. Handed over to a couple of boys, he was tor-

mented by their taunts and threats of mutilation. At last, prodded beyond endurance, he trounced one of his guards and—
much to his surprise—won the admiration of the chief of his
captors, who rescued him. When they reached Adowa, the
Abyssinian king learned that Johnson was a physician and
offered him double his Egyptian salary and the governorship
of a province. Johnson hurriedly invented a wife and children
as the reason he must refuse the offer. He was freed and after
some weeks made his way back to Massawa.

After the battle the Egyptian army remained on the plain
of Gura, licking its wounds and trying to determine its next
move. On March 19, Colonel Lockett arrived at the post and
promptly advised the strengthening of the fort at Khaya
Khor, where Dye and Derrick had wanted to make a stand.
He found the native and foreign officers at loggerheads, snarl-
ing, unwilling to work together—each group filled with recriminations for the actions of the other. Each faction, think-
ing Lockett close to Stone, poured its grievances into his ears.
The Americans blamed the failure at Gura on the utter incapacity of the Egyptian soldiers and their subaltern officers
and the failure of Osman Pasha to send aid from Khaya Khor.
There had been no orders given during the battle, no maneu-
vering to meet its changing aspects, no skirmishes. The army—
officers and men—had been whipped as soon as it got outside
the fort. The Abyssinians were undoubtedly superior in spirit,
in courage, in fighting experience, in numbers—in everything,
in truth, except equipment and red tape.

On the other side, Lockett heard the complaints of the
Egyptians. Ratib grumbled that he was not given a chance to
be commander in chief. He never gave an order that Loring
did not oppose, and Prince Hassan often supported Loring.
Ratib said he had been forced to divide his army, keeping half
in the rear and going into battle with only part of his troops.
Moreover, complained some of the other Egyptians, Dye and
Loring were foolhardy in insisting that they meet the enemy
in the open. Had they defended the fort on the first day, King

John would have attacked them and—as the assault on March 9 proved—would have been beaten off. Such tactics would have discouraged the Abyssinians and inspired the Egyptian soldiers with confidence.

"Why," asked the Americans in counterargument, "did the Egyptians come to Abyssinia?" Was it not to avenge Arrendrup and to show King John that Egypt was powerful and to be respected? Could this be done by lying in wait for an attack? The Abyssinians would have considered them cowards and blockaded the fort until they starved.

Lockett listened to the charges of cowardice, bad judgment, and treachery, but he reserved his opinion. Outwardly he kept the post of impartiality, and privately he tried to be judicious. Having thought it over, he concluded that the foreign element in the army was a source of weakness. The Americans had shown ability, zeal, and devotion to duty, but "their manner of doing things," he confided to his diary, "their ideas of military discipline, of military honor, of all the requirements of soldierly duty were totally different." He thought of conventional symbols of incompatibility—oil and water, a race horse harnessed to an ox. Out of it he drew his own conclusions: the Americans were "bold, impetuous, straightforward"; the Arabs were "slow, timid, cautious, crafty." The Americans had come to defeat King John, and they wanted to fight and "be done with the business." The Egyptians preferred stratagem, preferred to use bribery and treachery rather than to risk losses. And, surmised Lockett, with their capacity for spreading *la couleur de rose* over their acts, they concocted a "presentable record for the world's eye."

After listening to recriminations and judiciously arriving at his own conclusions, Lockett built a fort. During the month of his labors other developments brought into clearer focus differences more fundamental than those Lockett had recognized. With his army disintegrating, King John sent an offer to negotiate a peace, saying that he did not wish to kill more Egyptians but only wished them to leave his country. To the amazement of the Americans, who knew that a battle was not a campaign and had seen many a campaign saved after an initial defeat, Ratib began to negotiate. For weeks emissaries passed from John's camp to Ratib's headquarters, exchanging gifts and over cigarettes and teacups slowly deliberating the terms under which the Egyptians might withdraw.

On April 19 Ratib abandoned Fort Gura and moved four thousand men to Khaya Khor. The rest of the army returned to Massawa, their retirement more confused than their advance had been. There were fewer animals now, and fewer burdens to bear, but the transportation system upon which Loshe and Field had tried to impose order was now completely disarranged. The soldiers, too, were disorganized, and rumor spread through the ranks that the Abyssinians were planning to attack them flank and rear as they marched. By the time the columns got to Bahr Reza, the rumors had excited panic, and the men broke and fled. They stumbled, exhausted and terror-stricken, into Massawa, and there their officers hustled them on vessels bound for Suez. Not since Bull Run had American officers witnessed such a scene.

XI

vvvvvvvvvvvvv

Aftermath of Gura

To the American officers reassembled at Massawa it seemed, indeed, as if a repetition of the events of the summer and winter of 1861 would take place. After the flight from the first battle of Manassas, as the Americans well remembered, the Army of the Potomac had reorganized, drilled, and reoriented itself to face the victorious Confederates. Now, at Massawa, the handful of Americans fully expected that fresh and less timorous soldiers, better drilled and better trained, would arrive to replace those who had lost the first battle in the campaign against Abyssinia.

While they waited, they made preparations. Lockett was busy strengthening the secondary outposts at Bahr Reza and Addi Rasso—the first in a series of frontier forts, like those in the American West, to hold the land against the savages. In Massawa the rains came, and night and day, day after day, the waters poured from the heavens. The Americans expected that the new campaign would wait until the end of the rainy season. But before the rains stopped falling, orders arrived from General Stone. Field was to explore as far as Sanheet, and Colonel Derrick was to begin surveying for a railroad from Massawa to Bahr Reza. Clearly this was the renewal of the campaign. Almost at once they received new orders: the expeditions were to finish their work quickly and prepare to return to Cairo. Late in June a ship arrived, and all but Lockett embarked for Suez.

The Americans arrived in Cairo to find in the war department as well as in the cafés an atmosphere of hostility. Mrs.

Lockett, during her vigil in Cairo, had noted that "Americans are below par" in Egypt; they had lost what esteem they had. In the first moments after Gura, the Egyptian government released an "official account" of a great victory over King John's hosts, an account fulsome in its praise of Egyptian valor. The Cairo populace, accustomed to reading such announcements as before a mirror, correctly interpreted this as admission of defeat. Then the troops came home and with one accord laid the blame squarely on the foreign officers. Ratib, who had control of the telegraph, censored—even stopped—official and personal mail so that American countercharges got no hearing. And Prince Hassan, too, who had supported Loring against Ratib, hid his own less-than-courageous conduct at Gura by attesting the blunders of the Americans. The war department requested decorations from the Turkish sultan for Egyptian officers, and General Stone, citing official propaganda and ignoring whispered criticisms of his countrymen, asked for medals for the members of his staff who had taken part in the "victory" at Gura. Eventually the Americans were given their decorations, though not all were satisfied with the honors the Sublime Porte saw fit to bestow.

More important, and vastly more annoying to the Americans, was the difficulty they had in collecting their pay. The khedivial finances were in bad shape; expeditions into the Sudan, the equatorial provinces, and Abyssinia had drained the treasury; trade had been disrupted; revenues were declining. The bankers of Europe had fastened a strangling grip upon Egypt, and it was the Americans who suffered. Before leaving for Massawa, Lockett drew four months' pay, plus an extra 20 per cent for field service, so that his family would not be deprived. Other families were less fortunate. Upon his return to Cairo, as the Gura expedition was about to leave, the ill and suffering Colston waited months for what was owed him, refusing to sign receipts for token payments. Chaillé-Long, returning from Juba in February, 1876, was forced to wait until June 12 for his first payment. Stone's secretary, a

civilian from Massachusetts named Barnard, took to sponging
his breakfasts from Colston until the Virginian stopped him
by having meals at odd hours.

Stone, too, went unpaid but was able to be philosophical
about it. "We are now passing through a terrible financial
crisis," he told Colonel Boyd, of Louisiana, in April. "I believe it is always the fate of a young and enterprising country
to pass through such financial pressure." Moreover, Stone's
own sense of idealism served to bolster him. "The khedive de-
sires so earnestly to do so much [that it] is a grand sight to see a
man striving as this sovereign does." It would indeed "inspire
true men with a desire to help him." When true men showed
less than his own good faith, Stone turned on them impatiently. Of Colston's loyalty there could be no doubt, but on one
occasion, when the colonel questioned the accuracy of Egyptian accounting, Stone replied with withering scorn. "Why
don't you leave this damned service?" he demanded. "If I
were *you* I would not stay in it." He added, brutally, that
Colston "ought to be thankful for receiving anything."

But this was a bad morning, and Stone had more than his
share of troubles with the war department and with the Egyptian officials. He was doing all that he could for his officers.
Within a month after their return from Massawa he managed
to wheedle a bit of money from the treasury and arranged
leaves of absence for some. Among those who benefited was
Colonel Dennison, whose wife was ill and anxious to return
to the States. He was granted four months' leave and enough
back pay to meet current expenses. Together with Derrick,
Dennison went to the paymaster's office to collect his money
and found he would have to take part of it in Egyptian piastres
—twelve hundred dollars' worth. Derrick found the ensuing
negotiations highly amusing. The two officers undertook to
exchange the Egyptian coins for gold and sought out the shop
of a money-changer. "It would have amused you," he wrote
his wife, "to have seen us sitting out in public at one of these
stands, trying to exchange a bushel of piastres for gold, and

counting out and examining the various coins offered by the cunning and dishonest dealer, whilst a crowd of curious Arabs, and blind, variously deformed and crippled beggars swarmed around eyeing, with envious glances, the glittering pile, and importunately crying for 'backsheesh' in the name of Allah. I was sometimes forced to use my sabre vigorously to keep them back at a respectful distance." Eventually, with much haggling and threats, the officers completed their transaction, and, Derrick recounted, "we went on our way rejoicing."

With seemingly little understanding of General Stone's problems, a goodly group of Americans—Colston, Dye, Chaillé-Long, Martin, Hall, and others—scattered over Europe to spend the summer and the fall. They fully expected that by the time they got back a reinvigorated army, under their command, would be ready to take the field to link the khedive's Central African provinces with the Red Sea.

Colston headed for Paris. For several months after his return from Khartoum, recuperating slowly and still wracked with pain, he had hobbled about Cairo trying to collect his pay and settle his accounts. As soon as he reached Paris his spirits and health improved. He found childhood acquaintances and retramped the streets remembered from his boyhood. He went to museums and to Notre Dame like other tourists. From Paris he went to Switzerland, to Florence, Milan, and Rome, enjoying the mountains and glaciers, the people, the arts—enjoying them resolutely, as if certain he would not live to see them again. But he could not escape Egypt. He was discouraged by letters from Mason, who reported that the money situation in Cairo was worse. He was saddened by news that Dr. Pfund, the naturalist, had died in the desert. One morning, in Paris, he met Wilburn Hall on the stairs of his hotel. Hall was on leave, improving his time—under his wife's nagging—to apply for work in the United States. A day or two later Chaillé-Long appeared and relayed the information that Hall was going home full of stories of

Stone's "outrageous villanies" against the Americans. Chaillé-Long was to spend his furlough in the United States on a lecture tour. During his absence he arranged for the publication of his book *Central Africa: Naked Truths of Naked People*, which succeeded in making Chaillé-Long's lake larger than Baker's. In Geneva, Colston saw Martin—the very day after the annoyed Mrs. Martin presented her husband with a son.

In Geneva Colston talked with Dye, who was recuperating from the foot wound he had received at Gura and daily growing more rancorous as he nursed his grievances. After the battle, Loring had been particularly solicitous of Dye and as quickly as possible sent him off to Massawa with an officer, six soldiers, and two servants as personal escort, an arrangement which did not insure him a comfortable journey. Four of the soldiers made off with the food and camels and had to be caught and brought back under guard. They threatened to desert again, until Dye—on his knees because he could not stand on his wounded foot—flourished a revolver. In Geneva, Dye forgot Loring's solicitude and, sitting at sidewalk cafés, filled the ears of any who would listen with denunciations of the cowardly incompetence of Ratib and the excitable tactlessness of Loring. He extended his bitterness to Stone. The chief of staff had promised to make him a brigadier general, he related, but where was his promotion? He would not, he added petulantly, accept the decoration for valor for which Stone had recommended him.

In Egypt, while the vacationers were enjoying, each in his own way, their furloughs, Stone, Loring, and the remainder of the staff prepared to continue the Abyssinian campaign. At Massawa, the Red Sea port, Colonel Lockett remained on duty—making a survey of the harbor, drawing maps, and designing a fort. The sun blazed with full summer fury. Lockett begged to be relieved that he might see his family and recuperate in the cool shades of Cairo. But it was late summer before General Stone allowed him to return. Earlier, in May, Colonel Graves, with orders direct from the khedive, joined Lockett in Massawa to supervise the construction of jetties to be used for the more efficient landing of an army. In July, Graves returned to check and regulate chronometers that Lockett would be using in surveys.

In Cairo, at the Citadel, the staff officers and their Arab apprentice-officers made maps, prepared estimates, and collated data against the day when Ismail would have consolidated his East African domains. All were sure that the Abyssinian campaign was about to be resumed.

In Alexandria, however, General Loring had not begun to drill and train a new army. He spent the summer untangling the snarled finances and settling the estate of old General Reynolds, who had died while the others were off fighting for the glory of the khedive. Old Gauley Reynolds' last months of life were far from happy ones. He had come early to Egypt, and his wife, his son Frank, and Frank's wife and son were with him. They had lived happily enough in Loring's palace in Alexandria. In 1874 Frank went back to the United States as inspector of arms which the Remingtons were selling to the khedive. With him went his wife and child. He died in Ilion, New York, in 1875, still attached to the Egyptian army. Soon after, Mrs. A. W. Reynolds, the general's wife, went home to Philadelphia, where she had spent the years her husband and son served in the Confederate Army. Within a few months, she died. In Alexandria, the bereaved general moved to a hotel and watched his last friend, Loring, depart for the Abyssinian campaign. The world of the genial and gregarious Old Gauley was falling apart. To add to his misfortunes, he had no money, his pay was in arrears, and the hotel proprietor demanded he settle his mounting bill. Lonely and broke, he shifted to a boarding house, selecting one with a none-too-savory reputation—run by a Mrs. Letitia Stevens. One day—it was May 26, 1876—he went to his room to wait for a friend with whom he was going for a drive. The friend arrived to find the old man dead in his bed. "His death was caused by *drink*," declared Colonel Graves when he heard of it. "He was never sober. It was so habitual with him that people did not know that he was drunk for they had never seen him sober. He was *full* all the time. Had been a hard, systematic drinker for many years." Gossips tried to make the demise of the lonely old man even more scandalous. Stone's secretary whispered salacious rumors to Colston. They buried Old Gauley in Alexandria.

When Loring returned to Alexandria, he and Consul General Elbert E. Farman tackled the complicated job of settling the Reynolds estate. There were arrears of pay to collect, hotel bills to pay, a loan of $1,000 to be repaid a Mrs. Margaret Porter, a friend of Loring's. There were claims, some legitimate and some fraudulent, to dispose of. One claim was rejected: Letitia Stevens presented a bill for £10. When they sent their first accounting to Frank Reynolds' widow, the two gentlemen carefully marked "boarding" in explanation of the claim.

In December, 1876, the Americans began to gather in Cairo, presumably reinvigorated for the tasks ahead and ready to lead a new army to new conquests. Colston got back at noon on Christmas Eve, and Mason met him with open arms at the train. Colston went immediately to General Stone's, where Miss Stone welcomed him heartily, delighted with the silver fish he had brought her from Florence. He gave coral pins to Mrs. Stone, a box of candy to the children, cuff links to the general. That night there was a great Christmas tree at the Stones'. The Martins, who had returned to Cairo with their three-month-old son, were not on hand, but all the other officers were there—Loring, Field, Mason, Derrick, Irgins, Ward, Loshe, Lockett, and Graves. Missing were Prout and Purdy in Central Africa and Chaillé-Long and Dye, not yet back from leave. Missing, too, were others who had been among them at the end of the Gura campaign. Hall had taken his complaining wife to the States; Dr. Wilson had resumed his commission in the U.S. Army; Dennison, too, had taken his unhappy wife back to New York and would resign within the week. David Essex Porter, son of Admiral David Porter, had left in October. He was, remarked Graves, "a Low, Un-principled, Drunken fellow [who had been] disgracing him-self ever since he came to Egypt a year ago," and now had been "*compelled* to resign"—this, after a long period in which he was known to be "getting drunk, abusing Egyptian gov-ernment from the khedive down in public places, . . . bor-rowing money upon false pretenses, and *swindling* right and left." Ismail demanded his resignation only after Porter had fed an English newspaper correspondent "a long string of lies" about the Abyssinian campaign.

With gossip about the absent to spice the holidays, the American homecoming in Cairo was filled with good spirits. They had dinner at the Locketts', an eggnog party at the Loshes', wine almost everywhere, and a feast aboard a yacht on the Nile with visiting American tourists. Even the Egyp-tians seemed to be mellowing. The day after Christmas was Kourban Bairam, and all the Americans went to the palace in their dress uniforms to mingle with princes, pashas, beys, and extravagantly garbed diplomats and to pay their respects to the khedive. Everyone was cordial. The only sour note, in fact, was the reception given for them by the consul general, Elbert E. Farman. A "very common affair," noted Colston. The "chief persons" there were the "missionary brethren—a set of village vulgarians without the least tincture of style." For the Virginia gentleman just returned from fashionable Paris and Florence, it was "disgusting to be thus represented."

As the holiday season passed, the American officers waited for their new assignments—waited expectantly, even impa-tiently. By January 3 Colston was ready for a change. "Life is becoming dull and tiresome. . . ." In the Citadel General Stone and his map makers were assembling data and the quarter-master's staff was assembling materiel preparatory to sending Alexander McComb Mason on an expedition into the equa-torial provinces.

Mason was now an old hand in Egypt and on the Upper Nile. He had arrived in 1870, behind him a respectable record of service in the Confederacy, and promptly went to work as commander of a khedivial steamer plying between Alexandria and Constantinople. He was an industrious fellow of a careful and scholarly mind and taciturn in manner. Because he spent so little time in Cairo, few of his associates came to know him well. He had a sensitiveness about his position, a considerable amount of ambition, and a willingness to work. Soon Stone took him off the Constantinople run and added him to the general staff. He learned Arabic quickly, and he got along well with the Egyptians and people in the interior, perhaps better than with most of his American associates. In 1874, Stone sent Mason on the expedition to Darfur as second in command to Purdy. Under Purdy's directions, Mason pushed his explorations to the south and into the mountainous region to the west of Lake Albert. He worked well, gathering the kind of scientific information that Purdy needed for his report, but he was thoroughly displeased by his commander's failure to give him the credit to which he felt himself entitled. In 1876, after more than a year and a half in the Sudan, he returned to Cairo. There he buttonholed any American officer who would listen to his grievances about Purdy. He lost heavily in the gambling hells of the capital—to the horror of the thrifty Colston, who alone among the Americans was fond of him. In addition, he earned the enmity of a certain Mme. Camille, who denounced him loudly to all of her acquaintances. Stone concluded that Mason was more valuable in the field than in the Citadel. He gave him an opportunity to tell a special meeting of the Khedivial Geographical Society at the Hotel d'Orient of the valuable geographic information he had gathered in Darfur. He was then, with Prout, sent off as deputy governor to the equatorial domain of Chinese Gordon. Early in February he left Cairo.

Whatever Mason's claims to a major share of the credit for Purdy's expedition, this time, working on his own, he made an incontestable contribution to knowledge. Early in June, 1877, he left Dufile on the White Nile and headed up the river toward Lake Albert. He mapped the river as far as Magungo; in the steamer "Nyanza" he started around the shores of the lake, following the western shore, overhung with lofty, precipitous mountains, and pushed inquiringly into every inlet. He discovered a large population living in the ravines, along the narrow shore, and in small valleys behind the cliffs. On his first night—it was June 14—he anchored in the shelter of a point, beyond which was a large banana plantation.

Hardly had he cast anchor when he was hailed from shore. There stood the chief of the village, wearing huge bracelets of a yellow metal, and leading a large sheep. The sheep was an offering, perhaps a bribe. The chief quickly got down to business. To the north, he explained, there were villages rich in cattle, and his villagers hankered to add beef to their diet of mutton and bananas. Would Mason help to attack them? Mason had been too long in Africa to be surprised or amused. He refused solemnly, even a bit unctuously—the chief could not expect him to accept—and advised the would-be warrior to keep the peace. Then he turned the talk to ivory. The chief had heard of Gordon's prohibition and denied that his village possessed a store of tusks. They parted in friendship, Mason with the sheep and a store of information about the farther reaches of the lake.

Another day brought Mason and the "Nyanza" to a bay. Natives told him that the bay and its shores and inlets were clogged with *ambatch*, a tall, lush-growing water plant. Discouraged but dogged, Mason crossed the bay and, at the southernmost end of the lake, found a river, followed it, and entered another large bay. Mason poked the bow of the little steamer into one promising pool after another, withdrawing when vegetation barred his progress. At last he discovered a way that was passable and, slowly, came to a broad river—the Semliki, connecting Lake Albert and Lake Edward—whose reddish waters flowed almost imperceptibly in a northerly direction. The river, about one hundred yards wide, with high forest-clad banks, was shallow, and the steamer constantly ran aground. Returning to Lake Albert, Mason discovered that his course lay to the east. Along the shore were mountains barren of vegetation and not so high as those on the west. The people here scurried like frightened gazelles at sight of the steaming water monster. Mason anchored, called out to a few of the trembling villagers, stilled their terror, and persuaded them to bring wood as fuel for the steamer. On the fifth day he returned to Magungo. He had circumnavigated the lake and could say that it was not nearly as large as Sir Samuel Baker, its discoverer, had claimed.

With justifiable pride Mason sent his report to Chinese Gordon. The governor, apt to be envious of the achievements of his subordinates, sent it off without comment to Stone and Ismail. Stone valued it both for the information it contained and as evidence that the Americans could prove themselves useful to the khedive. He published it proudly, but no sooner had it been seen in London than Baker found reason to cavil at Mason's figures. The American had made careful observations of latitude, longitude, and elevation; Baker challenged them all. Other Britishers took up the cudgels and tried in vain to dim the luster of Mason's star. The president of the American Geographical Society echoed the British critics and claimed that Stanley earlier had named Mason's southernmost bay the Beatrice Gulf and that Mason had not proved it a part of the lake. But such criticism was puerile, and Mason and Stone were content with the new discoveries. When Prout left the Sudan, Stone and Gordon appointed Mason deputy governor of Equatorial Africa.

The American officers in Cairo, who watched Mason leave for further adventures, greater contributions, and ensuing controversies were convinced that soon they would again take up the Abyssinian campaign and complete the connections between the Red Sea and the inland empire. Colston suggested to a New York newspaper reporter that there were reserves of forty to fifty thousand men whom the Americans might lead in the event, as he put it, of another Abyssinian war. Yet for all their eagerness to work and their readiness for a fight, the Americans saw no steps taken toward these objectives. Late in February, when Mason had been gone for almost a month, Graves noted that none of the officers were doing anything of importance and most made no more than a pretense of working. They were all "awaiting orders." Chaillé-Long, Colston, and Loshe were idle. Field was engaged in "busy work," writing a resumé of the current troubles in Turkey. Every day he went to the Citadel and put in his hours, but he had "not written six pages in six months." Ward was head of the "Torpedo Bureau," and there was not a torpedo in all of Egypt. Lockett, Martin, and Derrick were doing a little map work—and Stone himself found little enough employment.

There were rumors about that the khedive intended to dismiss the American officers from his service rather than send them out on another expedition. The Abyssinian boundary dispute had not been settled, and emissaries of the khedive were still engaged in protracted negotiations with King John. Until agreement was reached, the railroad surveys could not be made, the protecting line of forts established, or the road built. Meanwhile, there was no work for the Americans in the Egyptian army. And yet Ismail gave every assurance that he wanted their services. "The khedive," Graves wrote, "is a kind-hearted man, and that is the only reason he keeps us here. He invited us to come out and now he does not like to discharge us."

Ismail was indeed kindhearted and that may have been at the root of his reluctance to discharge men he could not put to use. More fundamental, in American eyes, was a defect in the khedive's character. Ismail, for all his progressivism, for all his effort to westernize and modernize his country, for all his high ambitions and his energetic actions, they decided, was an indecisive man. He could not make up his mind to use the Americans, to push King John out of the disputed area on the

Abyssinian border, to build the railroad which he needed to realize his imperialistic dreams. He was unable to resist pressure, to hold firm against vigorous opposition. Against the sultan of Turkey he stood up well enough, but he did not defy him. Instead, he yielded, resorted to negotiation, and emerged with face-saving rather than with a victory. He was yielding, little by little, to the pressure of the international bankers. Perhaps, indeed, he was more oriental than he seemed, and the same fatalism which his soldiers showed when they left the battlefield of Gura was revealed in his own character and expressed the fundamental difference between Egyptians and Americans. Lying beneath superficial differences in manner, mores, and religious observances—the basis of cultural conflict—was a difference in spirit. American optimism—the spirit which infused American aggressiveness—was in sharp contrast to Egyptian acceptance of all that Allah ordained. The American officers of the khedive would never understand why they should remain idle when there were worlds to conquer, work to do, glory and honor to be won. They came of a tradition that stressed fighting it out on the line if it took all summer, of fighting desperately, barefoot, ragged, and starving, even when an Appomattox was inevitable. Americans did not give up; Egyptians swayed and broke beneath the winds of adversity.

An illustration of the conciliatory nature of the Egyptian spirit came in the early months of 1877. The Americans, with no work to occupy them, gossiped and took sides in the controversy. In January Colonel Dye returned from leave to find himself facing court-martial. The case grew out of an episode on the road to Gura, wakening fresh reminders of the confusion, conflicts, and mismanagement of the campaign. Dye needed no reminder; he carried rancor in his soul for all who had been concerned in the Abyssinian debacle. Convalescence in Geneva had healed his wound but had not lessened his vehemence. He was even more profane in his denunciations of Loring and Ratib, and his diatribes became shriller when Ratib ordered him to stand trial for having struck Ibrahim Lutfi Effendi. Lieutenant Lutfi was a man of dignity, one of the khedive's more faithful officers, an exceptionally pious Moslem; as a gentleman and patriot he resented Dye's charge that he had carelessly left a valuable box lying in the road; as a proud Mohammedan he could not bear the indignity of having been struck by a dog of a Christian. During Dye's absence, Lutfi filed charges. Dye was furious, loudly proclaiming that he would not appear before the court. Ismail appointed Colston and Field to serve with the native officers; still Dye refused to appear. Colston begged him to defend himself or to appeal directly to the khedive. Instead, Dye sought protection in the American consulate. It developed that on entering the service Dye, alone of Ismail's American officers, had refused to waive his right to appeal for American protection. Asserting his immunity, he would not listen to arguments that he appear before the court. Field joined Colston in arguing the matter, but Dye replied that he did not trust General Stone. Ismail suggested that the board be composed of American, Egyptian, and European officers, half to be American, but Dye remained adamant. Having refused to stand trial, he applied for a discharge and back pay, commutation, and special compensation for his wounds. The affair was at a stalemate. The court heard Lutfi but no defense from Dye. No verdict, except in public opinion, was rendered.

Clearly, as his actions in this case revealed, the khedive was approachable and judicious. But he was not always accessible. In the beginning months of 1877 a series of crises made inevitable the eventual dismissal of the Americans and the khedive's own abdication. Once Ismail wryly commented to a friend that he was so busy that he had scarcely set foot in his harem for six months.

Americans who sought to speak to His Highness found themselves blocked by a clique about the court. General Stone himself was often the victim of palace treachery. Frequently he found that the clerks in the palace told him of an appointment at other than the hour at which the khedive wished to see him. His Highness was irritated by Stone's apparent tardiness and irresponsibility. Other Americans, finding the hierarchy of clerks and lesser officials confusing and harassing, abandoned the effort to climb the bureaucratic ladder to the audience chamber.

Troubling problems of finance kept the khedive inaccessible to Stone and forestalled his intention of using the talents of his American staff. The American officers were victims of a situation they did not understand—indeed, which was greater and more complex than Ismail could comprehend. Perhaps the khedive had picked the wrong Americans for his service: these American soldiers had had experience in the greatest war of their generation, but in no sense was the American tradition solely a military one. While a million veterans of the Civil War sat reminiscing in country stores throughout the United States, new giants of finance and industry strode the land. Had the khedive hired to advise him American tycoons instead of military men and had they been as loyal as the officers whom Sherman sent, Egypt's problems might have had a more promising solution.

As it was, Egypt's financial involvement with European and English bankers tied Ismail hand and foot. From his predecessor, Said, Ismail had inherited a sizable debt— £3,293,000. Each time he gained concessions from the Sublime Porte—the 1866 right of primogeniture, the title of khedive in 1867, territorial concessions on the Red Sea—he made large increases in his annual tribute to the Turkish overlord. Festivities at the opening of the Suez cost a great deal and so did feasts at the weddings of his children. He bought lands. He improved the country with railroads, canals, harbors, forts, steamship lines, agricultural machinery—and borrowed heavily in Europe to do so, pledging taxes, customs duties, and trade concessions in payment. He expanded his empire into the Sudan, into Darfur and Kordofan, into the equatorial provinces. Instead of bringing fresh revenue, the expansion disrupted the established channels of trade. Late in 1875 the pressure of his creditors forced Ismail to offer for sale 176,602 shares of Suez Canal stock. While a French syndicate was hesitantly raising the money, the British prime minister snatched the opportunity and hurriedly bought the shares. Thereafter the international bankers had the vital interests of the British government aiding them in Egyptian affairs.

It was the Abyssinian campaign that completed the wreckage. With the sale of the canal stock, Britain took the lead for her own and European bankers. Two commissions in 1876 investigated Egyptian finances, forced changes in financial administration, assumed control of parts of the revenue, and put an Englishman and a Frenchman into the Egyptian Ministry of Finance. By Egyptian (and American) computations, Ismail had not realized more than 60 per cent of the money he had borrowed. But the commissions, the bankers, and the new officials of the debt were interested in collecting the last penny of the nominal amount.

By the beginning of 1877 every public creditor was demanding his pay. The Americans suffered with the rest. Lockett complained that American officers were "dunned and abused by Arab washerwomen for a few francs" even as the British "minister of finance" was building himself a palace of three hundred chambers. Bootblacks on the streets did not bother to solicit the custom of Americans. "No cash," they mumbled, and saved their breath for paying patrons.

In the summer of 1877 the declining prestige of the Americans and the declining fortunes of the khedive were involved in still another imbroglio in which they had no direct concern. In 1876 the Turks massacred some twelve thousand Bulgarians. Russia, ever the self-appointed champion of Christianity and civilization against Ottoman savagery, declared war on Turkey. In turn, the Sublime Porte called on Egypt for aid. Ismail faced a dilemma. He could not afford to give help, but he saw that, ideologically, it was to be a war of the faithful against the infidel. Britain and France, either pro-Russian or pro-banker, told him that he could not divert to the support of troops in the Turkish armies money pledged to pay Egyptian debts. The Americans, some of whom had come originally to Egypt to fight Turkey, faced an ideological dilemma and resolved it by announcing that they would not fight Russia. A few Americans saw no problem at all. Colonel Graves gave his wife a measure of consolation. "Don't worry about Turkey," he said reassuringly. The sultan needed troops, and the Americans were all staff officers. Ismail reluctantly sent a token force to Constantinople and strained still further his failing credit. Even this gesture was turned against the Americans: the Egyptian soldiers whom the Americans had trained fought badly in Bulgaria, and native officers were quick to blame the American officers.

Troubles—both for Ismail and for the Americans—were mounting. As the Russian war continued, revolt broke out in Darfur and Kordofan, and again King John threatened the far outposts of Egypt in the still unsettled border regions to the south. Each demand cost money, and each in turn brought from the bondholders greater interference in Egypt's internal affairs. The foreigners in the Ministry of Finance negotiated a new loan with the Rothschilds and announced that Egyptian finances would be reordered. The new order would impose greater economies on government employees and reduce drastically government expenditures. The bondholders wanted their full interest, and it disturbed no one that efforts to build a stronger economic system in Egypt in time would produce even greater wealth for the moneylenders. In the end, all that resulted was a mounting tide of anti-foreign feeling.

The anti-foreign response caught the Americans on all sides. As employees of the khedive they suffered with the Egyptians; as foreigners they shared the general opprobrium visited on all exploiting outlanders; as army officers who had attempted to oust the pasha system and had failed to win a victory in the Abyssinian campaign they bore the special en-

mity of native officers; finally, as Americans they suffered
from the jealousy of the French, whom they replaced in the
army, and of the British, who envied their successes in exploration. Assailed on all sides, the Americans stood alone.

In the midst of mounting disaster both to the monarch
whom he served and to the Americans whom he led, General
Stone continued to push for fresh adventures in exploration
and surveying and building. He was optimistic, quite certain
that Ismail's Egypt would survive. Some others agreed with
him. Colonel Graves, who had lived frugally in Egypt, was
not overly concerned when months passed before the treasury
could pay salaries. He assured his anxious wife, who read
propaganda against the khedive's regime in London newspapers, "I have no fears that we shall not be paid. I am doing
very well myself." And he recounted how he had paid off the
most pressing of his debts at home and was saving money. "I
have not a cent of debt in Egypt. . . . I have paid for my room
. . . and will have after sending off the $35, money in pocket
to maintain me one month."

But Ismail's financial problems gave less-provident Americans another cause for complaint. In the long run the brunt of
their discontent descended on General Stone, whose position
as liaison officer became increasingly difficult. Everyone with
a grievance looked to Stone. Dye blamed the general for all
his misfortunes, and Chaillé-Long contended that once Stone
had offered to make him a brigadier general at £60 a month,
"like an Arab Pasha," but had never mentioned it again. Moreover, Stone had not published Chaillé-Long's report on the
expedition into Central Africa, and Chaillé-Long, jealous of
his fame, suspected that the chief of staff was waiting until he
could claim all the credit for himself. Unhappy at his inactivity, Chaillé-Long asked for his discharge and went home,
spreading word that Stone's "incompetence and imbecility"
had reduced the American mission to a pitiable state. Under
Stone, Chaillé-Long said, the Americans had lost "spirit and
ambition"; the trouble was that Stone Pasha had become a

"thorough Turk" and thought only of his private ends, "at the cost of the demoralization of the corps of American officers." Mason, too, who thought that Stone sided with his old companion Purdy, turned against the chief of staff.

At first Lockett made an effort to be judicious. Stone was, he thought, "a kind, polished gentleman, in his outward demeanor toward everybody." This, obviously, was his "natural character." Still, he had had "so much dealings with slipperiness in Egypt [that] he has become slippery himself." Lockett considered him to be active and energetic, devoted to duty. "His head is full of schemes . . . ," yet he began a new project before completing the first. He spent his own money to "push along" government work—"yet everyone believes him to be thoroughly selfish [and] doubts his sincerity in everything." He was, concluded his friend, "a batch of contradictions, seeming always to be one thing and universally believed to be the opposite." But by the summer of 1877 even Lockett had turned against the chief of staff. "Every man who has come out to Egypt has been deceived," he complained. No one was given the position he had been promised—"We are all mere tools in the hands of one man for *his* aggrandizement." Stone had not given credit to Lockett for his map of Abyssinia or for his explorations in Massawa. So saying, Lockett quit Egypt, more heavily in debt than when he came, for a new start in Knoxville at the Tennessee Agricultural and Mechanical College.

Grievances had a chance to grow because the Americans in Cairo lacked work to do. Before he left, Chaillé-Long had not had his uniform on for a year. Lockett spelled out the complaint in some detail: "I don't believe that any true, honest, upright, faithful man can or ought to stay in the public service of the Egyptian government." The "whole confounded thing" was a "miserable humbug—all show, all bunk, all make-believe. . . . I am styled Chief of the Engineer Section of the General Staff. Well, as such I have no more to do with the Engineering of the army than the chief of police." Under these circumstances men grew desperate. Colonel Derrick, a genial, friendly person with a wife and three children in Virginia, became morose and uncommunicative, sinking slowly into lethargy and gloom. He came to sit with Graves, smoking, saying nothing, then went off to eat alone. One of Derrick's children died of diphtheria, but the bereaved father did not mention it to his companions; heavyhearted, he seemed unable to respond.

A few saved themselves by finding new preoccupations. General Loring started to write his memoirs and became so fascinated with his literary endeavors that he forced everyone to listen to what he had written. Graves was given an assignment to survey the land of Goshen. He enjoyed being received as "the Great Engineer" by the village sheiks who came to pay him court. His duties were to run lines between native villages, but even so unimportant an assignment was better than remaining idle in Cairo. Besides—ever a powerful factor with him—he received extra pay and had no expenses while in the field.

Early in 1878 the Americans hoped for a restoration of some part of their prestige with the visit to Cairo of former President Ulysses S. Grant. In January General Grant, with Mrs. Grant, their son, and a retinue of reporters, arrived on a trip around the world. From the train Grant spotted familiar faces in the welcoming group. "Why, there's Loring, whom I have not seen for thirty years," Grant cried. "And there's Stone who must have been dyeing his hair to make it so white." The Americans bore Grant and his party to a banquet, where General Stone, Loring, Colston, Dye, and Graves vied with missionaries and diplomats in doing them honor.

The Grant dinner, for all that it served to emphasize that Confederates and Federals were united in their regard for a great commander, had at least one unexpected echo of the rancor of civil war. The Confederate officers professed only friendly feelings for General Grant, but the presence of the daughter of Robert E. Lee suddenly called back memories which the men of the Blue and the Gray had long since believed to be forgotten on the Nile. Miss Mary Lee, middle-aged, uninhibited, and with a mind of her own, was visiting in Egypt for a time. Already the American officers in Cairo were well acquainted with her. Immediately upon her arrival, she had commandeered Charles Iverson Graves as her escort. Graves, nearing forty, a handsome man who prided himself that he looked much younger, was embarrassed by the demands made on him, as of right, by Miss Lee. She expected him to get her money exchanged at the hotel—and bring it to her room; he must come to her bedroom to help her pack for a trip; he must window-shop with her along the Muski; he must join a group which she had corralled for a visit to the Pyramids; he must walk with her—very late, after the gates were locked—in the Ezbekiyeh Gardens. Her traveling companion was Mrs. Margaret Porter, a widow. Graves decided that Mrs. Porter vigorously seeking a husband and had settled on General Loring as a suitable match. Like Graves, Loring was a fine Southern gentleman of the old school, and he squired Mrs. Porter around Cairo as a gentleman should—but he was also a confirmed bachelor, and whatever may have been her matrimonial intentions, General Loring had no intention of joining the ranks of the benedicts.

Miss Lee was a great talker, as unrestrained in her speech as she was unconventional in her conduct, and possessed of a good sense of humor. Once she told Graves the tale of a suitor, a great hulk of a man, who had protested that he was pining away for love of her. When Miss Mary pointed to the discrepancy between his words and his avoirdupois, he replied, "I pine for you between meals."

Graves enjoyed her company but was sometimes embarrassed by her unpredictable behavior. "I am going tomorrow," he wrote his wife Chichi, "either to a seance of the Egyptian Geographical Society with Miss Mary Lee or to see the dancing Dervishes. Gen. Stone is going to read a paper before the society. . . . Miss Mary thinks the dervishes will be more entertaining than Gen. Stone; but she thinks she ought to go to hear him unless she can think of some better excuse for going to see the dervishes." At least one American in Cairo, Graves wrote, hit the nail on the head, saying, "Isn't she ugly, and isn't she smart?"

But Graves, fond as he was of her, was disturbed at Miss Mary's attitude toward the visiting Grants. She was "openly and freely" critical of their "style" and of their manners. And she flatly refused to meet them socially. When General Stone arranged the banquet, he duly sent Miss Mary an invitation. She refused. Embarrassed for his guests as much as for himself, Stone went to see her, urging her to reconsider. She would not budge. She was tired, she told him, from so much sightseeing, and she was pressed for time to prepare for a Nile trip. But to her escort Graves she unburdened herself without dissembling. "I wouldn't sit down at the same table with General Grant to save his life." Neither her sense of humor nor her undoubted "smartness" deterred her from waving the Confederate flag in the land of the Pharaohs.

General Grant's visit was no help in restoring the dimming glory of the Americans. The truth was that the Americans of the general staff in Cairo had outlived their usefulness. Ever since Gura there had been rumors that the khedive would send his American officers home. In March, 1877, without warning and without giving reason, orders came dismissing Colonel Field and Major Martin from the service. Martin left promptly, already disgusted, but Field could ill afford to return jobless to America. He stayed on a while, pulling wires to get reinstated. But even Stone, who had not known of the dismissal before it came, could do nothing for him. The other Americans fully expected the ax to fall, but no further orders came from the Citadel.

In the spring of 1878 a commission of inquiry, forced by Ismail's European bondholders, came out with a positive demand that the size of the army be reduced and the American officers dismissed. By that time the Americans, veterans now of another lost cause, had no defenders. They did not even defend themselves. "What is the use," asked one of them, "of remaining in a service where the future promises no advancement and the present sees you unpaid?"

June 30, 1878, was the terminal date. An official order set the time and provided that each should receive full pay, six months' pay as indemnity for the termination of the contract, and an additional £75 for expenses on the return to the United States. Two officers, Dye and Colston, had additional claims for injuries received in service, and a special commission considered their claims. Eventually each got £1,000.

A dozen were left at the end. Finally, only Stone remained in the Egyptian army. Mason, Purdy, and Prout, the explorers, accepted employment as civilians in the interior of Africa. Loshe wangled a new job—only to die alone in Suakin a few months later. The others, Colston, Dye, Derrick, Graves, Irgins, Ward, and Loring—two who had worn the Blue and five who had worn the Gray—left the delta of the Nile.

XII

wwwwwwww

Veterans of Misfortune

As they left the harbor of Alexandria, the men who had worn the Blue and their companions from the ranks of the Gray could look back upon a substantial record of accomplishment. The nine men who returned home after their brusque dismissal from the Egyptian army were but the last of half a hundred Civil War veterans who had served the khedive in his efforts to modernize his country and expand his empire. Taken as a group, their collective service extended from the last weeks of 1869 to the middle of 1878. Altogether, they had made distinct contributions to the advancement of Egypt. The explorers among them—Prout, Purdy, Mason, Colston, Chaillé-Long, Ward, Graves—had dropped plumb lines into the waters of the Red Sea and the Mediterranean, surveyed and taken barometric readings in the deserts of the Sudan. They had pushed outward the frontiers of Egypt, given pause to the trade in human beings, made contacts with savage chieftains, explored rivers, discovered lakes, opened routes where railroads might run. The catalogue of their achievements would run long in the annals of scientific knowledge. It was here, in an area where the frontier experiences of American soldiers could be of value, that they had chalked up their greatest success.

But they could look back as well to other achievements, other contributions. They had taught some of the lessons of Western science to younger officers of the Egyptian army, and, more importantly, they had established schools wherein the children of the fellahin might acquire some of the rudimentary tools of progress. In the years after the Americans left, nativist disturbances threatened to oust the agents of the bondholders who, unlike the Americans, had come to exploit rather than to serve. Colston, assessing the part that the Americans had played in Egypt, traced the impetus for later uprisings to the schools the Americans had established. The old army, explained Colston, was submissive, but with Stone's reforms it had become a school of instruction. "The schoolmaster was abroad even in that Moslem land," and education had encouraged the yearning for freedom.

Whatever the validity of Colston's speculations about the influence of the American-created schools, the American officers of the khedive brought to Egypt virtues more important, if less tangible, than forts, railroad surveys, explorations, and harbor improvements. Into a land where backsheesh was the rule and bribery and corruption the normal accompaniment of government employment, they brought a spirit of personal honesty and integrity. They believed that they were advancing the cause of civilization and of progress, and their own sense of duty and their loyalty stood in contrast to Egyptian fatalism and to the predatory designs of the European bondholders. It was in contrast, too, to the conduct of other Americans, also veterans of the Civil War, in the United States. These were the years of Reconstruction, and carpetbaggers ruled and exploited the South. The Americans in Egypt imitated neither the Americans who were imposing a new regime upon the Confederacy nor the Europeans in Egypt who were grasping for power and pelf. They gave to Egypt an example of dedication in the performance of duty.

The Egyptian service was not easy; more than a fair proportion of the Americans who went to Egypt lost their lives. By the time the end came, half a dozen had died in service. In 1873 Cornelius Hunt was killed in a fall from a horse. A year later Edmund Parys and William P. A. Campbell succumbed to fever in Central Africa. Both Frank and Alexander Reynolds died, and in November, 1876, Robert Lamson, an American in the Egyptian army but not a Civil War veteran, died in Darfur. Others who had been in Egypt died just as the "American mission" came to an end, and their deaths may be attributed, at least in part, to their Egyptian service. Walter Jenifer died in Baltimore in April, 1878; a few miles away Thomas G. Rhett, close to derangement, came to his end in August. In Liverpool, en route home, Henry Irgins, who had scouted the Abyssinians with the Abbé Duflot, passed away alone in a hotel room. A few months later Charles Loshe, who had remained to accept civilian employment under the Egyptian government, died in Suakin. Still another who remained as a civilian, Erastus Sparrow Purdy, survived three years. In 1881, harassed by creditors and discharged from his position, he succumbed in Cairo to the fever he had contracted in Darfur.

The hardships, whether of disease or of battle—or of financial distress, which kept them long months without pay and in debt—did not daunt them. The slow end of the American mission came through the weakness of Ismail, the lack of will, the too-ready acceptance of defeat. Here was the cultural gap between East and West which the Americans could not bridge.

Never, indeed, would the American officers completely understand the difference in spirit of the Egyptians. They did bring back to the United States some knowledge of Egypt and an insight into the conflicting forces that were rending the land they had tried to serve. In newspapers and magazines they wrote their stories, to gain recognition for themselves and to inform their fellows on Near Eastern affairs. Many of them delivered lectures on Egypt. Chaillé-Long told the story of his adventures whenever he could find an audience. Lockett prepared lectures on "Life among Egyptians of a Christian Family," "Housekeeping in Egypt," and "Women Enslaved and Women Free," and offered them to lyceumgoers—with no great financial success. Colston gave lectures on Egypt, complete with magic-lantern slides of his own skilful and mildly humorous drawings. Prout, who served some years as

governor in the equatorial provinces, came home in the 1880's
to write about his explorations for the *Engineering News,*
the *Journal of the American Geographical Society,* and the
Railroad Gazette, of which he became editor. Each time there
was a new crisis in Egypt, newspaper reporters sought out
veterans of the khedive's army; and each time the Americans
pointed the finger of suspicion toward perfidious Albion.
However blind they may have been to the social structure of
a Moslem land, the Americans had experienced the workings
of international politics and finance; and they identified England as one of the enemies of Egyptian freedom.

Five Americans who had served the khedive wrote books
which included accounts of their Egyptian days. Dr. Warren
wrote on the practice of medicine on three continents—without mentioning his personal quarrels with fellow Americans.
Late in his long life—he lived until 1928—James Morris Morgan told of his youthful escapades in *Recollections of a Rebel
Reefer.* Books by Colonel Dye and by General Loring were
devoted entirely to their Egyptian experiences, each defending himself against criticism of his conduct in Egypt. Their
books, moreover, bore a curious relationship: one was an
answer to the other.

Colonel Dye's book was published in 1880. After "dismissal day" he had waited in Egypt only long enough to collect damages for his Gura wound. Then, with the $5,000 he
had received, he hurried home to write his version of his stay
in Egypt. He had been a sour, critical, contentious person,
and *Moslem Egypt and Christian Abyssinia* was as sour and
critical as its author. Colonel Dye had no good word for either
Egypt or Abyssinia, Moslem or Christian. He gave a detailed,
factual description of Egypt, but he found nothing to praise
in it. He doubted the progressive intentions of the khedive,
finding Ismail both confused and deceptive; he suspected all
Egyptians; he denounced the British and the French; he had
caustic remarks to make about Americans; he was bitterly
critical of Stone. Much of his book was given over to the

Abyssinian campaign, to the confusion of the march, the incompetence of the Egyptians, the cowardice of the natives, both officers and men. He damned Ratib. And, along with the rest, he criticized the temperament, the judgment, the courage, and the leadership of General Loring. Yet, for all its bias, it was an able and convincing account.

General Loring had already begun to write the story of his life, but after Dye's work was in print he hurried to complete those parts relating to Egypt. He returned to America a leisurely year after "dismissal day" and took a room in a New York hotel. For the next seven years he lived in New York, in Florida, and, briefly, in Chicago. He was considered an authority on Egypt, and reporters liked to quote him and sought him out regularly for his opinions. Perhaps they liked his looks, his genial manner, his willingness to talk emphatically. He was a fine-looking man, tall and impressive, with iron-gray mustache and imperial beard. His bearing was military. He wore his left sleeve pinned to his breast, a rosette of red and green ribbons, emblem of his Egyptian honors, in his buttonhole. He spoke didactically—praising the khedive and damning the British and the French.

In 1884 Loring published *A Confederate Soldier in Egypt,* a detailed, rambling, discursive account of Egypt's recent history and problems and of his own experience in Egypt. It was intended to outline, he said, the "selfish, cruel policy" of France and England—especially England. But though he agreed with Dye on perfidious Albion, he did not share Dye's skepticism of Ismail. The khedive, said Loring, was sincerely progressive, eager to modernize his country and promote his people's well-being. He thought as little of Ratib as did Dye, but he had only praise for General Stone. He described the Gura campaign with its confusions and abject cowardice, but he found some Egyptian officers worthy of praise. He did not repay Dye's strictures in kind. He hardly mentioned Dye, but in case after case, incident after incident, his statement of the facts was precisely the opposite of Dye's account. He had gained a reputation for quick temper and a salty, vehement vocabulary, but in his book he displayed a gentle skill in exhibiting Dye as a liar. In these pages, at least, Loring was vindicated.

The search for vindication consumed the years of Charles Chaillé-Long, and with him it took the form of indignation and assault. He was disappointed because "his lake," as well as the rest of his work in Central Africa, had not received proper recognition. It was, he well knew, a British plot to denigrate him in favor of Britishers like Henry M. Stanley and Chinese Gordon. He wrote for geographic journals, the *New York Herald*, the *Chicago Times*, the press of France. He was outraged when British map makers changed the name of Lake Ibrahim to Kodjoe, Choga, Kioga. He complained to the king of England when a speaker before the Royal Geographic Society discussed fifty years of Nile exploration with praise for Speke and Baker but no word for Chaillé-Long, the greatest of them all. At last he got recognition in the United States. In 1910 the American Geographic Society conferred on him the Daly medal for "valuable additions to geographic knowledge." But even this did not satisfy him. Two years later Chaillé-Long published his last book, a two-volume autobiography called *My Life in Four Continents*. In it he denounced his traducers. He had blazed the way, he said, for later explorers. He excoriated Stanley, ridiculed his "finding" the not-lost Livingstone. He criticized Gordon. He damned the British. To the end of his life he believed that the selfishness of Stone, the jealousy of explorers, the pettiness of Gordon, and the outright opposition of a British-toadying State Department had denied him the honor that was his due.

Whatever their biases, the Americans who returned from Egypt furnished a critical balance to the overwhelming condemnation of Egyptian ways that came from the supporters of the bondholders. They spread a knowledge, and to some extent an understanding, of Egypt and of international intrigue.

A few of the khedive's American officers found their Egyptian experience useful in other foreign service. One of the first of these was Thaddeus Mott, who went back to Constantinople. There he survived a succession of sultans and was an active member of an anti-Ismail clique at the Porte. Carrol Tevis, an adventurer who had passed quickly through Egypt, became an officer in the Turkish army. Another was James Bassel, whose unfitness for Egyptian service was apparent from the day of his arrival; he left within the year and went on to equally unsuccessful stints in China and Japan. James Morris Morgan, failing as a planter in South Carolina, tried Mexico, first as a supervisor of mule trains carrying bullion from mines to the Pacific Coast, then as an attaché at the American legation in Mexico City. Eugene Fechet spent a year as a mining engineer in Venezuela, and for several years in the 1890's was a consul in Mexico. In the same decade Wilburn Hall was a consul at Nice. And Lockett, who died in Bogotá, spent the last year of his restless, improvident life as a railroad engineer in Chile. More important than these was the foreign service of Chaillé-Long and Dye—both of whom went to Korea. Chaillé-Long, in fact, returned to Egypt in 1882 at the time of the British bombardment of Alexandria. He assumed the duties of consul general and helped to rescue stranded Americans. As a reward he was given an appointment, not to Cairo for which he had hoped, but to Seoul, where he spent two years as consul general and secretary of the legation. Just before he left Seoul, William McEntyre Dye arrived as military adviser to the king of Korea—a post not so different from that held by Stone in Egypt. He remained for ten years, serving a monarch whose shifting fortunes were similar to those of Ismail, and faced problems that should have made him more sympathetic to General Stone.

The American actors returning from Egypt's drama faced the perennial problems of players after a play has closed. They were "at liberty," and each confronted the problem of finding employment. They found, in time, a variety of places, few making use of their experience in Egypt. Hall and Lockett, each perennially impecunious, taught school for a few years. Dr. Johnson, recuperating from his Gura wound and his Abyssinian captivity, returned to Tennessee in 1877 and practiced medicine in Clarksville for thirty years. Prout was successful as editor of the *Railroad Gazette* and as general manager of the Union Switch and Signal Company, but he lost his job in 1915 when faced with charges of attempting to bribe a public service commissioner to specify Union Switch signals for the New York subway.

Many of the Americans at the khedive's court wound up in some form of government service. James Dennison practiced law in upstate New York and for two years in the 1880's was deputy attorney general. In 1878, after a spirited debate over a Confederate veteran for such a post, Field was appointed doorkeeper of the House of Representatives. After three years he became a civil engineer on a government project, and from 1885 to 1889 he was superintendent of the Hot Springs Reservation in Arkansas. Chancellor Martin came back from Egypt to finish his medical education at Columbia University, but he did not practice. He joined the customs service in 1880, rose to be deputy collector for the Port of New York, and retired in 1908. Colston, who lost his European savings—plus the $5,000 "compensation" from the Egyptian government—took a place as clerk and translator in the surgeon general's office. In 1886 he was semiparalyzed and for the next six years remained at home and worked from his bed. After the Democratic victory in 1892, he lost his place. In 1894 friends supplied funds for his support and medical care, and he entered the Confederate Soldiers' Home in Richmond. He died there on July 29, 1896.

More important by far than the jobs they held, and more important than the contributions they made to Egypt, was the personal triumph which some of the Americans realized in their Egyptian service. It was bad luck and sickness that prevented Raleigh Colston from being a Stonewall Jackson during the Civil War, but his perseverance in the deserts of Darfur demonstrated clearly that he, too, might have been a stone wall at Manassas. Chaillé-Long was too young to play a distinguished role in the Civil War, but in Uganda and in the Makraka Niam-Niam he drove his frail and fevered body to triumphant feats of physical endurance.

One personal triumph was especially noteworthy. Charles Iverson Graves had gone to Egypt for "corn" for his family. He had only scorn for his improvident companions; he lived frugally, sent his money home to pay his debts, and was not frantic when payments were slow from the khedivial treasury. He had confidence that when "dismissal day" came there would be a strict settling of accounts. When it came in 1878, Graves was on an assignment. He had been sent to make a survey and to locate a site for a lighthouse on the Cape of Guardafui, a dangerous spot. Piratical beachcombers, profiting from the ships wrecked on the shore, wanted no aid given to navigators entering the Gulf of Aden from the Indian Ocean. But Graves seized as hostage a "prince" of the ruling family, forced him to serve as guide, and made his surveys in safety. His work kept him twenty days beyond the date when the other Americans left the service. He won a hearty commendation—and a decoration—from the khedive.

True to his expectations, Graves received his pay in full. But an experience he had had during the Civil War made him cautious. At the close of the Civil War his wife Chichi made frantic efforts to buy a dress with $1,000 in Confederate notes. No merchant would accept them—and thereafter both Graves and Chichi had a well-founded suspicion of paper money. When he came to get his pay at the Citadel, Colonel Graves demanded cash. The clerks and paymaster carefully counted out 514 golden sovereigns, 1,000 golden half sovereigns, and 500 Egyptian silver coins, weighing, altogether, twenty-four pounds. Carefully he placed the sum in a satchel, swung it to his shoulder, and marched forth in triumph with his "corn."

He received over $5,000, enough to lift the mortgage from his Georgia farm, refurnish the house, and build walls and dig the drainage ditches that would save it from another flash flood. He bought a bill of exchange on Liverpool, made his way to England, bought another bill on New York, and arrived home with a profit on each transaction. To the end of his life, to the delight of his grandchildren, he kept a donkey on his Georgia farm as a reminder of his years as a bey in Egypt.

But the greatest personal triumph of a member of the Egyptian mission was that of Charles Pomeroy Stone, the one among them who had entered the service under the darkest cloud. General Loring's wisdom and judgment had been questioned, but Stone was suspected of treason itself. Memories of defeat at Ball's Bluff, of six months' unexplained imprisonment at Forts Lafayette and Hamilton, of harsh and abrupt dismissal from command, made him feel first in the ranks of the soldiers of misfortune. Others who went to Egypt might seek glory, or vindication of their courage, their judgment, their competence—but Stone had his honor at stake.

In Egypt, Charles Pomeroy Stone, major general of United States Volunteers, and Liwa Pasha, gave the lie to all his detractors, including Abraham Lincoln and Edwin M. Stanton and crusty Ben Wade's Committee on the Conduct of the War. To all those who would cast aspersion of treason, Stone Pasha proved that as a man and as a soldier he was incapable of disloyalty.

It was after "dismissal day" that Stone's personal loyalty to the khedive was seen in boldest relief. Alone of the Americans, Stone retained his military position and title. He was still chief of staff and high in the councils of the khedive. In the next four years he proved himself incapable of intrigue, of betrayal, of treason. To the end he retained his belief in Ismail. "Egypt has been kind and generous to us all in her days of plenty," he once told Colston, "and will again when plenty returns to her as it surely will. . . . I am perfectly willing to cast my lot with His Highness for good or ill."

But plenty did not return to Egypt or to Ismail, and the khedive's own "dismissal day" came within the year. In August, 1878, Ismail turned his private property over to his creditors and accepted a new ministry imposed by the English and French. The new ministry determined to reduce the army from 60,000 to 7,800. The Egyptian officers, whose pay—like that of their American colleagues—was long in arrears, faced dismissal. Four hundred Egyptian officers rioted on February 18, 1879, surrounded the office of the Ministry of Finance, and attacked the British minister as he attempted to leave. The khedive appeared and quieted the rioters with promises. By his side, an example of loyalty, stood Stone Pasha. As a consequence of the meeting, Ismail dismissed his minister Nubar and his foreign ministers. In London, promptly echoed in the *New York Times*, appeared a story that Ismail had instigated the army mutiny. In Constantinople, the powers began to press upon the sultan. On June 25 an edict from the sultan deposed Ismail and named his son Tewfik Khedive in his place. Five days later, unable to resist the pressure or to rally support, Ismail abdicated.

The word came to Ismail in a manner that might have reminded General Stone of his last days in the Civil War. Late in 1864, at a time when lesser men were receiving promotions to high ranks in the Volunteer Army, Major General Stone received an order addressed to "Colonel" Stone—an abrupt order to report to his regular army regiment at his old rank. Ismail's news came in much the same way. The ceremonial message from the Ottoman monarch was addressed to "Ismail, ex-khedive of Egypt."

It was an abrupt end for a ruler who had dreamed the dream of a modern Egypt, with prosperous industries, rich trade, a far-flung frontier, and political independence. Ismail had built railroads and telegraphs, completed the Suez Canal, explored the interior, improved navigation, built public works on a magnificent scale. But the improvements he had made had only incited the cupidity of the imperial powers. He departed without honor—followed by the parting accusation of the British that he had stolen millions of pounds in order to maintain in exile his barbaric extravagance.

His successor, Tewfik, was the only one of Ismail's sons who had not been educated in Europe. He lacked his father's sparkling imagination, but he was not unintelligent, and he knew that he needed loyal advisers. At his request Stone Pasha stayed at his post and gave Tewfik the loyalty that he had given Ismail. The British and French had resumed their control of Egypt, and Stone tried to steer the new khedive's course between the European interlopers and the increasingly aggressive nativists.

In January, 1881, the nativists, powerful in the army, rose in revolt. A certain Colonel Arabi, with two others, protested against army promotions going to Turks and demanded the return of the previous war minister. For their pains the Khedive Tewfik placed them under arrest and made Stone president of their court-martial. But their regiments rescued them, literally snatched them from the court, and rough-handled Stone. Tewfik yielded to the colonels and made the cabinet changes they had demanded. Thereafter the colonels increased in power and in September of the same year staged an even more impressive revolt. This time Stone advised Tewfik to win the support of the regiments and to arrest Arabi and the others. Tewfik—with Stone at his side—appealed to the regiments, but Arabi was securely in favor. Truculently, Arabi told the khedive that his successor could easily be found. Within a few months Arabi controlled the war department and was able to defy both Tewfik and the Europeans. In May, 1882, the British and French consuls general demanded Arabi's retirement. The reaction was immediate: nativist riots began. To meet the threat of revolution, British and French warships anchored outside Alexandria. When Arabi began to strengthen the fortifications which Beverly Kennon and General Loring had built, the British protested. When Arabi refused to cease preparations for defense, the British opened fire on the city.

Throughout these developments Stone Pasha made every effort to preserve an orderly government. In November, 1881, he believed that Tewfik and his ministry were working out their problems. "If Europe will only mind her own business for a while, I think it will be better for all concerned." By the following May, however, he had given up hope of being useful to the khedive or of serving under Arabi and offered his resignation. But when the British bombarded Alexandria, Stone was still in office.

He was, in fact, in Alexandria itself. On July 6, taking his thirteen-year-old son John with him, he went to the port city. On July 9 the British naval commander announced he would open fire in twenty-four hours. Stone put his son aboard an American ship and hurried off to the suburban palace where the Khedive Tewfik, awaiting events, was installed.

In Cairo, the general's wife was called upon to demonstrate her own personal courage and, all unwitting, to give proof of Stone's high standing among the Egyptians. Nativist riots had placed Mrs. Stone and her three daughters in grave danger, and she appealed to the war department for protection. Promptly, staff officers and police were dispatched to guard the house, and Stone's two orderlies took up stations in the garden. Mrs. Stone called the three girls together, advised them of the precariousness of their situation, and told them how they must conduct themselves. They must use very sparingly what food supplies they had. They must be patient, cheerful, and brave; they must continue their studies, keep busy, and, if the worst came, trust her to save them. "We have firearms enough in the house to defend ourselves until we can get help from the staff officers; and if they fail us, you can be brave and face death like good soldiers. Only promise me never to let an Arab touch you. When it comes to that, remember I expect you to save yourselves by putting a bullet through your heart. Don't leave it to me to do it."

When a rumor reached Cairo that Tewfik had accepted protection from the British and that General Stone was remaining at the khedive's side, Mrs. Stone and her daughters feared for their own safety. "We have no claims upon them now for protection," said young Fanny Stone. "Even the staff officers may desert us." But they soon found that their concern was unfounded, for their Arab protectors continued to watch over them and saw to their welfare. Several offered the hospitality of their own homes. Mrs. Stone insisted that she could not and would not leave the city until she heard from her husband. By late July their home was the only one occupied in the entire European quarter. The staff officers maintained a constant guard, and Mrs. Stone planned the family's every action in the light of the impression it would make upon hostile Arabs in the city. Their only chance for safety, she told the girls again and again, lay in the courage they now displayed.

By late July the money General Stone had left with her had been spent. But Mrs. Stone was equal to the dilemma. The khedive's government owed money to her husband, and if Colonel Arabi had taken over the government, she reasoned, he could expect to face its responsibilities. On July 24 she sent to Arabi a demand that he forward to her the general's pay for the month of July. The staff officers, amazed at her audacity, were equally dumbfounded when, with kind words and gracious compliments, Colonel Arabi sent her a part of her husband's salary.

Flushed with her first success, Mrs. Stone two days later wrote Arabi again. She would like to leave Cairo, she told him. The staff officers who guarded the family told her she had done a perfectly useless thing. No, she explained emphatically, Americans believed that anything worth having was worth pursuing, and this was exactly what she had done.

While she awaited reply, she demonstrated American courage, Stone variety, in another action. On the evening of July 30 she announced to her daughters, Hettie, Fanny, and Todas Santas, that she planned to "reconnoiter" Cairo in an open carriage. Although the guards and servants begged her to reconsider, after dinner she ordered the open carriage and herded the girls into it. "One of the orderlies mounted on the box beside the coachman," Fanny remembered, "and away we went straight into the heart of the city, where thousands of Arabs were congregated on the sidewalks, eating, drinking and smoking, after their day of fasting. . . . We drove rapidly, as mama said it would not do to leave them a moment in which to recover from their surprise or we might be treated to a pistol shot. . . ."

On the evening of August 1 Mrs. Stone got an answer from Colonel Arabi. They would be permitted to leave. Arabi would also provide them with an escort to Ismailia. On the following morning Arabi's agent informed Mrs. Stone that Arabi had prepared a special train (the government to pay all expenses), and she might take any amount of baggage, which would not be examined. The Stones left Cairo and, by way of Ismailia, reached Alexandria, where the acting American consul, Chaillé-Long, had prepared a house for them.

Stone Pasha stayed by Tewfik's side throughout the bombardment and during the British campaign against Colonel Arabi and his supporters. When the British defeated Arabi and Tewfik reassumed active direction of his government, Stone began to prepare maps and reports for an expedition into the Sudan to suppress a nativist Mahdi, Mohammed Ahmed, who was encouraging rebellion. But the British managers forbade the spending of money on an army to save the empire.

Frustrated at every turn, Stone finally abandoned hope. He had seen his work, even to the schools for army children, scrapped by the new masters of Egypt. In February, 1883, with his family beside him, he left Egypt to return to the United States. In some of the things he had attempted he had failed. In others, he saw a new tyrant tearing down what he had built. Only one thing remained—honor. He had served well and faithfully, removing the blot of suspicion which had marred his record during the Civil War.

There was a fine irony in Stone's last employment in the United States. He had no difficulty in finding work, but, like other Americans who had served Ismail, he was not able to make use of his Egyptian experience. For a time he was chief engineer for the Florida Ship Canal and Transit Company, directing a survey for a route across the peninsula. Then, in 1886, came a strangely symbolic offer of employment. He was asked to design and construct the base for a huge statue to be executed by a Frenchman and presented to the United States by the schoolchildren of France. In the harbor of New York City, a quarter of a century before, General Charles Pomeroy Stone had lingered in prison on the mere suspicion of disloyalty to the government that now employed him to prepare the foundation for the Statue of Liberty. It was a fitting symbol of his success in removing the partisan stigma on his honor.

With hardly a thought of the sardonic fate that brought him to Bedloe's Island, Stone went to work, sometimes giving lectures on Egypt to help raise funds for the project. And, as if to compound the strange ways of destiny, he called on Samuel H. Lockett, once again jobless, to aid him in drafting the plans. Then one day in the street General Stone thought he recognized a familiar face. It was James Morris Morgan, whose adolescent exuberance had first fascinated and then annoyed the Khedive Ismail. Morgan, too, was out of a job. He had failed as a planter and in newspaper work, and he had been notably unsuccessful in Mexico. Stone offered him temporary refuge helping to erect the near-pyramidal base of the new Colossus. In October, 1886, the work was done, and fitting ceremonies brought Civil War generals and politicians to pose at the laying of the cornerstone. Stone rode in the rain at the head of the procession and stood bareheaded in the cold autumn storm that marred the day. Perhaps that too was a moment of irony.

After the cornerstone laying, the end came quickly—as dramatic proprieties might have dictated—for the two ranking officers who had faithfully served the khedive. In December, 1886, General Loring, who had spent the summer and fall visiting relatives in Chicago, came back to New York to continue work on the autobiography, "Fifty Years a Soldier." But before he could take up his pen, death came. On December 29 he had a sudden attack and sank rapidly. Chaillé-Long hurried to his bedside and watched during the eighteen hours that remained. On January 2, 1887, Chaillé-Long and Stone knelt together at the funeral of their old companion.

General Stone survived his fellow soldier of misfortune for less than a month. He had never recovered from the chill he had taken at the dedication of the Statue of Liberty. And with Loring's passing, his spirit as well as his body grew weak. In mid-January he caught cold, and on January 24 he passed away. From the requiem mass in St. Leo's Church, General William T. Sherman, John M. Schofield, and Fitz-John Porter escorted the body to its resting place in the national cemetery at West Point. The military rites were a fitting tribute to a faithful soldier's refurbished honor.

In New York harbor stood a monument which might be seen as a suitable encomium for Stone's work, his diligence, and his unswerving loyalty. But it was more. It was a symbol of a changing America. The statue whose base he laid marked the end of an American era. Through the years the Americans had dreamed that by example alone they would give refuge and hope to the poor and oppressed, that America's heritage of liberty would serve to enlighten the world. But by 1886 this concept was giving way to another. In the dockyards on the Atlantic a new steel navy was coming into being. The light that would gleam from the statue's upraised hand would guide seamen of all nations to a safe port. Already men with a new dream were fashioning an American empire and in little more than a decade the United States would be fairly launched as a world power. Other men like Stone would spread the doctrines of democracy throughout the world.

The Blue and the Gray on the Nile

The veterans of the Blue and the Gray who worked for the Khedive Ismail on the Nile were far more than refugees seeking employment, far more than knights-errant seeking a crusade. They were the advance guard of a newly invigorated nation whose representatives—technicians, soldiers, salesmen, cultural agents, missionaries, administrators—would soon go forth to every part of the world.

wwwwwwww

Appendix
Egyptian Muster: Americans on the Nile

VANDERBILT ALLEN
(Civil War record: brevet major, U.S. Volunteers)
1870: Arrived in Egypt.
Member of Loring's staff.
1872: Resigned.

JAMES BASSEL
(Civil War record: U.S. Military Academy, 1863–67; 2d lieutenant, U.S. Army)
1874: Arrived in Egypt.
Resigned.

WILLIAM P. A. CAMPBELL
(Civil War record: lieutenant, Confederate States Navy)
1870: Arrived in Egypt.
In charge of khedivial steamers between Alexandria and Constantinople.
1874: To Sudan with Gordon; died in Khartoum on October 10.

CHARLES CHAILLÉ-LONG
(Civil War record: captain, Maryland First Eastern Shore Regiment, U.S. Volunteers)
1870: Arrived in Egypt.
Member of Loring's staff.
1871: General staff, orders and correspondence section.
1872: Aide to visiting General William T. Sherman.
1874: To Sudan with Gordon; to Uganda and the lake region.
1875: To Makraka Niam-Niam country; to Juba River country.
1877: Resigned.

253

RALEIGH E. COLSTON
(Civil War record: brigadier general, Confederate States Army)
  1873: Arrived in Egypt.
    Assigned to teach at military college in Cairo.
    Expedition to explore and map military road from Kenneh on Nile to Berenice on Red Sea and to make geological survey and prepare maps of desert between Nile and Red Sea and from Kenneh to Berber.
  1874: Expedition with Purdy and Mason, a hydrographic survey of bay and harbor of Berenice, exploration and mapping of Bishereen Desert between Berenice and Berber, Colston to conduct special survey of ancient gold mines at Derehib in Wadi Allakee, all to return via Korosko Desert and city.
    Expedition to Kordofan.
  1875: Continued exploration in Kordofan.
  1878: Discharged.

JAMES A. DENNISON
(Civil War record: private, U.S. Army; U.S. Military Academy, 1866–70; 2d lieutenant, U.S. Army)
  1875: Arrived in Egypt.
    Arrendrup expedition to Abyssinia.
  1876: Gura campaign; left Egypt December 31.

HENRY C. DERRICK
(Civil War record: captain, Confederate States Army)
  1875: Arrived in Egypt.
  1876: Gura campaign, chief engineer; with Lockett and civilian employee of the khedive to explore and map region southwest of Massawa; with Egyptian officer to explore and map districts of Berber and Harrar.
  1878: Discharged.

WILLIAM W. DUNLAP
(Civil War record: colonel, Confederate States Army)
  1871: Arrived in Egypt.
    Artillery school at Damietta.

WILLIAM McE. DYE
(Civil War record: brevet brigadier general, U.S. Volunteers)
  1873: Arrived in Egypt.
    General staff.
  1876: Gura campaign.
  1878: Discharged.

OSCAR EUGENE FECHET
(Civil War record: U.S. Military Academy, 1864–68; 2d lieutenant, U.S. Army)
1872: Arrived in Egypt.
General staff.
1873–74: Chief of reconnaissance and survey in Nubia and Sudan, from Aswan to Khartoum, Cairo to Suez.
1874: Left Egypt February 14.

CHARLES W. FIELD
(Civil War record: major general, Confederate States Army)
1875: Arrived in Egypt.
Inspector general on Ratib's staff.
1876: Gura campaign.
1877: Discharged.

CHARLES I. GRAVES
(Civil War record: lieutenant, Confederate States Navy)
1875: Arrived in Egypt.
Assigned to Third Section to draw maps for fortifications in various regions of Egypt.
1876: Gura campaign, port officer at Massawa.
1877: Surveying east of Cairo.
1878: Surveying for lighthouse at Cape Guardafui.
Discharged.

WILBURN B. HALL
(Civil War record: lieutenant, Confederate States Navy)
1874: Arrived in Egypt.
General staff.
Survey of Lower Egypt.
1875: Chief of military construction after Arrendrup defeat.
Supervised education of three of Ismail's sons.
Visitor and inspector of government military schools.
1877: Resigned.

CORNELIUS HUNT
(Civil War record: master's mate, Confederate States Navy)
1870: Arrived in Egypt.
1871: Assigned to teach in military school at Aboukir.
1873: Died February 28 of injuries sustained in fall from horse.

HENRY IRGINS
(Civil War record: sergeant, U.S. Volunteers)
1876: Arrived in Egypt.
Gura campaign; assistant to chief engineer.
1878: Discharged; died in Liverpool en route to U.S.

WALTER H. JENIFER

(Civil War record: colonel, Confederate States Army)

1870: Arrived in Egypt.

Inspector of cavalry at Alexandria.

1871: Resigned.

THOMAS D. JOHNSON

(Civil War record: private, Confederate States Volunteers; signal corps, aide to Major General Henry Heth)

1875: Arrived in Egypt.

1876: Gura campaign; staff surgeon.

1877: Resigned.

BEVERLY KENNON

(Civil War record: lieutenant, Confederate States Navy)

1870: Arrived in Egypt.

Worked on coastal defenses.

1871: Survey party to Aswan.

1874: Resigned.

ROBERT S. LAMSON

(Civil War record: none)

1875: Arrived in Egypt.

Member of Ratib's staff.

1876: Gura campaign.

To Darfur, and died there in November.

SAMUEL H. LOCKETT

(Civil War record: colonel, Confederate States Army)

1875: Arrived in Egypt.

General staff.

1876: Gura campaign; *see also* Derrick note for this year.

1877: Directed preparation of the Great Map of expanded Egypt.

Resigned, September.

WILLIAM W. LORING

(Civil War record: major general, Confederate States Army)

1870: Arrived in Egypt.

Inspector general of infantry.

1871: In charge of coastal defenses.

1875: Preparations for Gura campaign.

1876: Gura campaign: chief of staff to Ratib.

1878: Discharged.

CHARLES F. LOSHE
(Civil War record: lieutenant, U.S. Volunteers)
1875: Arrived in Egypt.
1876: Gura campaign; chief of transportation, quartermaster, and commissary.
Surveying on Red Sea coast.
1878: To Red Sea coast; died at Suakin in October.

HARRY McIVOR
(Civil War record: none)
1870: Arrived in Egypt.
General staff.

CHANCELLOR MARTIN
(Civil War record: U.S. Military Academy, 1864–68; 2d lieutenant, U.S. Army)
1874: Arrived in Egypt.
General staff.
1877: Resigned.

ALEXANDER M. MASON
(Civil War record: lieutenant, Confederate States Navy)
1870: Arrived in Egypt.
1871: Assigned to work related to khedivial steamers between Alexandria and Constantinople.
1872: Expedition to map Fayum and the Oasis of Siwa.
1874: *See* Colston note for this year.
1874–75: Ascended Nile to New Dongola and explored route to El Fasher, capital of Darfur; corrected maps for true position of El Fasher.
1877: With Gordon in equatorial provinces.
Discovered Semliki River; circumnavigated Lake Albert and corrected maps for its true size.
1878: Discharged.

JAMES M. MORGAN
(Civil War record: midshipman, Confederate States Naval Academy)
1870: Arrived in Egypt.
Loring's staff.
1871: Ratib's staff.
1872: Returned to U.S.; resigned.

The Blue and the Gray on the Nile

THADDEUS P. MOTT
  (Civil War record: colonel, U.S. Volunteers)
    1869: Arrived in Egypt.
          Khedivial chamberlain.
    1870: Escorted first recruits to Egypt.
          General of division of cavalry and artillery.
    1871: In U.S. as agent of the khedive.
    1875: Retired to Turkey.

EDMUND PARYS
  (Civil War record: acting ensign, U.S. Navy)
    1871: Arrived in Egypt.
          Signal corps.
    1874: Died in Egypt, April 13.

DAVID E. PORTER
  (Civil War record: brevet captain, U.S. Army)
    1875: Arrived in Egypt.
    1876: Gura campaign; assistant to chief engineer.
          Resigned.

HENRY G. PROUT
(Civil War record: with Massachusetts Volunteers)
    1872: Arrived in Egypt.
    1874: General staff; chief of Third Section.
    1875: Prepared map and profile of Suakin to Berber route.
          Took over Colston's command at El Obeid in June.
          Mapped Kordofan and joined Mason to map most of
          Darfur.
    1876: Governor-general of equatorial provinces in Gordon's
          absence.
    1877: In equatorial provinces.
    1878: Discharged.

E. SPARROW PURDY
  (Civil War record: brevet lieutenant colonel, U.S. Volunteers)
    1870: Arrived in Egypt.
    1871: Expedition to map area between Cairo and Suez and be-
          tween Kenneh on the Nile and Kosseir on the Red Sea.
    1874: *See* Colston note for this year.
    1878: Discharged.
          Civilian employee of khedive until death, June 21, 1881.

HORATIO B. REED
  (Civil War record: brevet lieutenant colonel, U.S. Volunteers)
    1874: Arrived in Egypt.
    1875: To Kordofan with Colston.
          Sick leave to U.S.; never returned.

ALEXANDER W. REYNOLDS
  (Civil War record: brigadier general, Confederate States Army)
    1870: Arrived in Egypt.
          Loring's staff.
    1876: Died in Alexandria, May 26.

FRANK A. REYNOLDS
  (Civil War record: lieutenant colonel, Confederate States Army)
    1870: Arrived in Egypt.
          Loring's staff.
    1873: To U.S. as inspector of arms purchased by khedive.
    1875: Died in Ilion, N.Y., still in Egyptian service.

THOMAS G. RHETT
  (Civil War record: major, Confederate States Army)
    1870: Arrived in Egypt.
    1871: Set up powder works in Cairo.
    1872: Six months' sick leave.
    1873: Six months' sick leave.
    1874: Resigned, April.

ROBERT ROGERS
  (Civil War record: captain, U.S. Volunteers; U.S. Military Acad-
      emy, 1863–67; 2d lieutenant, U.S. Army)
    1874: Arrived in Egypt.
          Colonel of engineers.
    1875: Resigned, March.

RICHARD SAVAGE
  (Civil War record: U.S. Military Academy, 1864–68; brevet 2d
      lieutenant, U.S. Army)
    1872: Arrived in Egypt.
          Military secretary to general staff.

HENRY H. SIBLEY
  (Civil War record: brigadier general, Confederate States Army)
    1870: Arrived in Egypt.
          Chief of artillery at Rosetta.
    1873: Discharged.

The Blue and the Gray on the Nile

CHARLES P. STONE
(Civil War record: brigadier general, U.S. Volunteers)
1870: Arrived in Egypt.
1871: Chief of staff (remained until 1883).

CARROLL TEVIS
(Civil War record: brevet brigadier general, U.S. Volunteers)
1872: Arrived in Egypt.
1873: Resigned.

WILLIAM H. WARD
(Civil War record: lieutenant, Confederate States Navy)
1871: Arrived in Egypt.
Torpedo experiments.
1872: Aide to visiting General Sherman.
1875: Reconnaissance of Island of Thasos.
Hydraulic survey of harbor of Kismayu.
With Juba River expedition.
1877: Surveying on coast of Red Sea.
1878: Discharged.

EDWARD WARREN
(Civil War record: surgeon general of North Carolina, Confederate States Army)
1873: Arrived in Egypt.
Chief surgeon of staff.
1876: Discharged.

D. G. WHITE
(Civil War record: major, Confederate States Army)
1875: Arrived in Egypt.
Surveying east of Cairo.
Deserted, December.

WILLIAM H. WILSON
(Civil War record: assistant surgeon, Thirteenth Ohio Cavalry, U.S. Volunteers)
1875: Arrived in Egypt.
1876: Gura campaign; surgeon of staff.
1877: Resigned.

wwwwwwww

Notes

I SOLDIERS OF MISFORTUNE

Sketches of Stone's pre-Civil War military experience appear in George W. Cullom, *Biographical Register of the Officers and Graduates of the U.S. Military Academy at West Point, N.Y., from Its Establishment, in 1802, to 1890, with the Early History of the United States Military Academy* (6 vols.; Boston and elsewhere, 1891–1920), Vol. II, 214–16; Francis B. Heitman, *Historical Register and Dictionary of the United States Army from Its Organization September 29, 1789, to March 2, 1903* (2 vols.; Washington, 1903), Vol. I, 928–29; William McE. Dye, *Moslem Egypt and Christian Abyssinia; or, Military Service under the Khedive, in His Provinces and beyond Their Borders, as Experienced by the American Staff* (New York, 1880); *New York Tribune, New York Times*, both for January 25, 1887.

Stone's military career in the Civil War to Ball's Bluff may be traced in *The War of the Rebellion: A Compilation of the Official Records of the Union and Confederate Armies* (128 vols.; Washington, 1880–1901), Ser. 1, Vol. V, 15–16, 32–34, 282–99, 557–58, 568–69; Vol. LI, Part I, 389, 455. See also Louis B. Starr, *Bohemian Brigade: Civil War Newsmen in Action* (New York, 1954), pp. 37–38; Fred H. Harrington, *Fighting Politician, Major General N. P. Banks* (Philadelphia, 1948), p. 113; Henry G. Pearson, *Life of John A. Andrew* (2 vols.; Boston, 1904), Vol. I, 312–15; *Congressional Globe*, 37th Cong., 2d sess. (1861–62), p. 139.

For the Ball's Bluff disaster and its results for Stone see *Official Records*, Ser. 1, Vol. V, 341–46; Ser. 2, Vol. III, 292–94, 449, 599; *Congressional Globe*, 37th Cong., 2d sess. (1861–62), pp. 1732–42; Richard B. Irwin, "Ball's Bluff and the Arrest of General Stone," in Robert Johnson and Clarence Buel (eds.), *Battles and Leaders of the Civil War* (4 vols.; New York, 1884–87), Vol. II, 123–33. See also the papers of Horatio G. Gibson, Stone's counsel, in the State Historical Society of Wisconsin. Stone's assignments during the remainder of his Civil War experience are detailed in *Official Records*, Ser. 1, Vol. XXXIV, Part I, 178–79, Part II, 756, Part III, 175, 235; Vol. XLII, Part II, 372; Cullom, *Biographical Register*, Vol. II, 217–18. See also M. A. DeWolfe Howe (ed.), *Home Letters of General Sherman* (New York, 1909), p. 424.

For Stone's character, personality, and troubles see George B. McClellan, *McClellan's Own Story* (New York, 1887), p. 139, and T. Harry Williams, "Investigation, 1862," in *American Heritage*, Vol. VI (December, 1954), 17–21.

The story of Stone's preparations for Lincoln's inauguration is told by Stone in "Washington on the Eve of the War," in *Battles and Leaders*, Vol. I, 7–25.

Loring's military career has never received special and separate study. For his army experience before and during the Civil War, see Clement A. Evans (ed.), *Confederate Military History* (13 vols.; Atlanta, 1899), Vol. II, 58; Vol. VII, 123–24, 142–45; Vol. XI, 203–6; Heitman, *Historical Register*, Vol. I, 642; Richard Hill, *A Biographical Dictionary of the Anglo-Egyptian Sudan* (Oxford, 1951), p. 217; Theodore F. Rodenbough and William W. Haskin (eds.), *The Army of the United States, Historical Sketches of Staff and Line with Portraits of Generals-in-Chief* (New York, 1896), pp. 200–201; Jacob D. Cox, "McClellan in West Virginia," in *Battles and Leaders*, Vol. I, 147; Joseph E. Johnston and Samuel H. Lockett, "Jefferson Davis and the Mississippi Campaign," *ibid.*, Vol. III, 475–95; Earl Schenck Miers, *The Web of Victory* (New York, 1955), pp. 170–71; *New York Herald*, July 17, 1872; *Official Records*, Ser. 1, Vol. IV, 55–58; Vol. IX, 56 ff., 437, 469; Vol. X, Part I, 504, 508, 561, 603; Vol. XI, Part III, 664; Vol. XII, Part I, 804 ff., 940, 949, Part II, 129, 756–57, Part III, 901, 940, 949; Vol. XVII, Part II, 800 *et passim*; Vol. XIX, Part I, 1068–90 *passim*; Vol. XXI, 636; Vol. XXIV, Part I, 38, 90, 253–65, 412–18; Vol. XXX, Part IV, 717, 754–56; Vol. XXXI, Part III, 153; Vol. XXXII, Part II, 719; Vol. XXXVIII, Part IV, 776. At the time of Loring's death, obituary notices in New York papers, especially the *World*, *Herald*, *Times*, and *Tribune* of December 31, 1886, gave varying accounts of his pre–Civil War career.

Loring's experience in Jackson's command was set forth by John D. Imboden, "Stonewall Jackson in the Shenandoah," in *Battles and Leaders*, Vol. II, 282–83, and Evans, *Confederate Military History*, Vol. III, 204–6. A highly pro-Jackson account is related by Jackson's admiring staff officer and first biographer, Robert L. Dabney, in *Life and Campaigns of Lieut.-Gen. Thomas J. Jackson* (New York, 1866), pp. 249–84. The orders and correspondence are in *Official Records*, Ser. 1, Vol. V, 968–82, 984, 988–89, 1040–41, 1053–71. See also Jackson's summary report, *ibid.*, 389–95.

A number of people have described Loring's physical appearance and personality. For the way he looked to a reporter who interviewed him in 1882, see the *New York Herald*, September 8, 1882. A British visitor, Lt. Col. J. A. L. Freemantle, who saw Loring in Mississippi in 1863, also describes him in Walter Lord (ed.), *The Freemantle Diary* (Boston, 1954), pp. 99–100, 268. Dye, *Moslem Egypt*, p. 177, gives a vivid picture of Loring in a tantrum. See also Elbert E. Farman, *Egypt and Its Betrayal* (New York, 1908), p. 194;

Leslie's Illustrated Weekly, August 1, 1863; Miers, *The Web of Victory*, pp. 190–91.

Thaddeus P. Mott's career is outlined in Heitman, *Historical Register*, Vol. I, 732. His Civil War activities are recounted in Frederick Phisterer, *New York in the War of the Rebellion* (6 vols.; Albany, 1912), Vol. II, 987–88, 996, 1565–66, 1568; Vol. V, 4431; and Thomas H. Townsend, *The Honors of the Empire State* (New York, 1889), pp. 263, 277–78. See also William B. Hesseltine (ed.), *Three against Lincoln* (Baton Rouge, 1960), pp. 179–80; *The Union Army, A History of Military Affairs in the Loyal States 1861–1865* (2 vols.; Madison, 1908), Vol. II, 193–94, 223; *Official Records*, Ser. 1, Vol. V, 166–68; Charles Chaillé-Long, *My Life in Four Continents* (2 vols.; London, 1912), Vol. I, 16, 231–33; Dye, *Moslem Egypt*, pp. 2, 4; *New York Herald*, February 7, February 28, June 17, 1870; November 30, 1873; July 28, 1874; *New York Times*, August 26, 1870; July 27, 1871; November 27, 1894.

Sketches of Henry Hopkins Sibley are in Cullom, *Biographical Register*, Vol. I, 721–22; Heitman, *Historical Register*, Vol. I, 886; Evans, *Confederate Military History*, Vol. X, 315–16. See also Chaillé-Long, *My Life in Four Continents*, Vol. I, 16, and Pierre Crabites, *Americans in the Egyptian Army* (London, 1938), pp. 6, 8.

William McEntyre Dye's history is detailed in Cullom, *Biographical Register*, Vol. II, 548–50; Heitman, *Historical Register*, Vol. I, 392; *Dictionary of American Biography*, Vol. V, 579–80; Hill, *Biographical Dictionary*, p. 118; William H. Powell, *A History of the Organization and Movements of the Fourth Regiment of Infantry, United States Army, from May 30, 1796, to December 31, 1870: Together with a Record of the Military Service of All Officers Who Have at Any Time Belonged to the Regiment* (Washington, 1871), p. 114. His Civil War experience is in S. H. M. Byers, *Iowa in War Times* (Des Moines, 1888), pp. 191, 519–21; Lurton D. Ingersoll, *Iowa and the Rebellion* (Philadelphia, 1866), pp. 340–57. See also William W. Loring, *A Confederate Soldier in Egypt* (New York, 1884), p. 362; *New York Times*, January 2, 1874, quoting the *Chicago Times* (n.d.); *New York Herald*, March 29, 1869.

For Cornelius Hunt's Civil War career, see *Register of Officers of Confederate States Navy 1861–1865* (Washington, 1931), p. 95; Crabites, *Americans in the Egyptian Army*, p. 10; *New York Times*, August 8, 1870.

Cullom, *Biographical Register*, Vol. III, 22–23; Heitman, *Historical Register*, Vol. I, 159; Dye, *Moslem Egypt*, p. 497; *New York Herald*, September 22, 1871; July 31, August 1, 1884; and *New York Times*, March 12, 1898, give information on Vanderbilt Allen.

Biographical sketches of Charles W. Field are in *DAB*, Vol. VI, 356–57; Heitman, *Historical Register*, Vol. I, 418–19; Cullom, *Biographical Register*, Vol. II, 390–91. His Civil War career is in Evans, *Confederate Military History*, Vol. IX, 236–37; *Official Records*, Ser. 1, Vol. XII, Part II, 217–18; Vol. XXI, 542 *et passim*; Edward A. Pollard, *Lee and His Lieutenants* (New York,

1868), pp. 520–21; John Pope, "The Second Battle of Bull Run," *Battles and Leaders*, Vol. II, 477; E. M. Law, "From the Wilderness to Cold Harbor," *ibid.*, Vol. IV, 124–26 ff.; Fitz John Porter, "Hanover Court House and Gaines's Mill," *ibid.*, Vol. II, 335; W. B. Taliaferro, "Jackson's Raid around Pope," *ibid.*, Vol. II, 511; W. Roy Mason, "Marching on Manassas," *ibid.*, Vol. II, 528–29; Allen C. Redwood, "Jackson's 'Foot Cavalry' at the Second Bull Run," *ibid.*, Vol. II, 530; P. G. T. Beauregard, "Four Days of Battle at Petersburg," *ibid.*, Vol. IV, 543–44; James Eldridge MSS, Box 37, Field Folder, Henry E. Huntington Library, San Marino, California.

Sketches of William P. A. Campbell are in *Register of Officers of Confederate States Navy*, p. 29; Hill, *Biographical Dictionary*, p. 95; Edward W. Callahan (ed.), *List of Officers of the Navy of the United States and of the Marine Corps from 1775 to 1900 Comprising a Complete Register of All Present and Former Commissioned, Warranted, and Appointed Officers of the United States Navy and of the Marine Corps, Regular and Volunteer* (New York, 1901), p. 99; *Confederate Veteran* (40 vols.; Nashville, 1893–1932), Vol. XXVII, 397; Evans, *Confederate Military History*, Vol. VIII, 260. Additional information is in James M. Morgan, *Recollections of a Rebel Reefer* (New York, 1917), pp. 169–70, 188–95, and *New York Herald*, July 17, 1872.

Heitman, *Historical Register*, Vol. I, 826, and *National Cyclopedia of American Biography*, Vol. IV, 167, give summaries of Thomas G. Rhett's career. His Civil War experience can be traced in *Official Records*, Ser. 1, Vol. II, 574; Vol. V, 1075 ff.; Vol. XI, Part I, 444; Vol. XV, 1062.

Walter H. Jenifer's biography is in Heitman, *Historical Register*, Vol. I, 571; Cullom, *Biographical Register*, Vol. I, 213; Evans, *Confederate Military History*, Vol. III, 187. His activities in the Civil War are indicated in *Official Records*, Ser. 1, Vol. V, 305–7, 313–14, 349, 352–53, 368–72, 509, 998, 1025, 1044–45; Vol. X, Part II, 514; Vol. XI, Part III, 670. See also *New York Herald*, January 18, 1870.

Cullom, *Biographical Register*, Vol. III, 122–23, details Chancellor Martin's career. See also the *New York Times* for January 4, 1874.

For the general story of the recruitment of the Americans, the terms of their contracts with Ismail, and their reception upon arrival in Egypt see Chaillé-Long, *My Life in Four Continents*, Vol. I, 16–17, 22–27, 38–39; Dye, *Moslem Egypt*, pp. 1–6, 76–77; Crabites, *Americans in the Egyptian Army*, pp. 6–10, 15; Samuel H. Lockett to David F. Boyd, June 11, July 7, 1875, both in Boyd MSS, Louisiana State University Library, Baton Rouge; *New York Herald*, January 21, 1879; *New York Times*, June 4, 1870; January 8, January 19, April 25, 1875; August 11, 1878. The story of the doctor who bought a fake commission is in the April 25, 1875, issue of *New York Times*. The story of the officers who refused the offer to go to Egypt is in Chaillé-Long, *My Life in Four Continents*, Vol. I, 203; Crabites, *Americans in the Egyptian Army*, p. 7; *Harper's Weekly*, May 14, 1870; *New York Herald*, September 14, 1875.

Union Army, Vol. III, 430; Cullom, *Biographical Register,* Vol. III, 112–13; and Heitman, *Historical Register,* Vol. I, 416, have biographical material on Oscar Eugene Fechet. See also R. Ernest Dupoy, "West Point Officers in Egypt," *Army-Navy-Air Force Register,* July 13, 1957.

For Robert Morris Rogers see Cullom, *Biographical Register,* pp. 89–90; Heitman, *Historical Register,* Vol. I, 843; *New York Times,* January 4, 1874, August 11, 1878; Chaillé-Long, *My Life in Four Continents,* Vol. II, 515–16.

For the career of Charles F. Loshe see Byers, *Iowa in War Times,* pp. 560–62; Ingersoll, *Iowa and the Rebellion,* pp. 637–39, 664–68; Heitman, *Historical Register,* Vol. I, 642.

Information on Dr. William Wilson is in Hill, *Biographical Dictionary,* p. 380; Loring, *Confederate in Egypt,* pp. 393, 405–6, 415–16, 418, 430; Dye, *Moslem Egypt,* pp. 166, 173, 226, 425, 461, 477, 499.

II THE VISION OF ISMAIL

Histories of Egypt in the nineteenth century have largely revolved about the questions raised by the British occupation after 1882, and furnish no sure guide to the personalities and events involved. The Earl of Cromer's *Modern Egypt* (2 vols.; London, 1911) is largely a justification of the British regime, and the information on Ismail is colored by his official position. Donald A. Cameron, *Egypt in the Nineteenth Century* (London, 1898), Edward Dicey, *The Story of the Khedivate* (New York, 1902), and J. Carlile McCoan, *Egypt under Ismail* (London, 1889), are based largely on British official accounts. On the other hand, critics of the British were no less biased. Wilfrid S. Blunt, *Secret History of the English Occupation of Egypt* (New York, 1922), is critical and frequently inaccurate. Edwin DeLeon, once an American consul in Egypt, wrote *The Khedive's Egypt, or, The Old House of Bondage under New Masters* (New York, 1878), and J. Seymour Keay followed the bombardment of Alexandria with *Spoiling the Egyptians: A Tale of Shame Told from the British Bluebooks* (New York, 1882). Elbert E. Farman, *Egypt and Its Betrayal* (New York, 1908) was the work of the American consul general who shared the pro-Ismail views of his friends William Wing Loring and Charles Pomeroy Stone. Pierre Crabites, an American judge on the Mixed Tribunals, defended Ismail in *Ismail the Maligned* (New York, 1933). George Young's *Egypt* (New York, 1927) and H. W. Jervis' *Pharaoh to Farouk* (New York, 1956) are brief summaries which largely follow the evaluations of British and European critics of Ismail's regime.

Descriptions of Ismail, together with various and conflicting estimates of his character, are in Elbert E. Farman, *Egypt and Its Betrayal,* p. 237; Clara E. C. Waters, *Egypt* (Boston, 1880), p. 419; Loring, *Confederate in Egypt,* pp. 77, 148; Edward Dicey, "The Egyptian Crisis," *Nineteenth Century,* Vol. V (April, 1879), 675–77; Dicey, *Story of the Khedivate,* pp. 50–57; Dye,

Moslem Egypt, pp. 8–10; and DeLeon, *Khedive's Egypt*, pp. 164–65, 170–72. For newspaper commentary see *New York Herald*, August 18, 1872, and *London Times*, June 21, 1879.

Ismail's varied interests and accomplishments are detailed in Dicey, *Story of the Khedivate*, pp. 24, 53–54; DeLeon, *The Khedive's Egypt*, pp. 98–99; and *New York Times*, September 24, 1868, June 5, 1869. But the British consul general at Cairo, Colonel Edward Stanton, was not impressed. He told Foreign Secretary Earl Granville (October 12, 1872) that nothing the khedive did could compete with England and that "there is no cause to fear." Stanton Report, No. 44. Turkey (Egypt) Consular Reports. Foreign Office Papers (FO 78–2139). Public Records Office, London.

For the story of the troubles which developed between Ismail and his Turkish overlord because of Ismail's ambitious plans, see Ismail to the Grand Vizier, answering protests of the sultan, in Abdin Palace (Cairo) Archives, Archives Européenes, Période Ismail, 34/3, No. 54, August 18, 1869. See also Keay, *Spoiling the Egyptians*, p. 13; Dicey, *Story of the Khedivate*, pp. 59–65; *New York Times*, May 28, 1866, June 23, June 27, 1869; *New York Herald*, July 20, 1868; and Dye, *Moslem Egypt*, p. 6.

Loring, *Confederate in Egypt*, pp. 245–46, 332; Dicey, *Story of the Khedivate*, pp. 25–38; Crabites, *Americans in the Egyptian Army*, pp. 4–5; and issues of the *New York Times* for October 22, 1866, February 5, February 7, March 14, June 8, June 12, August 4, August 17, 1867, relate the story of English and French interest in Egyptian problems during the early years of Ismail's rule.

The concern of the U.S. State Department for the recruitment of Americans for the khedive's army was discussed by Consul Charles Hale in a letter to Secretary Hamilton Fish (February 2, 1870). Egyptian Dispatches, American, in the Abdin Palace (Cairo) Archives, Division No. 194.

For the festivities and ceremonies which Ismail arranged in celebration of the opening of the Suez Canal, as well as the subsequent troubles which his arrangements caused between Egypt and Turkey, see Loring, *Confederate in Egypt*, p. 247; Dicey, *Story of the Khedivate*, pp. 73–78; and *New York Times*, August 6, August 9, August 12–13, August 21, September 1–2, September 4, September 6, September 13, September 16, September 22, November 17–18, November 20, November 24, December 2, December 10, December 15, 1869; and January 1, 1870.

III THE LAND OF THE PHARAOHS

Complete descriptions of places, antiquities, population, living conditions, customs, and social life in the Egypt of the 1870's are set forth in Kurt Baedeker (ed.), *Egypt: Handbook for Travellers* (London, 1885); DeLeon, *The Khedive's Egypt*; Georg M. Ebers, *Egypt: Descriptive, Historical and Picturesque*

(2 vols.; New York, 1884); *Egypt and How To See It* (New York, 1907); Stanley Lane-Poole, *Cairo* (London, 1893); Lane-Poole, *Egypt* (London, 1881); Lane-Poole, *Social Life in Egypt* (New York, 1884); Charles G. Leland, *The Egyptian Sketch Book* (New York, 1874); J. Carlile McCoan, *Egypt* (New York, 1900); McCoan, *Egypt as It Is* (New York, 1877); Bayard Taylor, *Egypt and Iceland in the Year 1874* (New York, 1874); and Isaac Taylor, *Leaves from an Egyptian Note-Book* (London, 1888). See also Farman, *Egypt and Its Betrayal*, pp. 1–5; C. B. Klunzinger, *Upper Egypt, Its People and Its Products* (New York, 1878), p. 125; Charles Dudley Warner, *My Winter on the Nile* (Boston, 1884), pp. 34–36, 41–42, 45, 49, 58, 61–64; M. L. Whately, "Life in Egypt," *Leisure Hour*, Vol. XIV (May 27, 1865), 325–27; *London Times*, November 27, 1872, March 4, 1873, April 17, 1878; *New York Herald*, January 2, July 5, 1870; and *New York Times*, April 5, 1873.

The transliteration of Arabic terms presents special difficulties. In this book the spellings are those used most commonly by the Americans in Egypt and by contemporary English-language newspapers. In some cases place names follow Baedeker's handbooks. In a few cases the names appear as on modern maps.

For statements by some of the Americans on life in Egypt see Raleigh E. Colston, "Modern Egypt and Its People," *Journal of the American Geographical Society of New York*, Vol. XIII (1881), 133–64; Dye, *Moslem Egypt*, pp. 19–40; Chaillé-Long, *My Life in Four Continents*, Vol. I, 42; Loring, *Confederate in Egypt*, pp. 6–8, 50–51, 80–86, 105, 114–25, 143–44; Samuel H. Lockett, "The Valleys of the Nile and the Mississippi," Charles Woodward Hutson mss, Louisiana State University Library, Baton Rouge; Morgan, *Rebel Reefer*, pp. 275–77; Colston to Joseph Byrne, in clipping from the *Daily Journal* (Wilmington, N.C.), September 5, 1873, in Raleigh E. Colston mss, Southern Historical Collections, University of North Carolina Library, Chapel Hill; Graves to his wife, in Charles I. Graves Letters, No. 11 (August 7, 1875), No. 12 (August 14, 1875), No. 25 (October 8, 1875), No. 29 (October 28, 1875), No. 30 (November 6, 1875), No. 79 (July 8, 1876), and No. 264 (February 21, 1878), all in possession of his granddaughter, Miss Margaruite Graves, Columbia, S.C.

For the Americans' reception by the khedive and their subsequent appraisals of him, see Crabites, *Americans in the Egyptian Army*, pp. 39–43; Morgan, *Rebel Reefer*, pp. 270–72, 296; Graves to his wife, Letters, No. 11 (August 7, 1875), No. 13 (August 21, 1875); Chaillé-Long, "Egypt under the Viceroys," *The Era*, Vol. II (March, 1903), 253–55; Loring, *Confederate in Egypt*, pp. 64–67, 273–77, 360–62, 446–48; *New York Herald*, October 20, 1871; *New York Times*, October 31, 1871; and Farman, *Egypt and Its Betrayal*, p. 278. For Loring's criticism of the British see Loring, *Confederate in Egypt*, pp. 16–17.

IV THE AMERICANS AT WORK

Several of the Americans who later wrote of their experiences in Egypt told of the job assignments given them and their countrymen upon their arrival in Egypt. Chaillé-Long dealt with the matter in *My Life in Four Continents*, Vol. I, 39–42, 54–55, 58–59, 64, 156–57, 231; in *The Three Prophets: Chinese Gordon, Mohammed-Ahmed (El Mahdi), Arabi Pasha, Events before and after the Bombardment of Alexandria* (New York, 1884), pp. 28, 85, 189; in *Central Africa: Naked Truths of Naked People* (New York, 1877), p. 201; and in "Egypt under the Viceroys," *The Era*, Vol. II (March, 1903), 256–57. William McE. Dye mentioned job assignments in *Moslem Egypt*, pp. 77–79, 165, 498. Loring wrote of the Americans' first tasks in *Confederate in Egypt*, pp. 12, 27, 67–71, 298–99, 360–62, 365–66, and James M. Morgan referred to them in *Rebel Reefer*, 290–91. See also Samuel H. Lockett, "Arabi and His Army," *Nation*, Vol. XXXV (September 28, 1882), 257; Edward Warren, *A Doctor's Experience in Three Continents* (Baltimore, 1885), pp. 442–44, 544; Lockett to Boyd, November 19, December 25, 1875, November 4, 1877, all in Boyd MSS; and Raleigh E. Colston's open letter in *Century Magazine*, Vol. XXVIII (September, 1884), 788–89. References to the assignments are also made in biographical sketches of individual Americans. See Cullom, *Biographical Register*, Vol. I, 723; Vol. II, 213, 550, 716, 836; Vol. III, 23; *DAB*, Vol. XI, 420–21; Vol. XV, 516; Evans, *Confederate Military History*, Vol. VII, 678–79; Vol. X, 315; Vol. XI, 203–6; and Hill, *Biographical Dictionary*, pp. 102, 142, 217, 311.

Although Pierre Crabites' entire book, *Americans in the Egyptian Army*, deals with the Americans' work in Egypt, material especially relevant to this chapter is to be found on pages 10, 13, 49–50, 53, 64, 175, 229, 243, 247, 336. Newspapers also reported from time to time on the activities of the Americans in the khedive's service: *New York Herald*, May 31, December 20, 1870; September 22, 1871; July 17, 1872; March 23, May 25, June 21, 1873; August 2, 1875; September 8, 1882; *New York Times*, August 26, 1870; July 27, 1871; January 19, 1875; *London Times*, June 1, 1877; and Richmond (Va.) *Weekly Times*, July 30, 1896. For British interest in the mission of the Americans see Stanton Report, No. 43. Turkey (Egypt) Consular Reports. Foreign Office Papers (FO 78–2139). Public Records Office, London.

Beverly Kennon's hectic career in the Civil War can be followed in Callahan, *Officers of the Navy of the U.S.*, p. 311; *Register of Officers of Confederate States Navy*, p. 107; J. H. Gilman, "With Slemmer in Pensacola," *Battles and Leaders*, Vol. II, 31 f.; *Official Records*, Ser. 2, Vol. I, 514–31, 559–60, 563, 566–68, 775–79, 797; and Eldridge MSS, Box 72, Beverly Kennon Folder. Chaillé-Long refers to Kennon in *My Life in Four Continents*, Vol. I, 16, 18–19.

Sketches of the life of Alexander W. Reynolds are in Cullom, *Biographical Register*, Vol. I, 723; Heitman, *Historical Register*, Vol. I, 824; Lyon G. Tyler, *Encyclopedia of Virginia Biography* (4 vols.; New York, 1915), Vol. III, 84; Evans, *Confederate Military History*, Vol. III, 655–56; and *DAB*, Vol. XV, 516.

His Civil War experience may be traced in Walter Clark (ed.), *Histories of the Several Regiments and Battalions in the Great War 1861–65* (5 vols.; Goldsboro, N.C., 1901), Vol. III, 436; *Official Records*, Ser. 1, Vol. V, 1026, 1042; Vol. X, Part II, 658; Vol. XVI, Part I, 436, 535, 829; Vol. XVII, Part II, 821, 831; Vol. XXIV, Part I, 231–32. A sketch of Frank A. Reynolds is in Cullom, *Biographical Register*, Vol. II, 836, and there are references to him in summaries of his father's career. See also Crabites, *Americans in the Egyptian Army*, p. 13.

James Morris Morgan gives a detailed account of his life in *Rebel Reefer*. See also *Register of Officers of the Confederate States Navy*, p. 137; Chaillé-Long, *My Life in Four Continents*, Vol. I, 43; and Morgan's "Brood of the Constitution," U.S. Naval Institute *Proceedings*, Vol. XLII (January-February, 1916), 138.

For Edmund Parys see Heitman, *Historical Register*, Vol. I, 772; Dye, *Moslem Egypt*, p. 499; Chaillé-Long, *My Life in Four Continents*, Vol. I, 231; *New York Times*, August 26, 1870; and *New York Herald*, September 22, 1871.

Erastus Sparrow Purdy's Civil War career is sketched in Phisterer, *New York in the Rebellion*, Vol. III, 2103–4, 2106, 2112; Vol. V, 4300; Heitman, *Historical Register*, Vol. I, 809; *Union Army*, Vol. II, 71–72; Loring, *Confederate in Egypt*, pp. 299–300; Fort Dalles MSS, No. 1206, Henry E. Huntington Library; *Official Records*, Ser. 1, Vol. V, 545. See also Crabites, *Americans in the Egyptian Army*, pp. 13, 55–59; Chaillé-Long, *My Life in Four Continents*, Vol. I, 231; *New York Times*, August 11, 1878; and *New York Herald*, January 4, August 2, 1875.

Short biographies of William H. Ward are in Tyler, *Encyclopedia of Virginia Biography*, Vol. V, 900; Callahan, *Officers of the Navy of the U.S.*, p. 569; *Register of Officers of the Confederate States Navy*, p. 203; and Evans, *Confederate Military History*, Vol. XII, 48–61, 105. See also *New York Times*, August 26, 1870. An account by Frederick J. Cox, "The American Naval Mission in Egypt," *Journal of Modern History*, Vol. XXVI (1954), 173–78, deals with Ward's and Kennon's assignment to work with John L. Lay, American submarine expert, in preparing Egyptian coastal defenses. Ward outlined a course of instruction for a projected submarine and torpedo school.

Callahan, *Officers of the Navy of the U.S.*, p. 227; *Register of Officers of Confederate States Navy*, p. 74; Hill, *Biographical Dictionary*, p. 142; and Dye, *Moslem Egypt*, p. 173, have material on Charles Iverson Graves. See also Graves to his wife, Letters, No. 279 (March 28, 1878), No. 287 (April 26, 1878), No. 289 (May 22, 1878), No. 292 (July 6, 1878), and Stone to Graves, March 29, 1878; all in Graves Letters.

Sketches of Raleigh E. Colston's life are in Tyler, *Encyclopedia of Virginia Biography*, Vol. III, 49–50; and *DAB*, Vol. IV, 317. See also *Papers Relating to the Foreign Relations of the United States Transmitted to Congress with the Annual Message of the President* (44th Cong., 1st sess., Executive Document No. 1,

Vol. II, Part I, Serial No. 1673, Washington, 1875), p. 1332; and *New York Herald*, May 25, 1873.

General Stone's ascendancy over Thaddeus P. Mott in the confidence of the Khedive Ismail, the problems which the Egyptian "pasha system" posed for Stone and all foreigners in the Egyptian service, and the story of Stone's problems in reorganizing the Egyptian army can be traced in Dye, *Moslem Egypt*, pp. 4, 41–65, 69–79, 169–70, 357–58; Loring, *Confederate in Egypt*, pp. 349–58; Crabites, *Americans in the Egyptian Army*, pp. 14, 51–52; DeLeon, *The Khedive's Egypt*, pp. 163, 176–77, 249–50, 357–58; Morgan, *Rebel Reefer*, p. 302; Colston, "Modern Egypt and Its People," *Journal of the American Geographical Society of New York*, Vol. XIII (1881), 143–45, 147–48; Lockett to Boyd, September 29, 1875, Boyd mss; Stanton Report No. 43. Turkey (Egypt) Consular Reports. Foreign Office Papers (FO 78–2139). Public Records Office, London; *New York Herald*, September 26, 1870; March 22, May 30, September 19, 1882; March 13, 1883; February 15, 1884; *New York Times*, August 26, 1870; July 27, 1871; January 19, April 25, December 6, 1875; and *London Times*, April 3, 1874; January 3, February 16, June 1, 1877; February 11, September 20, 1878.

For David F. Boyd's interest in going to Egypt, Lockett's efforts to help him, his eventual disappointment, and General Stone's subsequent explanation of why Boyd was not appointed, see Lockett to Boyd, June 11, July 1, September 29, November 19, December 17, December 25, 1875; November 4, 1877; Stone to Boyd, September 21, 1875; July 7, 1876; and Stone to Sherman, September 24, 1875; all in Boyd mss.

V DELTA DAYS

Charles I. Graves told his wife about his working conditions, living accommodations, and meals, and described other American officers and their families in Letters, No. 2 (July 15, 1875), No. 3 (July 16, 1875), No. 6 (July 25, 1875), No. 11 (August 7, 1875), No. 12 (August 14, 1875), No. 13 (August 20, 1875), No. 14 (August 26, 1875), No. 18 (September 17, 1875), No. 20 (September 21, 1875), No. 21 (September 24, 1875), No. 22 (October 1, 1875), No. 25 (October 10, 1875), No. 29 (October 28, 1875), No. 33 (November 20, 1875), No. 36 (December 10, 1875), No. 37 (December 16, 1875), No. 79 (July 7, 1876), No. 81 (July 16, 1876), No. 93 (August 29, 1876), No. 96 (October 2, 1876), No. 97 (October 6, 1876), No. 98 (October 9, 1876), No. 99 (October 14, 1876), No. 101 (October 22, 1876), No. 145 (March 19, 1877), No. 146 (March 25, 1877), No. 201 (September 20, 1877), No. 209 (October 14, 1877), No. 212 (October 22, 1877), No. 269 (March 4, 1878), No. 275 (March 18, 1878), all in Graves Letters.

For additional observations on the Americans' life in Egypt, see Graves to H. W. Miller, August 12, 1875, Graves Letters; Samuel H. Lockett, "Housekeeping in Egypt," Samuel H. Lockett mss, Southern Historical Collections,

University of North Carolina Library, Chapel Hill; and Lockett to Boyd, December 25, 1875, Boyd mss.

Official Records, Ser. 1, Vol. XXII, Part I, 273; John G. Walker, "Surprise and Withdrawal at Shiloh," *Battles and Leaders*, Vol. I, 604–6; and Samuel H. Lockett, "The Defense of Vicksburg," *ibid.*, Vol. III, 482–92; concern Lockett's Civil War career. The story of Stone's offer and Lockett's decision to go to Egypt can be followed in Lockett's letters to David F. Boyd, August 22, September 8, October 3, 1874; January 17, February 12, March 28, May 6, May 29, June 11, June 20, June 30, July 7, July 16, 1875; and in James A. McWhorten to Lockett, May 14, 1875; all in Boyd mss. See also the *Atlanta Constitution*, September 25, September 29, 1874; and Loring, *Confederate in Egypt*, pp. 334–35.

Wilburn Briggs Hall is identified in Callahan, *Officers of the Navy of the U.S.*, p. 240; *Register of Officers of Confederate States Navy*, p. 79; and *National Cyclopedia of American Biography*, Vol. VIII, 269–70. See also his "Capture of the Slave-Ship Cora," *Century Magazine*, Vol. XLVIII (May, 1894), 115–29.

For sketches of Dr. Edward Warren's career, see Hubert A. Royster, *The Adventurous Life of Edward Warren Bey* (Address . . . Section on History of Medicine of the Richmond Academy of Medicine, April 13, 1937); *Confederate Veteran*, Vol. IV, 172–73. For the story of his conflicts in Egypt see Warren, *Experience on Three Continents*, pp. 53–54, 362, 370–90, 393, 396–403, 411, 422–24, 447–52, 456–60, 484; Warren to Jenifer, December 14, 1874, Seth Barton mss, Library of Congress; Colston Diary, May 7, 1874, Colston mss; Warren to Dr. Lamson, April 11, 1871; Note from Stone, June 13, 1875; Stone to Farman, June 14, 1876 in U.S. Department of State, Official Correspondence of the Consulate General of the United States, Alexandria and Cairo, 1869–75, National Archives; Lockett to Boyd, December 25, 1875, Boyd mss; Loring, *Confederate in Egypt*, p. 251; Dye, *Moslem Egypt*, p. 178; and Graves to wife, letter 78, June 19, 1876, Graves Letters.

VI PROBLEMS OF A PASHA

Morgan tells of his escapades in his *Rebel Reefer*, pp. 277–81, 297–300, 310–15, and Chaillé-Long mentions them in *My Life in Four Continents*, Vol. I, 40–46.

Cornelius Hunt's stay in Egypt is recorded in Official Correspondence of the Consulate General, 1869–75, November 15, 1870, October 30, November 10, 1871; Crabites, *Americans in the Egyptian Army*, p. 10; and Chaillé-Long, *My Life in Four Continents*, Vol. I, 54–56.

The story of the Dunlap uniform is in a letter from Gott to the consul, April 10, 1874, Official Correspondence of the Consulate General, 1869–75. See also *Confederate Veteran*, Vol. XVII, 509.

Sibley's problems are aired in bills from Victor Philip (no date); Robertson and Co., January 21, 1871, July 1873; and in a letter from Butler to Tinne, April 30, 1872, Official Correspondence of the Consulate General, 1869–75. See also *New York Herald*, December 9, 1873, and Warren, *Experience on Three Continents*, p. 443.

Lockett told of his getting an advance payment of salary before he left for Gura in a letter to David F. Boyd, November 19, 1875, Boyd MSS.

Crabites, *Americans in the Egyptian Army*, pp. 55–59, tells of Purdy's unpaid hotel bill.

The trouble over Hall's leased home is detailed in Farman to F. W. Seward, July 26, 1877, Official Correspondence of the Consulate General, 1869–75.

The story of the creditor who pressed Stone for debt payment is in Crabites, *Americans in the Egyptian Army*, p. 52, and Lawyer to Consul, June 30, 1875, Official Correspondence of the Consulate General, 1869–75.

The Rhett troubles are in Bill, November 3, 1873; N. D. Comanos to Fish, September 19, 1874; Beardsley to Fish, December 18, 1874; Rhett to Beardsley, December 30, 1874; Beardsley to Fish, July 28, 1875; and Rhett to Farman, June 8, 1877, Official Correspondence of the Consulate General, 1869–75. See also *New York Herald*, May 25, 1873.

Consular correspondence on the Butler problems includes George H. Butler to Cherif Pasha, May 20, 1870; Butler to T. P. Mott, June 27, 1870; Butler to G. Lansing, November 10, 1870, and June 19, 1871; Butler to Nubar Pasha, July 8, 1871; Butler to Stone, April 9, 1872; Stone to Fish, April 20, 1872; Bill, February, 1871, Official Correspondence of the Consulate General, 1869–75. See also Stanton Report, No. 48. Turkey (Egypt) Consular Reports. Foreign Office Papers (FO 78–2139). Public Records Office, London.

Private correspondence on the Butler affair includes George Butler to Allen, September 26, 1871; George Butler to B. F. Butler, and Mott to B. F. Butler, both July 15, 1872; Mott to B. F. Butler, July 18, 1872; and B. F. Butler to Fish, July 26, 1872; all in Butler MSS, Library of Congress.

Newspaper reports are in *New York Herald*, September 24, 1870; July 31, October 7, November 10, 1871; June 8, July 14, July 17, July 18, September 23, 1872; *New York Times*, March 16, July 14, July 17, July 18, August 22, 1872. See also Chaillé-Long, *My Life in Four Continents*, Vol. I, 60.

For the story of Major White see Graves to his wife, Letters, No. 12 (August 14, 1875), No. 13 (August 20, 1875), No. 25 (October 10, 1875), No. 36 (December 10, 1875), Graves Letters.

VII EXPLORING THE SUDAN

For the earliest expeditions sent out by General Stone see Chaillé-Long, *My Life in Four Continents*, Vol. I, 39–41, Vol. II, 540; and Raleigh E. Colston, "Stone Pasha's Work in Geography," *American Geographical Society Bulletin*, Vol. XIX (1887), 48–50.

Although a number of foreign governments showed interest in the presence of the Americans in Egypt, Britain evinced real concern over it. Her diplomats were as suspicious of the activities of the "American mission" as many of the Americans were of British designs. Stanton Reports, Nos. 20 and 56. Turkey (Egypt) Consular Reports. Foreign Office Papers (FO 78–2139). Public Records Office, London; Crabites, *Americans in the Egyptian Army*, pp. 44–45; Chaillé-Long, *My Life in Four Continents*, Vol. I, 41; Dye, *Moslem Egypt*, p. 82; and *New York Times*, September 13, 1869.

The story of Ismail's interest in the Sudan, his instructions to Sir Samuel Baker, and Baker's activities in the Sudan may be followed in Baker, *Ismailia: A Narrative of the Expedition to Central Africa for the Suppression of the Slave Trade* (New York, 1875); *Report on the Egyptian Provinces of the Sudan, Red Sea and Equator* (London, n.d.); Loring, *Confederate in Egypt*, pp. 254–55, 268, 270, 289–92; Dye, *Moslem Egypt*, pp. 81, 121, 123; Crabites, *Americans in the Egyptian Army*, pp. 29–31; U.S. Dept. of State, *Papers Relating to the Foreign Relations of the U.S. . . .* (43d Cong., 1st sess., Executive Document No. 1, Vol. II, Part I, Serial No. 1595, Washington, 1873), p. 1123; *ibid.* (43d Cong., 2d sess., Executive Document No. 1, Part I, Serial No. 1634, Washington, 1875), pp. 1164, 1167–70; Georg Schweinfurth, *Heart of Africa* (2 vols.; New York, 1874), Vol. I, 4–5; and *New York Times*, June 23, 1869; September 7, November 27, December 29, 1872; January 22, April 25, 1875.

In 1873 there were rumors that the projected Baker Relief Expedition was a "diplomatic cloak" to cover an Egyptian mission to counteract the damage to Egyptian trade which Baker's handling of affairs in the Sudan occasioned. The Egyptian government never gave an official reason for the cancellation of the expedition, but the rumors so disturbed Baker that he used the columns of a London newspaper to justify his actions. *London Times*, May 10, 1873; December 28, 1876; *New York Times*, August 2, November 29, 1872; U.S. Dept. of State, *Papers Relating . . .* (43d Cong., 2d sess., Executive Document No. 1, Part I, Serial No. 1634, Washington, 1875), pp. 1164, 1167–69, 1202–8; *ibid.* (44th Cong., 1st sess., Executive Document No. 1, Vol. II, Part I, Serial No. 1673, Washington, 1875), p. 1332; Reginald Coupland, *The Exploitation of East Africa 1856–1890* (London, 1939), pp. 276–77; and Chaillé-Long, *My Life in Four Continents*, Vol. I, 54.

In the alumni files of the Virginia Military Institute there is a statement by Colonel G. A. Porterfield, dated January 29, 1909, which tells a weird legend about the birth of Colston. The story goes that some years after his marriage Dr. Colston "made a protracted visit to his former home in Berkeley County. Upon his return to France, his wife, knowing his wish to have an heir, presented him with a child (of respectable parentage which she had procured in his absence) as his son. Mrs. Colston made this confession to a priest upon her deathbed. Colston received information of this while at VMI and it had a very depressing effect on him." The yarn also appears in William Channing Paxton, *The Marshall Family* (Cincinnati, 1885), pp. 112–13. Legend gives the name of Victor Boucher to the changeling child. See also William Couper, *One Hundred Years at V.M.I.* (Richmond, 1939), and an undated entry referring to Colston's early life in his Diary, Colston MSS.

Colston's military career has never received special and separate study. For his Civil War experience, see *Official Records*, Ser. I, Vol. V, 390–92; Vol. XI, Part III, 481; Vol. XVIII, 207 *passim;* Vol. XXV, Part I, 890, 902, 940–42, 1003–9; Part II, 705, 830; Vol. XXXV, Part I, 361–65, 530–32; Vol. XXXVI, Part II, 317–19, 1007–8; Raleigh E. Colston, "Watching the Merrimac," *Battles and Leaders*, Vol. I, 712–14; August V. Kautz, "Operations South of the James River," *ibid.*, Vol. IV, 535; Evans, *Confederate Military History*, Vol. III, 586–87; and Jennings C. Wise, *The Military History of the Virginia Military Institute from 1839 to 1865* (Lynchburg, 1915), pp. 100, 132.

For Campbell's Egyptian experience see U.S. Dept. of State, *Papers Relating* . . . (43d Cong., 2d sess., Executive Document No. 1, Part I, Serial No. 1634, Washington, 1875), p. 1327; George B. Hill (ed.), *Col. Gordon in Central Africa 1874–1890* (London, 1881), pp. 16, 40–41; Crabites, *Americans in the Egyptian Army*, p. 99; Dye, *Moslem Egypt*, pp. 79–81; Chaillé-Long, *My Life in Four Continents*, Vol. I, 116, 231; Chaillé-Long, *Three Prophets*, p. 32; Chaillé-Long, *Central Africa*, p. 210; Stone to Consul, October 10, 1874, Official Correspondence of the Consulate General, 1848–79; Chaillé-Long, "Uganda and the White Nile," *Journal of the American Geographical Society of New York*, Vol. VIII (1876), 299; *New York Herald*, September 22, 1871; July 16, 1872; and *London Times*, April 28, June 5, August 10, August 11, 1874; February 15, 1875.

James M. Morgan has told of his experience with the "Rappahannock" in his *Rebel Reefer*, pp. 169–70, 188–95.

A detailed account of Colston's first expedition in Egypt is in *Report on Northern and Central Kordofan* . . . (Cairo: Office of the General Staff, 1878). See also Colston Diary, January, 1874, Colston MSS. Colston referred to the 1873 expedition in "The Land of the False Prophet," *Century Magazine*, Vol. XXIX, 657 (March, 1885), and Oscar Eugene Fechet wrote about it in *Journal of the March of an Expedition in Nubia, between the Assouan and Abouhamid* (Cairo, 1878). In "Life in the Egyptian Deserts," *Journal of the American Geographical Society of New York*, Vol. XI (1879), 301–33, and "Modern Egypt and its People," *ibid.*, Vol. XIII (1881), 133–64, Colston combined details of the 1873 and the 1874–75 expeditions. See also Chaillé-Long, *Central Africa*, p. 10; Chaillé-Long, *Three Prophets*, p. 30; *New York Herald*, June 8, 1872; *New York Times*, August 15, 1874; and Graves to his wife, Letters, No. 12 (August 14, 1875), No. 14 (August 26, 1875), Graves Letters.

For Alexander McComb Mason see *Register of Officers of the Confederate States Navy*, p. 128; Dye, *Moslem Egypt*, p. 77; Hill, *Biographical Dictionary*, 95; *New York Times*, July 27, 1871; and *Washington (D.C.) Post*, March 18, 1897.

Consul General Richard Beardsley outlined the 1874 troubles in the Sudan for Secretary of State Hamilton Fish in U.S. Dept. of State, *Papers Relating* . . . (44th Cong., 1st sess., Executive Document No. 1, Vol. II, Part I, Serial No. 1673, Washington, 1875), pp. 1330–31, 1339–41. See also Taylor, *Egypt and Iceland in 1874*, pp. 56–57, and *New York Times*, February 19, September 28, 1874.

In 1872 Beardsley talked with Ismail about the khedive's plans for Egypt. He subsequently reported that Ismail believed that the railway system of Lower Egypt was at that time extensive enough to warrant his expanding the system into Upper Egypt and Nubia. U.S. Dept. of State, *Papers Relating* . . . (43d Cong., 2d sess., Executive Document No. 1, Vol. II, Part I, Serial No. 1595, Washington, 1873), p. 1123. See also *New York Times*, October 31, 1871.

Sketches of Horatio B. Reed are in Hill, *Biographical Dictionary*, pp. 315–16, and Heitman, *Historical Register*, Vol. I, 820. His Civil War record is in Phisterer, *New York in the Rebellion*, Vol. II, 1065–66, 1076; Vol. V, 4434; *Official Records*, Ser. 1, Vol. XI, Part II, 288; *Union Army*, Vol. II, 197–98; and Townsend, *Honors of the Empire State*, p. 265. See also *New York Herald*, March 15, 1870; September 3, 1875; September 9, 1897; and *New York Times*, January 4, 1874; August 11, 1878. Stone expressed his displeasure with Reed in a letter to Colston, March 31, 1874, Colston MSS. For the Warren story see his *Experience on Three Continents*, pp. 460–66.

For Henry G. Prout's career see Hill, *Biographical Dictionary*, pp. 309–10, and *New York Times*, January 4, 1874.

Both Colston and Prout made detailed reports on the 1874–75 expedition: Colston, "Itinerary from Debbe to El Obeiyad . . . ," *Proceedings of the Royal Geographical Society*, Vol. XX (London, 1876), 257–362; Prout, *General Report on the Province of Kordofan* (Cairo, 1877) and "Report of Col. H. G. Prout on his Reconnaissance from Khartoum to El Obeiyad," *Journal of the American Geographical Society of New York*, Vol. IX (1877), 157–58. See also U.S. Dept. of State, *Papers Relating* . . . (44th Cong., 1st sess., Executive Document No. 1, Vol. II, Part I, Serial No. 1673, Washington, 1875), pp. 1330–33; Dye, *Moslem Egypt*, pp. 84–98, 103; Loring, *Confederate in Egypt*, pp. 298–300; Crabites, *Americans in the Egyptian Army*, pp. 34, 72–76, 79, 81–87; *London Times*, October 22, 1874; *New York Herald*, January 2, January 4, August 2, 1875; and *New York Times*, January 11, January 19, April 14, October 13, 1875; June 9, 1878.

VIII CHAILLÉ-LONG IN CENTRAL AFRICA

Charles Chaillé-Long's writings cover every phase of his career in various parts of the world. His assignments and accomplishments in Egypt are detailed in *Central Africa*, in *My Life in Four Continents*, Vol. I, 39–40, 53, 61, 64, 89–115; *The Three Prophets*, pp. 7–38, 55, 85; "Chaillé-Long's Work on the Nile," *American Geographical Society Bulletin*, Vol. XXXVI (1904), 346–52; "The Part of the Nile Which Colonel Chaillé-Long Discovered," *ibid.*, Vol. LXI (1909), 222–24; "England in Egypt and the Sudan," *North American Review*, Vol. CLXVIII (May, 1899), 570–80; "Uganda and the White Nile," *Journal of the American Geographical Society of New York*, Vol. VIII (1876), 285–304. See also *DAB*, Vol. III, 591–92; *Union Army*, Vol. II, 275; Crabites, *Americans in the Egyptian Army*, p. 13; and *New York Times*, January 11, 1875.

For other considerations of Chaillé-Long and his work see Crabites, *Americans in the Egyptian Army*, pp. 96–97, 100–52; DeLeon, *The Khedive's Egypt*, pp. 295–96; Loring, *Confederate in Egypt*, pp. 269, 291; Coupland, *Exploitation of East Africa*, p. 274; Edwin S. Balch, "American Explorers of Africa," *The Geographical Review*, Vol. V (April, 1918), 276–78; U.S. Dept. of State, *Papers Relating . . .* (44th Cong., 1st sess., Executive Document No. 1, Vol. II, Part I, Serial No. 1673, Washington, 1875), pp. 1326–30; and Dye, *Moslem Egypt*, pp. 79–81.

Chaillé-Long's activities made good news copy, and he was always more than obliging in giving information to the newspapers. See *New York Herald*, November 12, 1874; January 15, 1875; *New York Times*, December 8, 1874; January 8, January 11, January 19, April 13, 1875; *New York Semi-Weekly Times*, February 19, 1875; and *London Times*, January 1, March 27, 1875.

Britain's interest in Africa, with particular reference to Abyssinia and the area around the Gulf of Aden, are discussed in Dicey, *Story of the Khedivate*, pp. 89–96; Dye, *Moslem Egypt*, pp. 82, 120–28; Hill, *Gordon*, pp. 204–5; *Report on the Sudan*, pp. 16 ff.; *New York Times*, January 6, July 3, November 13, November 25, 1872; January 6, January 30, April 27, June 16, July 15, 1873; November 3, 1874; January 15, 1876; December 10, 1879; *New York Herald*, October 15, 1868; June 16, 1873; *New York Semi-Weekly Times*, November 5, 1872; January 10, 1873; and *London Times*, December 28, 1876.

Charles G. "Chinese" Gordon's service in Central Africa and his relations with Chaillé-Long can be followed in the latter's *My Life in Four Continents*, Vol. I, 64–70, 76–87; *Three Prophets*, pp. 7–39, and *Central Africa*, pp. 4–36. See also Lord Elton, *Gordon of Khartoum* (New York, 1955), pp. 124–27, 135–37, 145–46, 151; Hill, *Gordon*, pp. 3, 16, 41, 54–55, 62–65, 115–16; Bernard M. Allen, *Gordon and the Sudan* (London, 1931), pp. 14–18, 36–37; James W. Buel, *Heroes of the Dark Continent and How Stanley Found Emin Pasha* (Philadelphia, 1890), pp. 237, 296–302; U.S. Dept. of State, *Papers Relating . . .* (43d Cong., 2d sess., Executive Document No. 1, Part I, Serial No. 1634, Washington, 1875), p. 1185; *ibid.*, (44th Cong., 1st sess., Executive Document No. 1, Vol. II, Part I, Serial No. 1673, Washington, 1875), p. 1326; *London Times*, April 28, May 19, August 20, 1874; *New York Times*, March 27, 1875; September 7, 1898; Colston, "Land of the False Prophet," *Century Magazine*, Vol. XXIX (March, 1885), 647; and Loring, *Confederate in Egypt*, pp. 275–77.

IX THE ROCKY PATH OF EMPIRE

For Chaillé-Long's Paris visit and subsequent criticism of his work see his *My Life in Four Continents*, Vol. I, 162; *London Times*, March 27, 1875; *New York Semi-Weekly Times*, February 19, 1875; *New York Herald*, January 15, 1875.

Chaillé-Long told of his Juba River experience in *My Life in Four Continents*, Vol. I, 157–94; *Central Africa*, p. 67; "Col. Chaillé-Long on the Juba," *Journal of the American Geographical Society of New York*, Vol. XIX (1887), 194–98; *Chicago Times Sunday Magazine*, June 7, 1885. See also Allen, *Gordon and the Sudan*, p. 43; Elton, *Gordon of Khartoum*, pp. 158–59; Hill, *Gordon*, pp. 146, 151; Coupland, *Exploitation of East Africa*, pp. 279–80; Crabites, *Americans in the Egyptian Army*, pp. 173–85; Loring, *Confederate in Egypt*, pp. 292–96; Dye, *Moslem Egypt*, pp. 81–83; *New York Herald*, January 15, July 6, December 18, December 19, 1875; *New York Times*, September 20, December 2, December 3, 1875; January 7, February 2, March 27, 1876; *London Times*, March 27, 1875; *New York Semi-Weekly Times*, February 19, 1875.

The story of the Arrendrup invasion of Abyssinia and the part which Americans took in it can be followed in U.S. Dept. of State, *Papers Relating . . .* (43d Cong., 1st sess., Executive Document No. 1, Vol. II, Part I, Serial No. 1595, Washington, 1873), pp. 1119–21; *ibid.* (44th Cong., 1st sess., Executive Document No. 1, Vol. II, Part I, Serial No. 1673, Washington, 1875), pp. 1349–50; *ibid.* (44th Cong., 2d sess., Executive Document No. 1, Part I, Serial No. 1741, Washington, 1876), pp. 594–96, 600–601; Dye, *Moslem Egypt*, pp. 104–51, 499; Loring, *Confederate in Egypt*, pp. 289–92, 301–5, 341, 347–48; Chaillé-Long, *My Life in Four Continents*, Vol. I, 75; Crabites, *Americans in the Egyptian Army*, pp. 187–91; "The Egyptian Campaign in Abyssinia," *Littell's Living Age*, Fifth Series, Vol. XIX (August 4, 1877), 278–87; Hill, *Biographical Dictionary*, p. 112; Cullom, *Biographical Register*, Vol. III, 148; Samuel H. Lockett, "Notes on the Abyssinian Campaign of the Egyptian Army, 1875–1876," Lockett MSS; Lockett to Boyd, September 29, 1875, Boyd MSS. See also *New York Times*, January 7, August 5, August 31, September 3, September 25, 1872; November 20, December 4, 1874; August 13, September 1, October 3, November 30, 1875; October 13, November 7, 1876; *London Times*, December 13, 1875; October 12, October 17, October 25, November 11, November 14, 1876; May 25, 1877; *New York Herald*, August 28, 1872; October 25, 1876.

James A. Dennison arrived just in time to accompany the Arrendrup expedition in the fall of 1875. See Hill, *Biographical Dictionary*, p. 112; Dye, *Moslem Egypt*, pp. 131–32, 173, 207, 237, 259, 467; Loring, *Confederate in Egypt*, pp. 301, 433. A summary of Henry Clay Derrick's career is in *Confederate Veteran*, Vol. XXIII, 417. See also *Official Records*, Ser. 1, Vol.

IX, 43, and Dye, *Moslem Egypt*, p. 165. Heitman, *Historical Register*, Vol. I, 563, outlines the military career of Norwegian-born Henry A. Irgins. Thomas D. Johnson, a Tennessee physician, joined Ismail's service in 1875. He had served with the Army of Northern Virginia and studied medicine after the war, practicing in Clarksville until his departure for Egypt. See *Tennessee, the Volunteer State* (4 vols.; Chicago, 1923), Vol. III, 921–22; Charles I. Graves to his wife, Letter No. 138 (February 26, 1877), Graves Letters, For Robert S. Lamson see Chaillé-Long, *My Life in Four Continents*, Vol. I, 231; Dye, *Moslem Egypt*, pp. 166, 172–73, 499. David Essex Porter, a United States Army veteran and son of David Dixon Porter, arrived in Egypt late in 1875. See Richard W. West, Jr., *The Second Admiral, a Life of David Dixon Porter 1813–1891* (New York, 1937), pp. 43–44, 82, 113, 165, 310; Guy V. Henry, *Military Record of Civilian Appointments in the U.S. Army* (2 vols.; New York, 1871), Vol. I, 418–19; Heitman, *Historical Register*, Vol. I, 799.

Preparations for the invasion of Abyssinia, which got under way late in 1875, the participation of Americans in it, and the initial move to Massawa are discussed in U.S. Dept. of State, *Papers Relating* . . . (44th Cong., 2d sess., Executive Document No. 1, Part I, Serial No. 1741, Washington, 1876), pp. 594–96, 600–601; Dye, *Moslem Egypt*, pp. 151–79, 186–93, 211–30, 237, 425, 499; Farman, *Egypt and Its Betrayal*, pp. 193–95; Loring, *Confederate in Egypt*, pp. 329–47, 357–73, 405; Hill, *Biographical Dictionary*, pp. 209, 380; Crabites, *Americans in the Egyptian Army*, pp. 191–95; Morgan, *Rebel Reefer*, pp. 301–2; Lockett Diary, August 25, 1876, Lockett MSS; Derrick to Graves, January 16, 1876, Graves Letters; *London Times*, January 8, January 26, November 11, December 14, 1876; *New York Herald*, August 28, 1872.

X GURA

In their books on their experiences in Egypt, both Dye and Loring gave detailed reports on the second Abyssinian campaign of late 1875, which culminated in the Egyptian defeat at Gura: Dye, *Moslem Egypt*, pp. 120–28, 173, 189, 193, 201–459; Loring, *Confederate in Egypt*, pp. 323–446. An article entitled "The Egyptian Campaign in Abyssinia," identified only as having been written from the notes of a "staff officer," is in *Littell's Living Age*, Fifth Series, Vol. XIX, (August 4, 1877) 278–87. Lockett, in "Arabi and His Army," *Nation*, Vol. XXXV (September 28, 1882), 257, makes brief reference to Gura, as does Colston in "Modern Egypt and Its People," *Journal of the American Geographical Society of New York*, Vol. XIII (1881), 145, and "The British Campaign in the Soudan for the Rescue of Gordon," *ibid.*, Vol. XVII (1885), 206.

Newspaper accounts of the Gura campaign are in *New York Times*, March

6, July 2, November 7, 1876; December 12, 1879; *New York Herald*, October 25, 1876; September 23, 1879; *London Times*, March 30, October 12, October 25, 1876.

See also Lockett, "Notes on the Abyssinian Campaign of the Egyptian Army 1875–1876," Lockett MSS; Lockett to Boyd, December 17, December 25, 1875; June 5, 1876; in Boyd MSS; Farman, *Egypt and Its Betrayal*, pp. 196–98; Hill, *Gordon*, pp. 205–7; Crabites, *Americans in the Egyptian Army*, pp. 197–200.

The official reports, orders, and correspondence of the Gura campaign are in the Abdin Palace (Cairo) Archives, Archives Generale, Periode Ismail, État Generale.

XI AFTERMATH OF GURA

The reports that the Egyptians had defeated the Abyssinians circulated in the days immediately following the battle of Gura. The true story came a few weeks later. See *New York Herald*, March 14, March 15, April 17, April 19, August 17, October 25, 1876; February 19, 1877; *New York Times*, March 14, March 30, June 21, 1876; *London Times*, March 14, May 15, November 1, 1876; *New York Semi-Weekly Times*, April 21, 1876. See also U.S. Dept. of State, *Papers Relating . . .* (44th Cong., 2d sess., Executive Document No. 1, Part I, Serial No. 1741, Washington, 1876), pp. 602–3; Comanos to Fish, April 21, 1876, U.S. Dept. of State, Official Correspondence, Consulate General, 1869–75; Loring, *Confederate in Egypt*, pp. 396–97, 430–36; Hill, *Gordon*, pp. 204–6; Dye, *Moslem Egypt*, pp. 433–39, 465–67; Colston Diary, May 29, 1876, Colston MSS; Lockett, "Notes on the Abyssinian Campaign of the Egyptian Army 1875–1876," Lockett MSS.

From the moment of defeat at Gura the Americans faced increasing antagonism toward their participation in Egyptian affairs. Even the rigors of their detention at Massawa, however, did not prepare them for the anti-foreign atmosphere which they found upon their return to Cairo. See Dye, *Moslem Egypt*, pp. 194–200, 448–49, 460–72, 477–92, 496. Loring, *Confederate in Egypt*, p. 436; Farman, *Egypt and Its Betrayal*, p. 195; Chaillé-Long, *My Life in Four Continents*, Vol. I, 197; Mrs. Samuel H. Lockett to David Boyd, March 3, June 5, 1876; Lockett to Boyd, September 10, September 24, October 8, 1876; November 4, 1877; and Charles P. Stone to Boyd, April 9, 1876; all in Boyd MSS; Mrs. Lockett to Boyd, August 12, 1876, Charles Woodward Hutson MSS, University of North Carolina Library; "The Egyptian Campaign in Abyssinia," *Littell's Living Age*, Fifth Series, Vol. XIX (August 4, 1877), 282–85; Colston Diary, April 29, May 14, May 27, 1876; *New York Herald*, April 23, June 25, 1876; *New York Times*, April 23, 1876.

The activities and problems of the Americans in the months after the

Gura campaign can be followed in Colston Diary, April, 1876, through February, 1877; Graves to his wife, Letters, No. 76 (May 27, 1876), No. 78 (June 19, 1876), No. 79 (July 7, 1876), No. 82 (July 23, 1876), No. 83 (July 24, 1876), No. 85 (July 29, 1876), No. 88 (August 13, 1876), No. 89 (August 23, 1876), No. 90 (August 24, 1876), No. 93 (August 29, 1876), No. 94 (September 22, 1876), No. 96 (October 2, 1876), No. 99 (October 14, 1876), No. 129 (January 26, 1877), No. 138 (February 26, 1877), No. 141 (March 10, 1877), No. 143 (March 14, 1877), No. 145 (March 19, 1877), No. 146 (March 25, 1877), No. 147 (March 26, 1877), No. 148 (March 31, 1877), No. 152 (April 11, 1877), No. 160 (May 12, 1877), No. 170 (June 3, 1877), No. 269 (March 4, 1878), No. 272 (March 11, 1878); Field to Graves, May 10, 1877; all in Graves Letters; Chaillé-Long, *My Life in Four Continents*, Vol. I, 193–208, 214–16, 239; Dye, *Moslem Egypt*, pp. 224, 266–67, 282, 393–422, 440–60, 488–89, 491, 495; Mrs. Lockett to Boyd, June 5, 1876; Lockett to Boyd, October 8, 1876; June 27, November 4, December 30, 1877; Stone to Boyd, April 9, July 7, 1876; all in Boyd MSS; Mrs. Lockett to Boyd, August 12, 1876, Charles Woodward Hutson MSS; Stone to Colston, March 3, 1876, Colston MSS. Dennison's pay difficulties are recounted from the H. C. Derrick MSS by Annie L. Etheredge, "An Alabamian in Abyssinia," unpublished thesis, University of Alabama, 1957. See also U.S. Dept. of State, *Papers Relating . . .* (45th Cong., 3d sess., Executive Document No. 1, Part I, Serial No. 1842, Washington, 1878), pp. 915–16, 924; Farman, *Egypt and Its Betrayal*, pp. 195–96; *New York Times*, August 17, September 30, 1876; May 25, November 11, 1877; February 6, March 3, May 6, 1878; *New York Herald*, August 17, 1876; January 6, January 9, February 15, March 2, 1878; March 10, 1879; *Baltimore American and Commercial Advertiser*, September 28, 1876; *St. Louis Dispatch*, October 23, 1876.

The Reynolds story can be followed in consular correspondence: Farman to Mrs. Frank Reynolds, May 26, 1876; November 5, 1877; January 15, 1878; February 12, 1879; Farman to Evarts, June 11, 1877; Stone to Farman, October 28, 1877; Farman to executor of last will and testament of Mrs. A. Reynolds, March 29, 1878; all in Official Correspondence of the Consulate General, 1869–75; T. Ludwig to Consul, March 6, 1877, and Consular agent to Farman, March 17, 1877, both in U.S. Dept. of State, Egyptian Dispatches, Consulate General, 1848–79. See also Graves to his wife, Letter No. 79 (July 8, 1876), Graves Letters.

Charles I. Graves explained the Porter dismissal to his wife, Letter No. 96 (October 2, 1876), Graves Letters. For Mason's expedition see "Report of a Reconnaissance of Lake Albert, made by order of His Excellency General Gordon Pacha, Governor-General of the Soudan, by Colonel Mason-Bey," *Proceedings of the Royal Geographical Society*, Vol. XXII (London, 1878),

225–29; Crabites, *Americans in the Egyptian Army*, pp. 215–25 and *Journal of the American Geographical Society*, Vol. XII (1880), 86.

For the story of Miss Mary Lee in Egypt, Graves to his wife, Letters, No. 161 (May 14, 1877), No. 257 (February 4, 1878), No. 258 (February 6, 1878), No. 274 (March 16, 1878), No. 275 (March 18, 1878), No. 276 (March 20, 1878), No. 279 (March 28, 1878); Field to Graves, May 10, 1877; all in Graves Letters.

The serious financial situation in Egypt in 1876 not only brought payless paydays to the Americans, it curtailed every activity of the Egyptian government. U.S. Dept. of State, *Papers Relating* . . . (43d Cong., 1st sess., Executive Document No. 1, Vol. II, Part I, Serial No. 1595, Washington, 1873), pp. 1119–23, 1126–27, 1178–81; *ibid.* (44th Cong., 1st sess., Executive Document No. 1, Vol. II, Part I, Serial No. 1673, Washington, 1875), pp. 1349–50; *ibid.* (44th Cong., 2d sess., Executive Document No. 1, Part I, Serial No. 1741, Washington, 1876), pp. 596–97; *ibid.* (45th Cong., 3d sess., Executive Document No. 1, Part I, Serial No. 1842, Washington, 1878), pp. 925–26; *ibid.* (46th Cong., 2d sess., Executive Document No. 1, Part I, Serial No. 1902, Washington, 1880), pp. 994–96; Farman, *Egypt and Its Betrayal*, pp. 154–59, 196–220, 236–46, 252–55, 280–84; Loring, *Confederate in Egypt*, pp. 148, 165–81, 245–47; Chaillé-Long, *My Life in Four Continents*, Vol. I, 195, 209–15; Lane-Poole, *Egypt*, pp. 179–80; Crabites, *Americans in the Egyptian Army*, pp. 249–50, 255; Dicey, *Story of the Khedivate*, pp. 47–78, 84–85, 89–96, 103–4, 132–41, 143–59, 166, 174–87; Keay, *Spoiling the Egyptians*, pp. 6–7; Cromer, *Modern Egypt*, pp. 11–15, 21, 27–28, 30, 33, 45, 47, 51, 55, 61–63; Dye, *Moslem Egypt*, pp. 8–13; Dicey, "The Egyptian Crisis," *Nineteenth Century*, Vol. V (April, 1879), 670–89; DeLeon, *The Khedive's Egypt*, pp. 236, 337–41, 362–68; Donald A. Cameron, *Egypt in the Nineteenth Century* (London, 1898), pp. 254–55; Lockett to Boyd, October 8, 1876; March 24, 1877; Mrs. Lockett to Boyd, June 5, 1876; all in Boyd MSS; Colston Diary, May 12, May 17, May 27, June 15, June 17, October 10, 1876; January 13, February 5, February 8, 1877; *London Times*, September 20, October 24, 1876; April 30, May 3, May 21–22, June 1, June 27, 1877; January 2–3, January 21, January 25–26, January 30–31, February 1, February 5, February 8, February 11–12, February 14, March 8, March 25–26, March 29, April 1, April 5, April 15, April 17, April 19, May 25, June 6, June 8, June 10, June 20–21, June 25, August 9, August 26, 1878; *New York Times*, August 4, 1869; April 19, 1870; September 30, December 20, 1872; September 14, October 4, 1876; February 24, April 29, May 17, May 25, June 17, August 7, August 20, October 13, 1877; September 6, November 15, 1879; *New York Herald*, October 4, 1876; April 29, May 17, June 2, August 7, 1877; September 26, 1878; April 5–6, May 6, June 12, September 6, September 26, 1879.

XII VETERANS OF MISFORTUNE

Miscellaneous information on the post-Egyptian careers of the Americans who served the Khedive Ismail can be culled from Cullom, *Biographical Register*, Vol. I, 722–23; Vol. II, 213, 389, 391, 550, 836; Vol. III, 90, 93, 108, 112–13, 123; Vol. IV, 92, 168, 177, 179–80, 185; Vol. V, 70, 139, 148, 151–52; Vol. VI A, 126, 134, 137; Evans, *Confederate Military History*, Vol. III, 656; Vol. VIII, 260; Vol. IX, 237; Vol. X, 316; *Confederate Veteran*, Vol. VI, 181; Vol. XVII, 509; Vol. XXIII, 417; Vol. XXXVI, 224; Tyler, *Encyclopedia of Virginia Biography*, Vol. III, 49–50, 84; *The Annals of Iowa*, Third Series, Vol. IV (January, 1900), 318; *National Cyclopedia of American Biography*, Vol. VIII, 270; Association of the Graduates of the U.S. Military Academy, *48th Annual Report* (June 12, 1917), pp. 88–90, and *56th Annual Report* (June 11, 1925), pp. 182–83; Hill, *Biographical Dictionary*, pp. 118, 125, 127, 215, 300–310; Crabites, *Americans in the Egyptian Army*, pp. 10, 13, 55–59, 188; "Monument to E. S. Purdy," *Journal of the American Geographical Society of New York*, Vol. XI (1879), 306–8. A number of Americans served most inconspicuously in Egypt. For Carroll Tevis see Heitman, *Historical Register*, Vol. I, 951; Cullom, *Biographical Register*, Vol. II, 389; *Union Army*, Vol. I, 523–24, Vol. II, 281; Crabites, *Americans in the Egyptian Army*, pp. 10, 14; Dye, *Moslem Egypt*, p. 495; *New York Times*, July 6, 1880. Sketches of James Bassel are in Cullom, *Biographical Register*, Vol. III, 93, Vol. VI A, 126; Heitman, *Historical Register*, Vol. I, 198. See also Dye, *Moslem Egypt*, p. 498, and *New York Times*, January 4, 1874.

The personal accounts of the participants contain material on the later events in their own and their companions' lives. See, in particular, Chaillé-Long, *My Life in Four Continents*, Vol. I, 16, 18–19, 37, 40, 53, 223, 231, 334; *Central Africa*, pp. 2, 218; Dye, *Moslem Egypt*, pp. 131–32, 142–45, 496–500; Loring, *Confederate in Egypt*, pp. 187–88, 208 ff., 298–305, 490–91; Farman, *Egypt and Its Betrayal*, pp. 66, 82, 89–90; Morgan, *Rebel Reefer*, pp. 316–482; Warren, *Experience in Three Continents*, pp. 443–45, 480–81, 484, 490, 532–37.

Colston's and Lockett's efforts at rehabilitation, with some incidental reference to other of their Egyptian colleagues, may be traced in their manuscript letters. See, especially, Samuel H. Lockett to David Boyd, October 8, 1876, November 4, 1877, August 9, 1878, September 8, 1885; all in Boyd MSS; Lockett, "The Valleys of the Nile and the Mississippi," Hutson MSS, Louisiana State University Library, Baton Rouge; Colston Diary, May 27, 1876; Stone to Colston, March 3, 1876; Colston to Stone, March 1, March 3, March 27, 1878; Prout to Colston, June 24, 1878; Long to Colston, August 17, 1878; Dye to Colston, September 10, 1878; Kemp Battle to Colston, November 26, 1881; all in Colston MSS. See also

Stone to S. S. Cox, November 24, 1881, Cox MSS, Brown University Library, Providence, R.I.; Colston to Marcus J. Wright, January 1, 1898, and Colston to James W. Eldridge (n.d.), both in Eldridge MSS; Colston Diary, January 8, January 28, 1877; "The Egyptian Campaign in Abyssinia," *Littell's Living Age*, Fifth Series, Vol. XIX (August 4, 1877), 278–79.

Magazine articles by the former soldiers of the khedive, some of them reminiscent, some biographical, most of them indicating that the ex-officers of the Egyptian army were "experts" on Egypt, include Lockett, "Arabi and His Army," *Nation*, Vol. XXXV (September 28, 1882), 257–58; "The Egyptian Disaster," *ibid.*, Vol. XXXVII (November 29, 1883), 442–43; Colston, "False Prophet of the Sudan," *ibid.*, Vol. III (February 15, 1884), 199–204; "The Land of the False Prophet," *Century Magazine*, Vol. XXIX (March, 1885), 643–62; "Life in the Egyptian Deserts," *Journal of the American Geographical Society of New York*, Vol. XI (1879), 306–8; Henry G. Prout, "A Central African Railroad," *ibid.*, Vol. XXIII (1891), 566–74; "From Suakin to Berber," *Science*, Vol. V (March 27, 1885), 254–56; "The British and the French on the Upper Nile," *New York Times*, February 14, 1898. Henry Prout also wrote articles on American foreign trade and on transportation. See "The United States as a Foreign Trader," *New York Times*, December 28, 1897, January 6, 1898; "The Motive Power of the City Railroads of New York," *ibid.*, July 24, 1898; "The Rapid Transit Situation in New York," *ibid.*, October 22, 1899; "The Pennsylvania's Great Hudson River Tunnel," *ibid.*, September 14, 1902.

Newspaper articles whose sources (either direct or indirect) were the repatriated Americans include the *New York Herald*, March 23, 1873; September 23, 1876; May 22, 1877; April 9, 1878; June 17, June 20, 1879; July 11, September 19, 1882; July 31, August 1, 1884; *New York Times*, July 19, 1877; April 9, May 6, July 28, August 11, 1878; March 12, 1879; July 6, 1880; July 11, August 6, August 16, August 29, October 17, November 22, December 31, 1886; January 3, March 17, 1887; November 22, 1890; April 9, 1892; November 27, 1894; August 3, 1896; October 26, November 14, 1897; March 12, 1898; November 14, 1899; October 12, 1903; June 30, 1914; December 18, December 19, 1915; October 29, 1916; August 23, 1918; April 23, 1928; *London Times*, February 15, 1875; July 23, 1881; *New York Tribune*, April 11, 1892; *Chicago Daily Inter Ocean*, December 30, 1886; *Richmond (Va.) Weekly Times*, July 30, 1896; *Chicago Times*, December 31, 1886.

For Graves's last-minute expedition to Cape Guardafui see Graves to his wife, Letters, No. 279 (March 28, 1878), No. 287 (April 26, 1878), No. 289 (May 22, 1878), No. 292 (July 6, 1878), No. 294 (July 13, 1878), No. 297 (July 23, 1878), No. 298 (July 24, 1878), No. 301 (July 29, 1878),

No. 302 (August 2, 1878); Stone to Graves, March 29, 1878; all in Graves Letters.

The departure of the Americans from Egypt occasioned considerable work for the American consul general. Matters of debts, settlement of accounts, and the death of several Americans produced routine correspondence that sometimes contained revealing details. See Comanos to Fish, September 19, 1874; Beardsley to Fish, December 18, 1874, July 28, 1875; Stone to Farman, April 26, April 30, June 18, June 20, June 21, June 23, 1877; William Wilson to Farman, May 19, 1877; Prout to Farman, June 23, 1877; James A. Dennison to Farman, June 24, 1877; all in U.S. Dept. of State, Egyptian Dispatches, Consulate General, 1848–79.

The official lack of interest of the State Department and the necessary concern of the Cairo consulate is revealed in Bill, November 3, 1873; Rhett to Beardsley, December 30, 1874, January 7, 1875; Rhett to Farman, June 8, 1877; Beardsley to Fish, October 20, 1875; Comanos to Fish, January 23, 1876; Farman to Evarts, April 4, June 24, July 3, July 9, July 15, 1878; all in U.S. Dept. of State, Official Correspondence of the Consulate General, 1869–75.

Details concerning the deaths and the disposition of the property of Americans sometimes involved tedious transmittal of papers. On the death of Major Loshe, see Charles G. Gordon (undated note); W. W. Faulkner to acting Consul, October 5, 1878; Stone to Consul General, October 9, 1878; Faulkner to acting Consul General, October 28, 1878; Stone to Vice-Consul, November 10, 1878; Mrs. Lillie Loshe to Farman, February 10, June 22, 1879. On W. P. A. Campbell, Stone to Farman, October 10, 1874; Warren to Farman, June 21, 1876. On Irgins, Brown to Consul, September 4, 1878. All such communications are in U.S. Dept. of State, Official Correspondence of the Consulate General, 1869–75.

For the career of Charles Chaillé-Long after the dismissal of the Americans in Egypt, see Chaillé-Long, *My Life in Four Continents*, Vol. I, vii–xvi, 40, 137, 165, 206, 215–25, 234–307; Vol. II, 209–574; *Three Prophets*, pp. 97, 104, 115–22, 136–43, 163–67, 186–89, 195–223; "Egypt under the Viceroys," *The Era*, Vol. XI (March, 1903), 258; "England in Egypt and the Soudan," *North American Review*, Vol. CLXVIII (May, 1899), 570–80; "From Corea to Quelpaert Island: In the Footprints of Kublai Khan," *Bulletin of the American Geographical Society of New York*, Vol. XXII (1890), 219–66; "New Arab Kingdom Takes Its Place among Near Eastern Nations," *New York Times Magazine*, March 4, 1917; "Stray Letters from General Gordon," *Chicago Times Supplement*, May 23, August 29, 1886; "Rivalry between Egypt, England and Germany for Supremacy on the East Coast of Africa," *Chicago Times Sunday Magazine*, June 7, 1885; Long to Colston, August 17, 1878, Colston MSS; Long to Cox, January 31, April 13, 1885,

Cox mss; Allen, *Gordon*, pp. 86–91; Crabites, *Americans in the Egyptian Army*, pp. 259–60; Hill, *Biographical Dictionary*, pp. 98–99; Farman, *Egypt and Its Betrayal*, pp. 314–21, 326; Archibald Forbes, "An American Criticism of the Egyptian Campaign," *Nineteenth Century*, Vol. XVI (August, 1884), 230; Elton, *Gordon*, pp. 159–63; *Bulletin of the American Geographical Society*, Vol. XLII (1910), 205–7; *Geographical Review*, Vol. III (April, 1917), 329; *London Times*, March 5, 1884; *Richmond Times Dispatch*, March 26, 1917; *New York Times*, June 9, 1878, November 5, 1882, March 26, 1917; *New York Herald*, May 29, 1878; January 23, September 17, 1880; July 26, November 12, 1881; June 17, June 19, July 4, July 11, July 14–15, July 25, August 20, 1882; September 6, 1884.

For the career of Charles P. Stone after the dismissal of the Americans in Egypt, see Cullom, *Biographical Register*, Vol. II, 215; Cromer, *Modern Egypt*, Vol. I, 184; *Journal of the American Geographical Society of New York*, Vol. XV (1883), 361–74; Farman, *Egypt and Its Betrayal*, pp. 317, 326; Hill, *Biographical Dictionary*, pp. 346–47; Loring, *Confederate in Egypt*, pp. 188–89; Dicey, *Story of the Khedivate*, p. 257; Chaillé-Long, *My Life in Four Continents*, Vol. I, 272–73; *Three Prophets*, pp. 179, 194; Fanny Stone, "Diary of an American Girl in Cairo during the War of 1882," *Century Magazine*, Vol. XXVIII (June, 1884), 288–302; Colston, "The British Campaign in the Soudan for the Rescue of Gordon," *Journal of the American Geographical Society of New York*, Vol. XVII (1885), 161–62; Stone, "The Climate of the Egyptian Sudan," *Science*, Vol. V (April 3, 1885), 268–71; "The Route from Suakin to Berber," *ibid.*, Vol. V (April 10, 1885), 290; "The Bombardment of Alexandria," *Century Magazine*, Vol. XXVIII (October, 1884), 953–56; C. F. Goodrich, "The Bombardment of Alexandria," *ibid.*, Vol. XXVIII (August, 1884), 635–36; Stone to Cox, November 24, 1881; Stone to Mrs. Cox, February 15, 1883; both in Cox mss; *New York Herald*, February 3, September 12, September 13, September 16, September 27, February 27, June 13, June 20, June 23, July 2, July 14–15, July 24, 1882; March 3, March 13, April 3, 1883; January 24, January 30, February 7, September 3, 1884; *New York Times*, January 25, January 28, 1887; *New York Daily Tribune*, January 25, January 28, 1887; *London Times*, January 13, 1880; February 15, September 20, December 21, 1881; January 10, May 13, 1882.

For a long survey of Egyptian affairs, from the late 1870's on, see Chaillé-Long, *My Life in Four Continents*, Vol. I, 225–28, 242, 266; *Three Prophets*, pp. 75–79, 87–117, 123–24, 144–61, 172–77, 182–83, 201; Loring, *Confederate in Egypt*, pp. 165–76, 183–86; Crabites, *Americans in the Egyptian Army*, pp. 257–58; DeLeon, *The Khedive's Egypt*, pp. 245–47; Dicey, *Story of the Khedivate*, pp. 208–19, 233, 251–78, 287–93, 299–306, 310; Farman, *Egypt and Its Betrayal*, pp. 247–65, 301–12, 321–24, 332–33, 337–48; W.

Basil Worsfold, *Egypt Yesterday and Today* (New York, n.d.), pp. 66–72; Cromer, *Modern Egypt*, Vol. I, 74–77, 83–105, 110–27, 135–41, 153–223, 337; Wilfrid S. Blunt, "The Egyptian Revolution: A Personal Narrative," *Nineteenth Century*, Vol. XII (September, 1882), 324–346; U.S. Dept. of State, *Papers Relating . . .* (46th Cong., 2d sess., Executive Document No. 1, Part I, Serial No. 1902, Washington, 1879), pp. 1005–10, 1013–14, 1016–18; *London Times*, February 19–20, February 22, June 28, July 7, July 21, August 8, August 11, August 13, August 18, August 21, September 3, September 6, September 10, September 26, September 28, November 19, December 21, December 29, 1879; February 23, 1880; *New York Herald*, June 27, September 19, 1879; September 10, November 10, 1881; March 22, September 9, 1882.

Index

The Blue and the Gray on the Nile

Farman, Elbert E., 218, 219, 282
Fechet, Oscar Eugene, 22, 120–21, 241, 255, 265
Field, General Charles W., 21, 96, 100, 183, 186, 187, 195–211 *passim*, 212, 218, 223, 225, 233, 242, 255, 263–64
Field, Mrs. Charles W., 96, 100
Fish, Hamilton, 117, 127, 128

Gordon, General Charles George ("Chinese"), 127, 135, 151–56, 165–69, 172–74, 220, 222, 240, 276–77
Grand New Hotel (Cairo), 47–48, 96, 114, 173
Grant, General Ulysses S., 16–17, 50, 231–33
Graves, Charles Iverson, 48, 53, 55, 59, 60, 61–62, 84–85, 91, 92–94, 96, 97, 99–102, 106, 118–19, 187, 216–19, 223, 228, 229, 231, 232–34, 235, 243–44, 255, 269, 270, 283–84

Halid Pasha, 151
Hall, Harriott Horry, 99–100
Hall, Wilburn B., 98, 115, 188, 215–16, 218, 241, 242, 255, 271, 272
Hamdy, Major, 144
Hassan, Prince, 190–93, 198, 202–5, 209, 213
Hood, General John B., 17
Hooker, General Joseph, 8
Houston, General Samuel, 23
Hughes, William, 103
Hunt, Cornelius, 21, 75, 83, 112–13, 117, 236, 255, 263, 271
Hussein (son of Ismail), 140, 186

Ingraham, Duncan, 99
Irgins, Henry, 183, 187, 194, 198, 201, 218, 234, 237, 278
Ismail, khedive of Egypt, 19, 23–41, 42, 47–50, 68, 71, 75–78, 80, 88, 110–12, 150, 154, 166–67, 180–81, 183–85, 223–29 *passim*, 238, 239, 244–46, 265–67

Jackson, General Thomas Jonathan, 11, 15, 66, 124, 186
Jenifer, Walter H., 21, 82, 103, 115, 237, 256, 264

John, king of Abyssinia, 181, 186, 193, 196–210 *passim*, 223, 228
Johnson, Dr. Thomas D., 183, 201, 206, 208–9, 242, 256, 278
Johnston, General Albert Sidney, 94
Johnston, General Joseph E., 14, 17, 20, 21, 66
Journal of the American Geographical Society, 238

Kassim Pasha, 103–4
Keba Rega (chieftain), 158, 162, 164, 175
Kennon, Beverly, 70–71, 75, 83, 256, 268
Khahin Pasha, 77–78, 80
Kirkham, John Charles, 181, 197

Laforge, Sitta Maria, 131
Lamson, Robert S., 187, 236–37, 256, 278
Lee, Mary, 231–33, 281
Lee, General Robert E., 5
Lesseps, Ferdinand de, 23, 26, 35
Letcher, John, 14
Levant Herald, 38
Linant, Auguste, 167
Linant, Louis, 129, 130
Lincoln, President Abraham, 5
Livingston, Dr. David, 152, 176, 240
Lockett, Samuel H., 16, 43, 58, 84, 85, 87–88, 89, 94–95, 96, 97, 114, 181, 183, 186, 187–88, 194–210 *passim*, 212–13, 216–17, 218, 219, 227, 230, 237, 241, 242, 250, 256, 265, 271, 272, 282–83
Lockett, Mrs. Samuel, 212–13, 223
Long, Charles Chaillé. *See* Chaillé-Long, Charles
Loring, General William Wing, 10–18, 43, 45, 51–52, 60, 61, 62–63, 65–77, 80, 89, 94, 104, 105, 108–9, 117, 134, 184–92, 194–208 *passim*, 216–18, 224, 231, 232, 234, 238–40, 251, 256, 262–63, 282
Loshe, Charles F., 22, 96, 100–101, 183, 187, 191–92, 195–211 *passim*, 218, 219, 223, 234, 237, 257, 284
Loshe, Mrs. Charles F., 100–101
Lutfi Bey, 73, 80, 189, 195, 225
Lyons, Lord, 77

The Blue and the Gray on the Nile

PRINTED IN U.S.A.

DATE DUE

MY 26 '65			
JAN 1 0 1966			
NOV 2 1966			
MAR 1 1967			
JAN 3 1968			
FEB 4 1970			
GAYLORD			PRINTED IN U.S.A.